R.E. LEE
REFLECTIONS

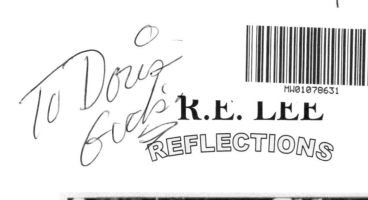

By
David Chaltas

'Protect My Men'
Black & white portrait
By Wendy Leedy
4048 Rocky Springs Rd
Bean Station, TN 37708
865-993-2952 (work) 865-933-7173 (home)
email: equineartistntn@cs.com
website: wendyleedy.com

R.E. LEE: *Reflections*

ISBN: ISBN-13: 978-1481002868
ISBN-10: 1481002864

Library of Congress: 92179105503

Designs of Merritt
654 Chahokia Drive
Rutledge, TN 37861
www.mariemerritt.com

Proudly Printed in America

DEDICATION

First, I must acknowledge the goodness of God's grace. I have been blessed with a joyous life rich life. To God goes the glory. He has fostered within my being a burning desire to write about the Christian character and lessons we can apply to our lives. It is to the Founder of the Feast that I dedicate this book. To those who believed in my work, I offer my sincere appreciation. Thank you for believing in me when I did not believe in myself. For my son; I pray that he finds his destiny. For my friends that encouraged me and supported my efforts, I offer my sincere thanks. To the lady who stood by my side, I will be forever grateful. Finally, I dedicate this book to our American heritage in honor of our heroes.

"Mr. President, Gentlemen of the convention, profoundly impressed by the solemnity of the occasion for which, I must say, I was not prepared. I accept the position assigned me by your partiality. I would have much preferred had your choice fallen on an abler man. But trusting to Almighty God, an approving conscience, and the aid of my fellow citizens, I devote myself to the service of my native State, in whose behalf alone will I ever again draw my sword." (Lee accepting command in the Senate Chambers building, Richmond, Virginia)

FOREWORD

He now rests in the land that he loved. And we pine for his presence once again. But there was a moment etched in time when a giant rode upon the land. There was an instance when a man of Christian character, values and mystery arose to become the very symbol of how to be a Christian during turbulent times. He was a man of sorrow, yet was filled with the joy and the spirit of living during a time of death and dying. He was a father, a son, a husband, and a soldier that served his country for over thirty years before resigning himself to a greater fate. There once existed a man, during a brief period, in which America stood upon a threshold of awakening-hesitating to be reborn, as one chose blue and one chose gray. This is my interpretation of his saga.

By all standards, Robert Edward Lee was no doubt one of the greatest generals of all times. His tenacity in battle, unique deployment of his men, ability to fight off an army with more resources and man power for four years is renowned. His love of country and genuine concern for his soldiers were all part of the dynamics that comprised his spirit. His sterling Christian character, humbleness of spirit, values, and devotion to duty are legendary. He was a man of God serving his convictions at a tremendously high personal expense. He lost everything while maintaining his principles and honor. Not once did he flinch from his duties and placed it all in the hands of God.

One of the many tributes paid to Lee was by General John Brown Gordon. He summated the essence of the man as seen by friend and foe. In his reminiscences, he stated, "Lee exhibited everywhere all those lofty characteristics which have made the name of Scipio immortal. He not only possessed true genius, the 'gift that Heaven gives and which buys a place next to a king.'-he had what was better than genius-a heart whose every throb was in harmony with the teachings of the Great Captain whom he served. He had a spirit naturally robust and aggressive, but he made it loyally obedient to the precepts of the Divine Master. In the combination of great qualities, he will be adjudged in history as measuring up as few commanders have ever done to Scipio's loft conception of the noblest soldier: the commander who could win victories, but who found more pleasure in the protection afforded defenceless citizens than in the disasters inflicted upon armed enemies." (Reminiscences of the Civil War; Gordon, John Brown; New York; C. Scribner's Sons, 1904)

Many things impressed this fielder's mind while researching Robert Edward Lee. I first started reading about his military exploits but quickly diverted my attention to the Christian Character of Lee. Here was a man of honor and beliefs! I remember reading of his self-denial as evidenced by General Ewell when the city of Petersburg was being evacuated. He had no time to eat and General Lee insisted that he take his lunch that was in a bag. It consisted of two cold sweet potatoes. He would only eat what his boys had simply stating, "I am content to share the rations of my men." He never possessed a home in his own name though his greatest aspiration was to be the owner of a small farm away from the public spotlight. He diplomatically turned down positions of honor and wealth. One of my favorite stories is of an insurance company that offered him a salary of $10,000 to compensate him for the use of his good name. He forcefully replied, "I am sorry, sir, that you are so little acquainted with my character as to suppose that my name is for sale at any price." Another company offered him $50,000 to go to New York and become president of a commerce company. A wealthy Englishman that was an admirer of his character offered Lee and his family a home in England with 3,000 pounds provided a year. Lee graciously declined all offers and instead took a job rebuilding a failing college but more importantly took upon his shoulders the task of rebuilding his beloved Virginia and the country. For Lee was a true patriot and had served the red, white, and blue for over thirty years. Even within the ranks of gray, he was still an American (A proud Confederate American!) fighting for his beliefs and honor, never relinquishing to the pressure of many but only to the verdict of his conscience. (Life & Letters of Gen. Robert Edward Lee; Jones, W.J.; Sprinkle Publications; Harrisonburg, Virginia; 1986; Neale Publishing Company in 1906; pages 444-446)

Not perfect by any measure, his life personifies a time of great turmoil. It is said that he possessed a hot temper but managed it so well that he was calm and quiet among his men. He was a man of God during an ungodly time. In all things, he prayed and prior to the battle, after spending countless hours with his Maker in prayer, he would give the outcome of the forthcoming battle into God's hands. He was a man to look up to and set standards by. He was of impeccable character and followed his Christian heart in all endeavors. He was a product of his childhood teachings. He followed the teachings of his beloved mother and learned the hard lessons of life as demonstrated by his father's ill-fated investments and choices. He firmly believed in the power of providence and that God knows all things.

He was a mortal man of morals, possessing a shy disposition and at times seemingly to be reserved with a graceful dignity. He was a man with a taste for buttermilk and sweet potatoes. He possessed a very keen wit and great sense of humor. He was a man that was surrounded by sorrow and death yet never failed to embrace life. A mortal man that touched immortality through his commitments to a cause long since disappeared, love of his state, and dignity during victories as well as defeats. He was a man of the ages that etched our nation by his struggle. He was a man that showed us all how to live humbly and was instrumental in the reunification of our country by his example of being a true American.

He was a man, an immortal in the mind of history: yet he was just a man; he was the legend, the legacy: Robert Edward Lee.

I Remain Your Obedient Servant,

David Chaltas
Box 41 Deer Branch Road
Jeremiah, Kentucky 41826
honestlee33@yahoo.com

ABOUT THE AUTHOR

David Philip Chaltas is a resident of eastern Kentucky. In the Summer of 2001, he was selected Teacher of the Year by the Kentucky Council of Children with Behavioral Disorders. He is the first recipient of the prestigious award in the state of Kentucky. His innovative Alternative Education and Day Treatment Program won the coveted 2000-2001 Program of the Year by the International Association of Directors of Pupil Personnel. His concepts have been featured in Forward in the Fifth; a paper designed to recognize excellence in educational programs. The Kentucky Center for Safe Schools has posted his model program on their website. He has been a State Consultant on Emotional Behavioral Disorders. He has conducted numerous seminars on behavioral management and has been a featured speaker nationally. He was a professor at Hazard Community College. He is a Kentucky Colonel. He spent six years working with Native Americans and compiled material for his book entitled Native American Customs, Sayings, and Prayers: A Rediscovery of Native American Truths. He is also the author of The ABC's of Appalachian Expression, Appalachian Recollections, Window to the World of Expressions, and The Alpha and Omega of Sayings. He has penned a book on behavioral management entitled, The Art of Teacher Behaviors. But his true love is writing about the War Between the States. He has written a delightful book entitled Fading of the Grey and his book of original Poetry of the Civil War; Poems of a By-Gone Era should be considered a must for the serious Civil War buff. His latest endeavor is the compilation of Confederate Kin I, II, III and IV.s destined to become a classic. He coauthored a book with fellow author (Richard G. Brown) regarding the stories of men and battles

9

from the mountainous regions of Appalachia entitled, "Appalachian Rebel."

His writings have been published in several magazines and newspapers including The Civil War Courier (a monthly newsletter with a national audience), The Kentucky Explorer, East Kentucky Magazine, Appalachian Quarterly (selected as the Civil War Correspondent), Lost Cause, and the Letcher County Historical Society publications. He served as the Commander of the Colonel Ben Caudill #1629 (Sons of Confederate Veterans), member of the Southern Guard Battalion, Hardees's Corp Chaplain, member of the Tennessee Valley Battalion, Army of the Tennessee Chief of Staff, Kentucky Cavalry Brigade, North/South Alliance, Aide De Camp for Cleburne's Division (Colonel Robinson), SCV Ky Division and SCV AOT Chaplain. He has been featured nationally in the persona of General Robert E. Lee at numerous reenactments, dedications, and engagements. He was chosen to represent General Lee at the 2005 National Reunion. He was selected to be the keynote speaker at the Lee/Jackson Day event, held in Lexington, Virginia, honoring the 200th birthday of Robert E. Lee.

"A nation which does not remember what it was yesterday does not know what it is today" *Lee*

AUTHOR'S NOTES

Why write about a man who has already been so widely reviewed? What could I possibly contribute that has not already been offered? Maybe it was because of my resemblance to him, or his Christian principles that he followed. Maybe it was due to his being one of my idols, as surely as the old Lone Ranger was dear to my heart. Could it possibly have been a spiritual kinship that drove me forward? Could it be the soliloquies in which I have been privileged to take on the persona of General Lee thanking his boys for their sacrifices? In order to portray him, I must first know him, therefore I felt compelled to discover the legend and the myths of the man.

At the very beginning of this project an author friend asked why try to rewrite history and had not the subject already been exhausted? I had to take exception to those comments. In no manner am I trying to redefine the man or to complicate matters with my feeble efforts. Never can we exhaust rediscovering men of Christian character and moral fiber. That is how we learn to live humbly and follow the teachings of our Lord.

I wish to compliment and honor a hero within our history. I believe the principles that the Christian knight endorsed and lived by draws one to the realization that it isn't to whom we are born or the circumstances, but it is by the manner in which we live and dignity of our suffering that matters. I had to write about this wonderful human being. It is as simple as that and I am humbled to be given the drive to follow my passion. I pray God will continue allowing me the opportunity to express my being via the magic avenues of written expression...

TABLE OF CONTENTS

For speaking engagements or if you wish to
purchase additional copies contact:

David Chaltas
Box 41, Deer Branch Road
Jeremiah, Ky. 41826
Cell # 335-1479   Fax-633-2459
honestlee33@yahoo.com

(Author at the Angle; Pickett's Charge, Gettysburg)

ROBERT EDWARD LEE
January 19, 1807-October 12, 1870

"Marse Robert"

"Bobby Lee"

"Uncle Bobby"

"Marble Model"

"King of Spades"

"The Great Tycoon"

"Granny Lee"

"The Old Man"

"Our Beloved General"

"He Lost a War and Won Immortality!"

THE MOLDING OF THE MAN OF MARBLE

Robert E. Lee was born at Westmoreland County, Virginia, on a plantation known as the Stratford estate. He was born in the master bedroom on the southeast side of the house. The original crib in which he was placed is still at that location. (In the Footsteps of Robert E. Lee; Johnson, Clint; John H. Blair Publisher; Winston-Salem, North Carolina; 2001; page 6) The area around the estate is located between the Potomac and Rappahannock Rivers and was known by the locals as the "Northern Neck." Thomas Lee built the mansion (it had burned once and was rebuilt with financial help allegedly from Queen Caroline of England and friends) between the years of 1725-1730. It was made of brick and shaped in the form of the letter H, with eighteen rooms and beautifully engraved woodwork. The large estate was in the center with four single brick buildings at each corner. They contained a kitchen, office, milk house and a stable. A Mr. Lossing reported that, "There is no structure in our country to compare with it. The walls of the first story are two and a half feet thick, and the second story two feet, composed of brick imported from England. It originally contained about one hundred rooms. Besides the main building, there are four offices, one at each corner, containing fifteen rooms. The stables can accommodate one hundred horses. Its cost was about $80,000." The house became the property of his half-brother when Robert was but a toddler (16 months of age). Into this setting, Robert Edward Lee was born. (Life & Letters of Gen. Robert Edward Lee; Jones, W.J.; Sprinkle Publications; Harrisonburg, Virginia; 1986; @ by Neale Publishing Company in 1906; page 16)

Robert Edward Lee was born into one of the most prominent families of the time. He was the fourth offspring of "Light Horse Harry" Lee (Cavalry Commander in the Revolutionary War, U.S. House of Representatives for two years, Continental Congress and Governor of Virginia from 1791 to 1794) and the third son of Ann Hill Carter of the prosperous Shirley Plantation. She was the great-granddaughter of Robert "King" Carter who during the colonial days had established an empire worthy of a king. Her father was Charles Carter and was from one of the wealthiest families of that era. Robert was named after his mother's two brothers, Robert, and Edward. His brothers (he had six siblings; one died during infancy) were Henry (known by the Lee family as Harry-Light Horse Harry's first son by his first marriage), Charles Carter (known as Carter) and Sidney Smith (Robert referred to him as Rose or Smith). He had two sisters by the name of Mildred and Anne. He would later name two of his daughters after his sisters. Harry Lee was descended from Launcelot Lee, Lionel Lee, and Sir Henry Lee. Two of his ancestors who were born in the Stratford mansion signed the Declaration of Independence. They were Richard Henry Lee and Francis Lightfoot Lee.

Harry received his nickname "Lighthorse" due to the many adventures while an outpost cavalry leader and his ability to sit light in the saddle. He joined the Virginia cavalry and was commissioned a captain. He later transferred to the Continental Army under General George Washington. He was soon General Washington's favorite and was sent on several guerilla missions where he performed brilliantly. He captured Paulus Hook (Jersey City) and guarded the retreat of General Nathanael Greene in South Carolina, making the life of the British almost unbearable. He was promoted to Lt. Colonel and was given a gold medal by Congress for his exploits. He retired from the military life at the youthful age of twenty-five citing ill health as the reason. But General Washington would continue to hold his favorite general in high esteem and it was said that among the Lee family only God was above the name of Washington. A letter of congratulations for the wedding of "Lighthorse" and Ms. Carter reveals Washington's level of respect for Lee as well as Washington's sense of humor. "As we are told that you have exchanged the rugged and dangerous field of Mars for the soft and pleasurable bed of Venus, I do in this as I shall in everything you may pursue like unto it, good and laudable, wish you all imaginable success and happiness."

After returning home from the Revolutionary War, Light Horse Harry became restless and overindulged himself to the point of being imprisoned due to his unpaid debts. For whatever reason, Light Horse Harry had left his wife during Robert's youth after losing most of the family fortune due to poor investments. The Lee's beloved Stratford was sold and Mrs. Lee with her children moved to 607 Oronoco Street in Alexandria, Virginia. He had invested heavily in a speculation upon an enterprise to purchase land to connect the Virginia-Maryland Great Falls area via a canal that never materialized. He had also loaned Robert Morris (one of the signers of the Declaration of Independence) the sum of forty thousand dollars that was never repaid. He had also invested monies as a farmer and the project yielded a disastrous return. At the onset of the War of 1812, he was given the rank of major general but due to an incident in Baltimore where he was badly beaten defending a friend's right of speech via the free press, he never realized his dream of serving. Due to related health problems, he sailed to a tropical climate and slowly the

16

recovery progressed well enough for him to try to return. In 1816 he wrote his son Charles Carter, "I begin to hope that I may live to see you, your dear mother and our other sweet offspring." But on the winds of change, as he stopped at the home of Nathanael Greene, his old commander on the Cumberland Island (a place called Dungeness), he took a turn for the worse and on March 25, 1818, he succumbed to the sweet surrender of the night. He was buried in the area owned by the daughter of his former commander, Nathaniel Greene. He was sixty-two years of age. The sailors from the U. S. Navy vessel *John Adams* offered a military salute at his funeral. (Robert E. Lee, A Biography; Thomas, Emory M.; W.W. Norton & Company; New York-London; 1995; page 36)

However Light Horse Harry Lee is judged by historians, his words spoken at the funeral of George Washington will forever connect him with American History; "First in war, first in peace, and first in the hearts of his fellow citizens." In 1913, Colonel Light Horse Harry Lee's remains were solemnly carried back to Ole Virginia (the land of Lees) and he was reunited with his family and their descendants. His remains now rest beside his famous son in the chapel of Washington and Lee College. All of his immediate family members now rest in that sanctuary.

Robert was only eleven years old at his father's passing. Fifty-two years later, the full circle of a son's affection is realized when General Lee, in the autumn of his years, went to Florida via rail and paid his last respects to his father's grave. Robert E. Lee paid the highest tribute to his father by choosing to edit and to write a biography of his father for the book entitled, The Revolutionary War Memoirs of General Henry Lee instead of writing his own memoirs. Such was the love and admiration he possessed for the man he briefly knew but always held so dear in his heart (as only a son can carry the love for his father), his idol, his friend, his father: Light Horse Harry Lee. The visit occurred just over a year prior to his demise and on October 12, 1870, he crossed the river of Jordan to be reunited with his loved ones. (The Boys' Life of Robert E. Lee; Horn, Stanley F.; Harper Brothers Publishers; New York and London; 1935)

As his mother's health steadily declined, Robert became the primary caretaker of his mother. "In her illness, he mixed every dose of medicine which she took" and nursed her both night and day. Robert was molded by his mother's natural calmness of spirit and she was another important role model for him to follow. Her Christian influence and gentle characteristics stayed with him throughout his life. She "taught him in his childhood to practice self-denial and self-control, as well as the strictest economy in all financial concerns." He was totally devoted to her offering her constant companionship and care. One of his cousins wrote that what had impressed the family the most was, "Robert's devotion to his mother." His mother wrote that, "You have been a son and daughter to me. The other boys used to drink from the glasses of the gentlemen but Robert never would join them. He was different." Even at a young age, Robert's mother knew that her son was a man of destiny and this fielder couldn't help but believe that she groomed him for his upcoming role. (Robert E. Lee Man and Soldier; Page, Thomas Nelson; Charles Scribner's sons; New York; 1926; pages 13-14)

"He was a Most Exemplary Student"

Several people were already taking note of this young man and his potential. One of his teachers by the name of Benjamin Hallowell recalled young Robert with admiration and affection. It was during the period of time that Lee waited to go to West Point (he received an appointment in March of 1824 but due to too many new students had to wait until July of 1825 to attend) that he received instruction from the schoolmaster. (Lee; Freeman, Douglas Southall; Touchstone Book; Simon & Schuster; New York; 1961, 1991; page 46) Mr. Hallowell noted in his journal that:

"He was a most exemplary pupil in every respect...He was never behind time at his studies; never failed in a single recitation; was perfectly observant of the rules and regulations of the institution; was gentlemanly, unobtrusive, and respectful in all his deportment to teacher and his fellow-students. His specialty was finishing. He imparted a finish and a neatness, as he proceeded, to everything he undertook."

"He Will Neither Disappoint Me or His Friends"

Robert decided to attend West Point but knew that it was by appointment and had to have someone recommend him. Several men offered their endorsement of the young Lee. Some of the men that offered their support were C. F. Mercer, George Tucker, R. S. Garnett, James Barbour, R. H. M. Johnson, David Holmes, and William Kelly. All of them were noted men of character and held prestigious positions within the community as well as within the country. One letter in particular addressed his educational background and his potential. The author was his former teacher, Mr. Leary.

"Robert Lee was formerly a pupil of mine. While under my care I can vouch for his correct and gentlemanly deportment. In the various branches, to which his attention has been applied, I flatter myself that his information will be found adequate to the most sanguine expectations of his friends. With me he has read all the minor classics in addition to Homer & Longinus, Tacitus & Cicero. He is well versed in arithmetic, Algebra & Euclid. In regard to what he has read with me I am certain that when examined he will neither disappoint me or his friends."

"The Young Gentlemen is Her Son"

A close friend of the family that had watched Robert develop into a promising young man wrote an eloquent letter that was addressed to the Secretary of War endorsing Lee's candidacy. It was written at Ravensworth on February 7, 1824. The man was W. H. Fitzhugh.

"My Dear Sir,

"I cannot permit the young gentleman, who will hand you this letter, to make his intended application, without carrying with him, such testimony in his behalf, as a long & an intimate acquaintance both with himself and his family, justify me in giving. He is the son of Gen. Henry Lee, with whose history, you are, of course, acquainted; and who (whatever may have been the misfortune of his latter years) had certainly established, by his revolutionary services, a strong claim to the gratitude of his country. He is the son, also, of one of the finest women the State of Virginia has ever produced. Possessed, in a very eminent degree, of all those qualities, which peculiarly belong to the female character of the

20

South, she is rendered doubly interesting by her meritorious & successful exertions to support, in comfort, a large family, and to give to all her children excellent educations.

"The young gentleman, whom I have now the pleasure of introducing to you, as a candidate for West Point, is her youngest son. An intimate acquaintance, & a constant intercourse with him, almost from his infancy, authorize me to speak in the most unqualified terms of his amiable disposition, & his correct and gentlemanly habits. He is disposed to devote himself to the profession of arms. But his final determination on this subject, must, of course, depend on the result of his present application, and you will find him prepared to acquiesce in whatever decision, circumstances may require you to make in his care. Next, however, to promising him the commission, which he asks, the greatest favor you can do him will be to tell him promptly if you think the obstacles to his success are insurmountable. His own age (eighteen I believe) and the situation of his mother require that he should lose no time in selecting the employment to which his future life is to be devoted.

"Accept, my dear Sir, the assurance of the very great respect with which I am your & C. W. H. Fitzhugh" Based on the recommendations and the merits of his continence he was appointed a cadet at the fabled West Point where he became a legend in regards to his sterling character. (The Gentleman Commander: A Character Portrayal of Robert E. Lee; Bishop, Merrill & Roemer, Joseph; The Economy Company: Oklahoma City; 1936: pages 14-18)

He was accepted into West Point and he graduated from West Point in the year 1829. Upon graduation, Cadet Lee left an impressive record. Not one demerit had he received during his four-year tenure! No wonder he was known as the marble model. He was promoted to cadet adjutant (the highest rank a cadet could obtain while at West Point). In the graduating class of 1829 Lee placed second to a Charles Mason. Mason would later resign his commission and move to Iowa. (Robert E Lee; A Biography; Thomas, Emory M.; W. W. Norton & Company; New York/ London; 1995; pages 51-52)

"He Received No Demerits"

His nephew, General Fitzhugh Lee wrote of his perception on his uncle's tenure at West Point. One can note the pride he possessed for his uncle as well as seeing him as a model of inspiration. Fitzhugh knew that he walked with destiny and he acknowledges that through his acclamations of his uncle. (Life & Letters of Gen. Robert Edward Lee; Jones, W.J.; Sprinkle Publications; Harrisonburg, Virginia; 1986; @ by Neale Publishing Company in 1906; pages 28-29)

"He had now four years of hard study, vigorous drill, and was absorbing strategy and tactics to be useful in after years. His excellent habits and close attention to all duties did not desert him; he received no demerits; was a cadet officer in his class, and during his last year held the post of honor in the aspirations of cadet life-the adjutant of the corps. He graduated second in a class of forty-six, and was commissioned second lieutenant in the Corps of Engineers. It is interesting to note that his eldest son, George Washington Custis Lee, also entered the Military Academy twenty-one years after his father, was also the cadet adjutant, graduated first in his class, and was assigned to the Engineer Corps. During his whole course at West Point, Robert was a model cadet, his clothes looked nice and new, his cross-belts, collar, and summer trousers were as white as the driven snow mounting guard upon the mountain top, and his brass breast and waist plates were mirrors to reflect the image of the inspector. He conscientiously performed his tours of guard duty, whether the non-commissioned officer of the guard was approaching his post or sleeping in his quarters. He never 'ran the sentinel post,' did not go off the limits to the 'Benny Havens' of his day, or put 'dummies' in his bed to deceive the officer in charge as he made his inspection after taps, and at the parades stood steady in line. It was a pleasure for the inspecting officer to look down the barrel of his gun; it was bright and clean, and its stock was rubbed so as to almost resemble polished mahogany." (<u>Life & Letters of Gen. Robert Edward Lee</u>; Jones, W.J.; Sprinkle Publications; Harrisonburg, Virginia; 1986; @ by Neale Publishing Company in 1906; pages 28-29)

"A Superiority That Everyone Acknowledged in His Heart."

Even his classmates and peers marveled at the man of marble. One of them was a man by the name of Joseph Johnston. Joseph was born in Abingdon, Virginia, and was given an appointment to West Point with Robert E. Lee. Joseph would later ride with the Confederacy as a general in his own right. When he was wounded while defending Richmond, Jefferson Davis appointed Lee to replace him. General Johnston remained a life long friend to the Lee family. He said of Lee that: "No other youth or man so united the qualities that win warm friendship and command high respect. For he was full of sympathy and kindness, genial and fond of gay conversation, and even of fun, while his correctness of demeanor and attention to all duties, personal and official, and a dignity as much a part of himself as elegance of his person, gave him a superiority that everyone acknowledged in his heart."

He returned home as a brevet second lieutenant and was assigned to Fort Monroe. But upon returning home young Robert was greeted with the devastating news of his mother's grave declining health. He had been the caregiver of the family as a young child and now that role would befall him for only a brief season. Shortly after Robert came home he lost the lady that he adored. On July 26, 1829, after a gallant life of long battle with frailness his beloved mother passed from this earth. She was only fifty-six years of age.

On June 30, 1831, two years after his graduation, he married his childhood sweetheart, Mary Ann Randolph Custis. She was the daughter of George Washington's adopted grandson, George Washington Parke Custis. She was the biological great granddaughter of Martha Washington. She was born into richness and distinction. She was of strong character, highly intelligent and refined in the ways of lady-like southern charm. The famous Arlington Plantation was where Mary spent her youth and young Robert visited her and the family on different occasions. Mary would become his life long companion and they would have seven children together during their forty-year marriage. Legend has it that Lee proposed to Mary underneath a large tree while she was at her maternal grandfather's plantation known as Chatham Manor (across the Rappahannock River from Fredericksburg) which was an estate previously owned by the family of Mary's mother. The year was 1830. The twenty-three-year-old Lieutenant proposed to the twenty-two-year-old Mary on the West side yard. This hill overlooking the city of Fredericksburg would be the scene of another engagement. Thirty-two years later Lee would be engaged in a major battle. This legend says that he proposed under the same tree that, years later he would search for through his binoculars during the battle of Fredericksburg. (In the Footsteps of Robert E. Lee; Johnson, Clint; John H. Blair Publisher; Winston-Salem, North Carolina; 2001; pages 7-8) The other proposal scenario came while he was visiting the Custis family at Arlington. It stated that Robert Edward proposed to Mary after reading an excerpt from a novel written by Walter Scott to her and his future mother in law. He noted an opportunity when Mary went into the dining room and in the presence of a fruitcake that was on the table; Lee followed the custom of the times and asked for Ms. Mary's hand in marriage. (Robert E. Lee, A Life Portrait; Eicher, David J.; Taylor Trade Publishing; Lanham, New York; 2002; page 15) In any event, the union on June 30, 1831, resulted in a lifelong commitment to one another and their seven children. Their children were named George Washington Custis (after Mary's father), William H. Fitzhugh, Robert Edward Jr., Mary, Agnes, Annie, and Mildred. Custis was born on September 16, 1832, and Mildred was born in the year 1846, equaling approximately 1 child per two-year span of time. Being a devoted father and filled with the joy of parenthood, Lee ordained each child with an affectionate pet name. Both Lee and Mary often referred to their children by the nicknames that had been given to them when corresponding to one another. Custis was called "Boo or "Mr. Boo";

Fitzhugh was known as "Rooney" or "Roon"; and Robert, his name-sake, was called "Rob," "Brutus," or "Robertus." His daughter Mary was known as "Daughter"; Eleanor Agnes was "Wigs"; Anne was "Gentle Annie or Raspberry (reference to her birthmark on her face)"; and Mildred was "Life" or Precious Life." The terms of affection clearly demonstrated the level of love that surrounded the family. (Robert E. Lee, A Biography; Thomas, Emory M.; W.W. Norton & Company; New York-London; 1995; page 145)

All three of his sons would follow the stars and bars during the four-year struggle of state rights and honoring their beliefs. Two of them would become generals and his youngest a captain. His nephew Fitzhugh (the son of Sydney Smith, Lee's brother) was a West Point graduate and served in the cavalry. He had obtained the rank of major general by the end of the war.

His children would later become his greatest legacy and most devoted followers, singing the praises of their father in their writings as well as their individual life. His example set such a standard that his children would hold it up as an example for all to strive for but with the realization that few could obtain that degree of character.

Lee served in the Army Corps of Engineers and directed projects along the Atlantic Coast, Mississippi River, and at New York City's Harbor. During the Mexican War, he was a captain under his mentor and confidant, General Winfield Scott. He also volunteered as a scout, receiving three brevets for bravery under General Scott, who was so impressed with the young officers' abilities that he publicly proclaimed on several occasions that Robert Lee was, "The greatest living soldier in America." He also stated of Lee that, "American success in Mexico was largely due to the skill, valor, and undaunted energy of Robert E. Lee…He was the very best soldier I ever saw in the field." (Jackson & Lee; Legends in Gray; Kunstler, Mort, paintings of; Text by Robertson, James I., Jr.; Rutledge Hill Press; Nashville, Tennessee; 1995; pg 19)

After the Mexican War, he was assigned to Fort Carroll in Baltimore's harbor. Lee was then chosen to be Superintendent of West Point and served in that capacity from 1852-1855. In 1855, Jefferson Davis (holding the position of U. S. Secretary of War) transferred Robert E. Lee to the Cavalry. Lieutenant Colonel Lee was assigned duty in Texas. His service in the West was cut short due to the death of his father-in law and he returned home to Arlington.

In 1859, he was sent to Harper's Ferry with a young cavalier that would become the eyes of his army. His name was JEB Stuart, destined to become one of the greatest cavaliers of all time. After assessing the situation and formulating a plan, John Brown was captured at Harper's Ferry by Lee's soldiers. In 1860, Colonel Lee was again assigned to Texas over the U. S. Army stationed in Texas. As the spirit of war tightened its grip upon the nation, Lee was recalled to Washington. (<u>A Commitment to Valor: A Character Portrait of Robert E. Lee</u>; Gragg, Rod; Rudledge Hill Press; Nashville; 2001)

The dark shadows of war filled the air as officers and enlisted men discussed the looming darkness. As the Angel of Sorrow cast her silhouette upon the land, the states desiring to remain on the side of states rights chose succession and it became apparent that the war was imminent. Lee was torn by the love of his state and the sense of duty toward the army that he served. If not for honor and the defense of his beloved Virginia, Lee may have not drawn his sword against the Union. But his decision would be forthcoming after being offered the highest honor that could be bestowed upon a soldier.

At the onset of the Civil War, Abraham Lincoln offered him the command of the Union army. Montgomery Blair, son of Francis P. Blair stated that the President authorized his father to offer Lee the position as commander of the Union forces. The Honorable Simon Cameron (former Secretary of War expressed in an interview published in the New York Herald that, "It is true that General Robert E. Lee was tendered the command of the Union army. It was the wish of Mr. Lincoln's administration that as many as possible of the Southern officers then in the regular army should remain true to the nation which had educated them. Robert E. Lee and Joseph E. Johnston were then the leading southern soldiers…in the moves and counter moves in the game of war and peace then going on, Francis P. Blair, Sr., was a prominent figure. The tender of the command of the United States forces was made to General Lee through him. Mr. Blair came to me expressing the opinion that General Lee could be held to our cause by the offer of the chief command of our forces. I authorized Mr. Blair to make the offer" (Robert E. Lee Man and Soldier; Page, Thomas Nelson; Charles Scribner's sons; New York; 1926; page 39)

After a long sleepless night consisting of prayer, lamentations of the spirit and much soul searching came the agonizing conclusion that he could not raise his hand against his beloved Virginia. General Lee, now president of Washington College wrote a letter three years after the war addressing the issue of being offered that position. In the correspondence, he puts to rest the question of whether the offer was ever made. It was written to Senator Reverdy Johnson and is dated February 25, 1868. "After listening to his remarks, I declined the offer he made me to take command of the army that was to be brought into the field, stating as candidly and as courteously as I could that, though opposed to secession and deprecating war, I could take no part in an invasion of the Southern States. I went directly from the interview with Mr. Blair to the office of General Scott, told him of the proposition that had been made me and my decision." (Life & Letters of Gen. Robert Edward Lee; Jones, W.J.; Sprinkle Publications; Harrisonburg, Virginia; 1986; @ by Neale Publishing Company in 1906; page 128) He resigned his commission on August 20, 1861, and went to serve in the defense of Old Virginia based on his agonizing conclusion that he could not raise his hand against his beloved state. "I could take no part in an invasion of the Southern states." (Robert E. Lee and the Road of Honor; Carter, Hodding; Randon House; New York; 1955)

During the first year of the war, he served in Western Virginia and South Carolina. Due to several factors, his campaign in the western portion of Virginia (now West Virginia) was considered a failure and the politicians around Richmond referred to him as 'Evacuating Lee'. Although the failure was not his burden to bear, he nevertheless took full responsibility for the lack of the campaign's success. He was called to Richmond and became the military advisor to President Davis. Because of the wounding of Joseph E. Johnston, Lee given the command of the army. General Lee stopped McClellan's advance on Richmond, defeated Pope at Second Manassas, and went on to Antietam, where the bloodiest battle of the war occurred up to that point. He led his men in the ignominious victory against General Burnside at Fredericksburg. A literal shattering of General Hooker's army at Chancellorsville followed a short time later. All this built upon the legend of Lee. But during that struggle in May of 1863, he lost what he referred to as his right arm of his army; General Stonewall Jackson was mortally wounded. A few weeks later at Gettysburg, his loss was evident and the turning of the tide began for the Confederacy. Though his actions after that battle of Gettysburg were primarily defensive in nature, he continued fighting and winning against overwhelming odds. When Grant broke the siege of Petersburg, Lee was forced to leave Richmond and try to regroup but was surrounded at Appomattox. After a brilliant performance of cat and mouse, he surrendered his Army of Northern Virginia and the cause to General Grant on April 9, 1865, within the now hallowed parlor of the McLean House. (Lee and Grant at Appomattox; Kantor, MacKinlay; Randon House; New York; 1950)

For a brief period of time, he was unemployed. Though offered several lucrative employment opportunities (he was even offered an estate in England to escape the ravishes of postwar), he graciously declined the offers, instead choosing to endure the same fate as his beloved boys. Upon hearing of Lee and his plight, the Board of Directors of Washington College voted to make him the next president. At first he was reluctant to accept the position but was convinced by friends and those interested in his leadership that he could do more through education in helping rebuild the nation than by setting in an exile state. The general did possess the expertise and experience to hold that office. He had held the position of Superintendent of West Point for four years and his numerous other educational qualities really made him overqualified, as some suggested. But the greatness of the man shown through as given in a testimonial by Bishop Wilmer (delivered at the University of the South, Sewanee, Tennessee on the death of Lee) as documented by Robert E. Lee Jr.:

"I was seated at the close of the day, in my Virginia home, when I beheld, through the thickening shades of evening, a horseman entering the yard, whom I soon recognized as General Lee. The next morning he placed in my hands the correspondence with the authorities of Washington College at Lexington. He had been invited to become president of that institution. I confess to a momentary feeling of chagrin at the proposed change (shall I say revulsion?) in his history. The institution was one of local interest, and comparatively unknown to our people. I named others more conspicuous which would welcome him with ardour at the presiding head. I soon discovered that his mind towered above these earthly distinctions; that, in his judgment, the CAUSE gave dignity to the institution, and not the wealth of its endowment or the renown of its scholars; that this door and not another was opened to him by Providence, and he only wished to be assured of his competency to fulfill his trust and this to make his few remaining years a comfort and blessing to his suffering country. I had spoken to his human feelings; he had now revealed himself to me as one 'whose life was hid with Christ in God.' My speech was no longer restrained. I congratulated him that his heart was inclined to this great cause, and that he was prepared to give to the world this august testimony to the importance of Christian education. How he listened to my feeble words; how he beckoned me to his side, as the fullness of heart found utterance; how his whole countenance glowed with animation as I spoke of the Holy Ghost as the great Teacher, whose presence was required to make education a blessing, which otherwise might be the curse of mankind; how feelingly he responded, how ELOQUENTLY, as I never heard him speak before--can never be effaced from memory; and nothing more sacred mingles with my reminiscences of the dead."

Another individual that keenly sought Lee's leadership was Judge Brockenbrough. He was actively involved in the committee that appointed Lee to that position. In a letter addressed to the former commander of the Confederacy, he reassured Lee that his name would only help the floundering institution of higher education. He stated concisely the drawing power that Lee would have in the fight for the preservation of the school. He simply stated, "You have only to stretch forth your powerful arm to rescue it…you alone can fill its halls, by attracting to them not the youth of Virginia alone but of all the Southern and some even of the Northern States." And their destinies were intertwined…

"It Was Most Uninviting"

32

A Professor of Washington College by the name of Edward Joynes added even more to the legend by his penning of his thoughts regarding Lee's acceptance and leadership of that institution. The wondering of why he accepted a position with such a run down obscure college confounded the doctor. Dr. Joynes's notions are captured in the reflections and writings of William J. Jones. (Personal Reminiscences, Anecdotes, and Letters of General Robert E. Lee; Jones, J. William; Appleton; New York; 1875; pages 197-198)

"There was absolutely nothing in this position that could have tempted him. Not only was it uncongenial with all the habits of his past life, and remote from all the associations in which he had formally taken pleasure, but it was, at that time, most uninviting in itself. The college to which he was called was broken in fortune and in hope. The war had practically closed its doors. Its buildings had been pillaged and defaced, and its library scattered. It had now neither money nor credit, and it was even doubtful whether it would be shortly reopened at all for the reception of students. The Faculty were few in number, disorganized, and dispirited...Under these circumstances the offer of the presidency to General Lee was well nigh presumptuous; and surely it was an offer from which he had nothing to expect either of fortune or fame."

"Of Quiet Usefulness Gentle Patriotism"

But it was probably the advisement given by William Nelson Pendleton, his chief of artillery during the war that carried the most weight and offered the final persuasion. The former general of his artillery, who was also an Episcopal priest, strongly beckoned him to the hills of the valley surrounding the fledgling town. He conveyed his thoughts upon the subject via the following oratory.

"I have thought Dear General while thus doing an important service to the State & the people you might be presenting to the world in such position an example of quiet usefulness gentle patriotism, no less impressive than the illustrious career in the field." It was settled. Lee would take the presidency of a little college ravaged by war and at the brink of financial ruin. What a difference his leadership would make.

PRESIDENT LEE

Captain Robert E. Lee Jr. (son of Lee) also recalls in his book a detailed description of General Lee's four-day journey to Washington College. In it he states: "In the latter part of September, he mounted Traveller and started alone for Lexington. He was four days on the journey, stopping with some friend each night. He rode into Lexington on the afternoon of the fourth day, no one knowing of his coming until he quietly drew up and dismounted at the village inn. Professor White, who had just turned into the main street as the General halted in front of the hotel, said he knew in a moment that this stately rider on the iron-gray charger must be General Lee. He, therefore, at once went forward, as two or three old soldiers gathered around to help the General down, and insisted on taking him to the home of Colonel Reid, the professor's father-in-law, where he had already been invited to stay. My father, with his usual consideration of others, as it was late in the afternoon, had determined to remain at the hotel that night and go to Mr. Reid's in the morning; but yielding to Captain White's (he always called him Captain, his Confederate title) assurances that all was made ready for him, he accompanied him to the home of his kind host." (Recollections and Letter of Robert E. Lee; Lee, Robert E. Captain; Doubleday, Doran, and Company; 1904, 1924) "Uncle Robert" took a brief well-earned trip to Rockbridge Baths (a hot spring resort) and returned on October 2, 1865. He was taken to a building known as the South Hall to receive the oath of office. Per a reporter from the New York Herald, Lee was, "dressed in a plain but elegant suit of gray" stripped of his rank. They opened their ceremony with a prayer, including a prayer for the President of the United States. Squire William White, the Justice of the Rockbridge

County Court administered the oath and offered the keys to the college to him. He signed two major documents on that day. One was the copy of the oath that he had just taken and the other was the oath of allegiance to the United States. Ironically, it ended up in the hands of William H. Seward (Secretary of State) and somehow it was not recorded but given to a friend as a souvenir. One hundred five years later it was discovered in a group of papers in the National Archives. (<u>Lee, The Last Years</u>; Flood, Charles Bracelen; Houghton Mifflin Company; New York; 1981; pages 98-100)

President Lee was very involved in all aspects of the college, from the refurbishment of the dilapidated buildings (from the war-torn ravages of General Hunter's raid) to redesigning the curriculum. Under his leadership, the institution blossomed, increasing drastically in enrollment and credibility. As the college flourished, the Board voted to raise President Lee's salary but he thanked them and declined the offer, stating that his present salary was enough.

When he was not busy with the affairs of the college, Marsh Robert could be seen riding his favorite companion through the beautiful valleys surrounding Lexington. Wherever he rode, his loyal followers would be beckoned to the area just to glimpse upon the legend that rode amongst them. Their idol and hero would tip his hat and always have a kind word to his faithful followers. These were indeed the happy days, those days of autumn in his life.

He always had a kind word about his boys. Although he never called them that in public, his demeanor towards his students has been likened unto a father to his children. He worried about them. He visited with them every chance that he had. He would check on each of their progress and talk to them in a fatherly fashion. In every aspect of the definition, Lee was a teacher. All sought the praise of Lee and shunned his discipline. His words of encouragement are evident by all that were honored to be under him as a president of a college. One man remembered vividly the manner of Lee. His name was Doctor T. Ashley.

The following description of Lee as President of Washington College was written by Dr. T. Ashley, a former student. His portrait of Marse Robert uncannily reveals the true nature of the man and offers insight into the humorous side of Lee. He begins his narrative with a small historical overview of the character of Lee and ends with personal antidotes that will bring a smile to the reader as they see the child within the man. Lee was truly a humble person that loved his boys and admired the girls. He is a man that we should all attempt to walk within his footsteps. (General R.E. Lee as a College President; Ashley, T.; Confederate Veteran; Volume XIII; No.8; Nashville, Tennessee; August, 1905)

"Almost every side of Gen. Lee's life work and character has been written upon by the historian. But little can be said about him as a soldier and citizen except in the nature of a personal reminiscence. I much doubt whether Gen. Lee's ability and renown as a soldier are more deserving of praise and admiration than his simple, natural, and inspiring life as a college president. In the larger and more renowned field of action as a soldier he exhibited all the ability and manliness of the hero and warrior. In the discharge of the quiet duties of a college president he manifested that sweetness, charm, and simplicity of character which only a great and noble soul can possess. As the leader of a great army, the pride and support of a great cause, he was no greater a man than when he undertook to guide the educational training of a small band of young men who gathered around him for instruction in the arts of peace. It will be recalled that after the surrender at Appomattox Gen. Lee was left without an occupation and almost without the means of support for himself and family. His property had been almost entirely swept away by war and confiscation. He was in the fifty-ninth year of his age and without training, except as a soldier. A number of propositions came to him, offering him positions with remunerative salaries for the use of his name and influence. He promptly rejected every suggestion looking to the improvement of his fortune through business ventures.

"On the 4th of August, 1865, the trustees of Washington College, located at Lexington, Va., elected him to the presidency of that institution. This college endowed by Washington and named after him, was at that time a school with only a local reputation and a small endowment. It enjoyed an honorable name and a favorable position in the rich Valley of Virginia. The selection of Gen. Lee as its President was a happy stroke of fortune for the college, and gave great satisfaction to Gen. Lee as well. The position and the surrounding circumstances were in harmony. Gen. Lee at once saw an opportunity to round out the closing years of his life in a work which would gratify his pride and result in advantage to the youth of the South. He recognized that his influence in such a position would do more to reestablish confidence among the Southern people and to restore their pride and loyalty toward constitutional government than any course of action he could take. With that firm but quiet resolution which was the foundation of his true greatness, he entered upon the duties of President in October, 1865. He began the work of reorganizing the college in all of its departments at once, and when the college session opened students from all over the South and a few from the North and Northwest flocked to the institution. In the first class, perhaps as many as twenty-five per cent of the students had been old soldiers who had carried a musket or held a commission in the Confederate army. A colonel, several majors, and a half dozen captains and lieutenants, besides numerous sergeants, corporals, and privates, made haste to enroll under President Lee as students of literature, science, and law.

"Never, perhaps, in the history of any institution in the world did such classes of young men assemble for an educational training. Most the students who had not carried arms in the Confederate service had seen war as boys under trying circumstances. The young men of the South under age to bear arms were for four years practically without school training. Many of them had been at work on farms and in factories, or were growing up in a training school of excitement and danger that poorly prepared them for college discipline.

"Indiscretions Brought Pain to the Heart of Our Noble President"

"When I entered Washington College, in February, 1867, I found an undisciplined and raw crowd of college classmates. Many of them, like myself, had seen war from the boy's standpoint in its most thrilling and exciting aspects. We had been in battle and on the firing line, and yet had not carried a musket or fired a shot at the enemy. We were only waiting for the age limit, when we would be better material for shot. Many of our friends and relatives, only a year or two older than ourselves, had enlisted in service and had found soldiers' graves. As rough, uncouth, and poorly trained as this class of young students were, they were almost without exception the sons of Southern gentlemen and boys of pride, ambition, and spirit. Many of them had made great sacrifices to obtain college training under "Marse Robert," as he was affectionately called. They were with few exceptions, industrious, earnest students, in each of whom Gen. Lee took the warmest personal interest. I recall many incidents which show the solicitude and anxiety of Gen. Lee over this large class of young men who had gathered around him. At times we were a wild and excitable crowd of youths. War and race prejudice still ran high and more than once some of our number were guilty of indiscretions that brought pain to the heart of our noble President. As much as we loved and admired him, as a student body there were among our number a few individuals that the most rigid discipline could not at all times hold in check. But retributive justice was sure to overtake the offender of college authority when he came into the presence and under the piercing eye of Gen. Lee. He was at once either subdued by his benevolence and fatherly tenderness or returned to his parents at home. No student could riot long or waste his time in idleness under Gen. Lee's observation. His sins were sure to find him out, and he either yielded to the superior influences exerted over him or ceased to be a member of our student body.

"Each year from October, 1865, to 1870 (the year of Gen. Lee's death) the class of students increased in number and in character. Crude and untrained boys were soon molded into educated and cultivated men. The corps of professors,

40

associates, and instructors was enlarged to meet the requirements of the students. College buildings, laboratories, and an endowment were rapidly built up under Gen. Lee's leadership. I know of no institution in this country which began with so little that accomplished so much in four years' time. Gen. Lee's death came in the midst of this great up building. He had set in motion an influence which extended far beyond the walls of the college. I refer to the influence exerted over the young men who became his students and over the people of the South, whose eyes were ever on him. He taught all the value of character, the simplicity and nobility of life, and the highest duties of citizenship.

"No student could come in contact with Gen. Lee without absorbing the influence of his personality. It is safe to say that he knew nearly every student in college by name, the character of his work, and his conduct. He corresponded regularly with the parents or guardians of every student. He sought by every method to stimulate the best thought and work, and to promote the moral as well as intellectual training of those under him.

"Did You Not Bring the Photographs of the Young Ladies?"

"To show his personal relations with the student, I shall mention a few incidents of a personal nature. Upon the occasion of my first meeting with him, February 2, 1867, the day after I entered college, I handed him a letter of introduction from my father. With a cordial shake of the hand and a personal reference to my family, he remarked: "I wish you to make as good a record at college as your namesake made in the army." On another occasion, a few weeks later, I carried to him a half dozen of his photographs for his autograph. He remarked: "Why did you bring these ugly pictures to me?" I replied that some young lady friends had requested me to send them his photograph with his autograph attached. "Why," said he, "did you not bring the photographs of the young ladies? I would much prefer to see them." He then turned to a cabinet and drew out his photograph with his autograph attached and presented it to me, with the remark that it was a better likeness than the one shown in the photographs I had brought to him. It is needless to say that I still value this photograph above all of my treasures. Upon other occasions when I had to call at the President's office he invariably inquired after the young ladies, and made some pleasant remarks that removed all embarrassment and made me feel his friendly interest in me.

"This is a Good Day for Ducks"

"Upon a rainy, muddy day I happened to meet him on the path leading from the college to his residence. We were alone. He halted me in the rain, inquired after my friends at home, wished to know how I was getting along with my work, and then suddenly changed the subject of the conversation with the remark: 'This is a good day for ducks. Good-by.' I happened to meet him on another afternoon, when it was as rainy and as wet under foot as one could imagine. My roommate and I had ridden horseback that day to the Natural Bridge and back, a distance each way of fourteen miles. The road was muddy, the horses were bad, and we were drenched in water and covered with mud. As we were returning from the livery stable in the town to our room in the college we met Gen. Lee face to face on the sidewalk he noticed at once our mud-stained appearance, and halted us. I thought that we would be rebuked for some violation of college rules. But he pleasantly remarked: "Where have you young men been to-day?" We replied: "We have been out to see the Natural Bridge for the first time." He said: "Did you walk out or ride out?" Our reply was "We rode out, of course, General." "Ah!" said he. "You should have walked out; it is such a fine day for marching."

"Whilst I Give Three Cheers"

"I might mention numerous incidents of this character, showing his pleasant humor and friendly interest in the student. I may be pardoned for relating an anecdote, perhaps known to many, which Gen. Lee told on himself. It so fully illustrates his quiet humor that it will hear many repetitions. On one occasion when Gen. Lee was riding along the road alone he met an old Confederate soldier on foot. The old veteran addressed the General, and remarked to him that he had one request to make of him; would he grant it? Gen. Lee replied that he would gladly grant any request within his power to an old soldier. The old veteran then said: "I wish you to dismount from your horse whilst I give three cheers for Gen. Lee." Accordingly, Gen. Lee dismounted, and in the public highway, with no one present but the two, the old private gave three long and loud cheers for his chief. The conditions were complied with, to the joy of the old soldier, and the General remounted and rode away. Could any scene be more touching and pathetic, and at the same time so full of genuine humor?

"Gen. Lee's interest in the moral as well as intellectual training of the student was manifested in many ways. He was a regular attendant upon the religious services conducted in the chapel every morning, and by his example encouraged the students to attend these religious exercises. He took a deep interest in the Young Men's Christian Association, and in all the college societies that tended to promote the morals and culture of the student. Violations of college discipline, evidences of bad conduct, and neglect of study upon the part of any student were sure to call from him a reprimand or suggestion which the offender was not likely to forget.

"Upon one occasion I was an innocent victim of one of his admonitions, which I have remembered since with great discomfort. One of the college rules forbade the students playing baseball during recitation hours on the college campus. This rule was frequently broken during Gen. Lee's absence from his office in the college building. The time selected was when he had gone home for his dinner. At such a time a few of the boys with ball and bat would exercise with the same. A student was usually posted to give the alarm on the appearance of Gen. Lee. On one warm day in June a few boys were batting and catching ball while the General was at dinner. The boys had failed to post a sentinel, and Gen. Lee made his appearance in an unexpected manner. As soon as his presence was known the offenders ran to hide in the college building. Gen. Lee followed them in their retreat. It happened that I had been in the rear of the building, and as I came out of the hall onto the portico I met Gen. Lee face to face. The day was exceedingly warm, and I was in my shirt sleeves. I was not aware that the boys were in hiding for breaking rules. I was at once taken by the General for one of the offenders. Calling me by name, he asked if I did not know it was a violation of college rules to play ball during recitation hours. In my embarrassment I pleaded that I had not been playing ball. The circumstantial evidence was against me. I have always felt that my answer was doubted; but the noble old gentleman simply remarked that the boys must not violate this rule, and then walked away. I was too stunned to think, and did not realize my position until some of the offenders had come from out of their hiding places and made the situation plain to me. During the remainder of my college life I was always careful when I ventured on the campus in my shirt sleeves.

"Gen. Lee was one of the most modest as well as one of the most diffident of men. Notoriety and applause were not only distasteful but painful to him. On commencement or public occasions he avoided publicity, and was embarrassed by remarks which referred to him in any way in person. He disliked display and ostentation of manner and speech. Whilst his heart was said to have been broken by the results of the war, he had the faculty of concealing his feelings to a degree seldom equaled. He was less emotional than any human being I ever saw, and yet possessed the most gentle and sympathetic nature. I never saw him smile or frown. The expression of his face was as calm and placid as a child's. His features were noble, his eyes soft and benevolent, but piercing, and expressive of both thought and feeling. He could express with his eyes an authority and command which volumes of words could not convey. His voice was soft and gentle, and seldom raised above a whisper, but with sound so clear and distinct that every word was clearly heard. His influence over those thrown in his presence was magnetic. His poise, expression, and bearing commanded respect and exercised an authority which no one dared to deny in his presence. The great secret of his character was its simplicity and manliness. He seemed to tower above the heads of every one by nobility of mind and heart, which created the feeling that greatness was personified in him.

"Whether on foot or horse, he looked the soldier that he was. Except on rare occasions, he wore the Confederate gray uniform without its trimmings and brass buttons. When mounted on Traveler, his old war horse, he wore high-top boots, which gave him a military bearing never to be forgotten by those who had seen him at the head of the army. He was devotedly attached to Traveler, and the horse and the man seemed to be made for each other---the one proud of the other---and inseparable in spirit and noble bearing.   Art has tried to represent these two noble specimens of the man and of the horse as they appeared in life, yet all that the genius of the artist could do was to present forms and colorings. The life and pride of spirit can never be shown on canvas as they are recalled by eyes which saw the reality. In good weather Gen. Lee rode Traveler almost daily. The exercise was beneficial to both, now growing old in years as well as in service. When death came to Gen. Lee, Traveler was not long in following his old master.

"I have only touched upon a few of the many impressions made upon a student by the greatest of all college presidents.   Years have rapidly passed by, and the students of Gen. Lee's day are growing fewer and fewer. Those of us who remain still recall the noble influence he exercised over our lives."

"You Make Three Other Mistakes"

Thomas N. Page made an interesting observation while a student at Washington College. The old gentleman did not like the rhetoric of the young men's speeches and tries to discourage their fanfare. Mr. Page would later discuss this in more detail in a book written about his hero.

"It was occasionally the habit of the young orators who spoke in public at celebrations to express their feelings by indulging in compliments to General Lee and their ladies, and the reverse of compliments to 'the Yankees.' Such references, clad in the glowing rhetoric and informed with the deep feeling of youthful oratory, never failed to stir their audiences and evoke unstinted applause. General Lee however, notified the speakers that such references were to be omitted. He said: "You young men speak too long, and you make three other mistakes: what you say about me is distasteful to me; what you say about the North tends to promote ill feeling and injure the institution, and your compliments to the ladies are much more valued when paid in private than in public."

"His Health Progressively Worsened"

While serving in this capacity, his health (he actually never fully recovered from his illness he acquired during the war) progressively worsened. But being true to his nature, he nevertheless continued until his doctors ordered him to rest and suggested a trip to Florida. He consented but found that as he traveled word of his arrival swept the countryside and at every depot, his loyal supporters were waiting. Some shouted, some cried, some wanted to show their children the man that they were named after and some sobbed unashamed at seeing their general for what they knew would be the last time. Such was his charisma and charm. The trip did not aid in his rejuvenation as hoped and he returned home to Lexington, Virginia. On the 28th of September, the ailing president and general attended a vestry meeting at Grace Church. The day was drab with a dampness that chilled the bones. As they discussed the affairs of the church, an issue of money to pay the Reverend Pendleton (former Commander of Lee's artillery) was addressed. The sum gathered was fifty dollars short of the amount desired by Reverend Pendleton. Being the man that he was, President Lee simply stated, "I will give that sum," and the meeting ended. As he walked reflectively to his home, the coldness of the evening must have made him shiver. Upon arriving and hanging his coat, he found that his family was seated at the dinner table awaiting his arrival. The time was 7:00. The exhausted general took his customary place at the head of the table and bowed his head to offer thanks and say grace to the Giver of the Feast. With an unspoken prayer upon his lips, to the dismay of his loved ones, he suddenly sank to the floor. His condition was so bad that the physician would not allow him to be moved from the couch. For two weeks, he barely clung to life, drifting in and out of awareness. On October 12th for the briefest of seconds, he rallied himself and called out, "Tell Hill he must come up!" and shortly thereafter uttered in peaceful tranquility, "Strike the tent!" before relenting to the sweet surrender of a new dawning. And the darkness of the storm-filled night brought the purification of the morning sunrise.

Our beloved general died on October 12, 1870, from complications of the heart (angina pectoris). One cannot doubt that his sorrow, remorse for his people and the self-sacrificing manner of the man contributed to his early demise. This author feels that his death may have been a direct result of all the stress creating a blockage of the coronary arteries; a broken heart not only for the lost cause but also for the men that he loved so well and one can never rule out that the general simply grieved himself to death. This fielder finds it befitting the mood that a record rain occurred during the period of transition. A total of fourteen inches fell within a thirty-six-hour period creating one of the worst, if not the worst flood in that area since weather data keeping had begun. On Wednesday morning, the sun finally broke through the forbidding horizon possibly signifying that a warrior had made it home.

In his book, Stanley F. Horn quotes a beautiful passage that was written by one who witnessed the chieftain's last battle. It captures the last fitting tribute to this man of dignity, courage, and character. The passage states, "As the old hero lay in the darkened room, or with the lamp and hearth-fire casting shadows upon his calm, noble front, all the massive grandeur of his form and face and brow remained; and death seemed to lose its terrors and to borrow a grace and dignity in sublime keeping with the life that was ebbing away." (The Boys' Life of Robert E. Lee; Horn, Stanley F.; Harper Brothers Publishers; New York and London; 1935; pg. 324)

On October 12, 1870, Fitzhugh and Robert E. Lee Jr. were on their way to their father's side when they received word of his passing. In his book, Recollections and Letters of Robert E. Lee, General Lee's namesake states that his father passed into the tranquility of the twilight through the following descriptive portal written by Colonel William Preston Johnston, an eyewitness of the general's last hours. (Personal Reminiscences of General Robert E. Lee; Jones, J. William; 1874)

"General Lee returned to his house, and finding his family waiting tea for him, took his place at the table, standing to say grace. The effort was valid;

the lips could not utter the prayer of the heart. Finding himself unable to speak, he took his seat quietly and without agitation. His face seemed to some of the anxious group about him to wear a look of sublime resignation, and to evince a full knowledge that the hour had come when all the cares and anxieties of his crowded life were at an end. His physicians, Doctors H. S. Barton, and R. L. Madison, arrived promptly, applied the usual remedies, and placed him upon the couch from which he was to rise no more.

"To him henceforth the things of this world were as nothing, and he bowed with resignation to the command of the Master he had followed so long with reverence. The symptoms of his attack resembled concussion of the brain, without the attendant swoon. There was marked debility, a slightly impaired consciousness, and a tendency to doze; but no paralysis of motion or sensation, and no evidence of suffering or inflammation of the brain. His physicians treated the case as one of venous congestion, and with apparently favourable results. Yet, despite these propitious auguries drawn from his physical symptoms, in view of the great mental strain he had undergone, the gravest fears were felt that the attack was mortal. He took without objection the medicines and diet prescribed, and was strong enough to turn in bed without aid, and to sit up to take nourishment. During the earlier days of his illness, though inclined to doze, he was easily aroused, was quite conscious and observant, evidently understood whatever was said to him, and answered questions briefly but intelligently; he was, however, averse to much speaking, generally using monosyllables, as had always been his habit when sick.

"On October 10th, during the afternoon, his pulse became feeble and rapid, and his breathing hurried, with other evidences of great exhaustion. About midnight he was seized with a shivering from extreme debility, and Doctor Barton was obliged to announce the danger to the family. On October 11th, he was evidently sinking; his respiration was hurried, his pulse feeble and rapid. Though less observant, he still recognized whoever approached him but refused to take anything unless prescribed by his physicians. It now became certain that the case was hopeless. His decline of October 12, he closed his eyes, and his soul passed peacefully from earth.

"General Lee's closing hours were consonant with his noble and disciplined life. Never was more beautifully displayed how a long and severe education of mind and character enables the soul to pass with equal step through this supreme ordeal; never did the habits and qualities of a lifetime, solemnly gathered into a few last sad hours, more grandly maintain themselves amid the gloom and shadow of approaching death. The reticence, the self-contained composure, the obedience to proper authority, the magnanimity, and the Christian meekness, that marked all his actions, still preserved their sway, in spite of the inroads of disease and creeping lethargy that weighted down his faculties." (Recollections and Letters of Robert E. Lee; Lee, Robert E. Captain; Doubleday, Doran and Company; 1904, 1924;)

The general planned to write his memoirs but most of his notes had been destroyed or confiscated after the war. He had corresponded with his generals for their input but for some reason, the book on the history of the Army of Northern Virginia was never written. He did put to pen an introduction of his father's book, "Memoirs of the War of '76 in the Southern States" as his only publication. But this was probably enough for Lee as a son paying tribute to his father that he idolized. (The Boys' Life of Robert E. Lee; Horn, Stanley F.; Harper Brothers Publishers; New York and London; 1935) This raises the question of what the great general might have expressed, how much bearing and influence his work would have on the interpretation of the Civil War. But he chose to say nothing except in his letters. This question will never be resolved, only contemplated...

Lee served as president of what is now known as Washington and Lee College until his death in 1870. At the time of his presidency, Washington and Lee consisted of four professors and around forty students. His salary was $1500 a year. (R. E. Lee, a Biography; Freeman Douglas Southall; four-volume; New York; Scribner; 1934-35)

One hundred and five years after his passing, the United States Congress saw fit to right a wrong committed against this noble American. Senator Harry Flood Byrd Jr. of Virginia introduced a bill with the purpose of restoring Posthumously Full rights of Citizenship to General R. E. Lee. (Second Session of the Ninety-Third Congress the Senate Joint Resolution 189) President Gerald R. Ford signed the bill on August 5, 1975. This great American hero can now rest with the prize his heart desired next to Godliness and honor: that of regaining his citizenship!

IMPRESSIONS OΓ LEE

The following documentations are the actual words of those individuals that had the privilege of having direct contact with the man called Lee. Some of those are biased family members; friends that paint a portrait of grace and elegance but the most impressive are those that were his adversaries. But all salute the man of marble and pay homage to his Christian character, his devotion to duty, the honor that he valued more than riches or fame and his persona as a human being. What better eulogy than the following for any person. Dear reader, I present for your consideration, the impressions of Lee.

"No Tickling, No Story!"

In his book, Robert E. Lee's son portrays him as a man of exceptional character. His mutual respect and admiration honors the memory of the man that so many followed unquestionably. His pride in his father is evident as the excerpts ascertain. (Recollections and Letter of Robert E. Lee; Lee, Robert E. Jr. Captain; Doubleday, Doran, and Company; 1904,1924)

"From that early time I began to be impressed with my father's character, as compared with other men. Every member of the household respected, revered and loved him as a matter of course, but it began to dawn on me that every one else with whom I was thrown held him high in their regard. At forty-five years of age he was active, strong, as handsome as he had ever been. I never remember his being ill. I presume he was indisposed at times; but no impressions of that kind remain. He was always bright and gay with us little folk, romping, playing, and joking with us. With the older children, he was just as companionable, and they have seen him join my elder brothers and their friends when they would try their powers at a high jump put up in our yard. The two younger children he petted a great deal, and our greatest treat was to get into his bed in the morning and lie close to him, listening while he talked to us in his bright, entertaining way. This custom we kept up until I was ten years old and over. Although he was so joyous and familiar with us, he was very firm on all proper occasions, never indulged us in anything that was not good for us, and exacted the most implicit obedience. I always knew that it was impossible to disobey my father. I felt it in me, I never thought why, but was perfectly sure when he gave an order that it to be obeyed. My mother I could sometimes circumvent, and at times took liberties with her orders, construing them to suit myself; but exact obedience to every mandate of my father was part of my life and being at that time. He was very fond of having his hands tickled, and what was still more curious, it pleased and delighted him to take off his slippers and place his feet in our laps in order to have them tickled. Often, as little things, after romping all day, the enforced sitting would be too much for us, and our drowsiness would soon show itself in continued nods. Then, to arouse us, he had a way of stirring us up with his foot—laughing heartily at and with us. He would often tell us the most delightful stories, and then there was no nodding. Sometimes, however, our interest in his wonderful tales became so engrossing that we would forget to do our duty—when he would declare, 'No tickling, no story!' When we were a little older, our elder sister told us one winter the ever-delightful 'Lady of the Lake.' Of course, she told it in a prose and arranged it to suit our mental capacity. Our father was generally in his corner by the fire, most probably with a foot in either lap of myself or youngest sister—the tickling going on briskly—and would come in at different points of the tale and repeat line after line of the poem—much to our disapproval—but to his great enjoyment.

"In Baltimore, I went to my first school, that of a Mr. Rollins on Mulberry Street, and I remember how interested my father was in my studies, my failures, and my little triumphs. Indeed, he was so always, as long as I was at school and college, and I only wish that all of the kind, sensible, useful letters he wrote me had been preserved.

"My memory as to the move from Baltimore, which occurred in 1852, is very dim. I think the family went to Arlington to remain until my father had arranged for our removal to the new home at West Point.

"My recollection of my father as Superintendent of the West Point Military Academy is much more distinct. He lived in the house which is still occupied by the Superintendent. It was built of stone, large and roomy, with gardens, stables, and pasture lots. We, the two youngest children, enjoyed it all. 'Grace Darling' and 'Santa Anna' were there with us, and many a fine ride did I have with my father in the afternoons, when, released from his office, he would mount his old mare and, with Santa Anna carrying me by his side, take a five or ten-mile trot. Though the pony cantered delightfully, he would make me keep him in a trot, saying playfully that the hammering sustained was good for me. We rode the dragoon—seat no posting, and until I became accustomed to it I used to be very tired by the time I got back.

"My father was the most punctual man I ever knew. He was always ready for family prayers, for meals, and met every engagement, social or business, now. He expected all of us to be the same, and taught us the use and necessity of forming such habits for the convenience of all concerned. I never knew him late for Sunday service at the Post Chapel. He used to appear some minutes before the rest of us, in uniform, jokingly rallying my mother for being late, and for forgetting something at the last moment. When he could wait no longer for her, he would say that he was off and would march along to church by himself, or with any of the children who were ready. There he sat very straight—well up the middle aisle—and, as I remember, always became very sleepy, and sometimes even took a little nap during the sermon. At that time, the drowsiness of my father was something awful to me, inexplicable. I know it was very hard for me to keep awake, and frequently I did not; but when he, who to my mind could do everything right, without any effort, should sometimes be overcome, I could not understand, and did not try to do so.

"My father always encouraged me in every healthy outdoor exercise and sport. He taught me to ride, constantly giving me minute instructions, with the reasons for them. He gave me my first sled, and sometimes used to come out where we boys were coasting to look on. He gave me my first pair of skates, and placed me in the care of a trustworthy person, inquiring regularly how I progressed. It was the same with swimming, which he was very anxious I should learn in a proper manner. Professor Bailey had a son about my age, now himself a professor at Brown University, Providence, Rhode Island, who became my great chum. I took my first lesson in the water with him, under the direction and supervision of his father. My father inquired constantly how I was getting along, and made me describe exactly my method and stroke, explaining to me what he considered the best way to swim, and the reasons therefor.

"I went to day-school at West Point, and had always a sympathetic helper in my father. Often he would come into the room where I studied at night, and, sitting down by me, would show me how to overcome a hard sentence in my Latin reader or a difficult sum in arithmetic, not by giving me the translation of the troublesome sentence or the answer to the sum, but by showing me, step by step, the way to the right solutions. He was very patient, very loving, very good to me, and I remember trying my best to please him in my studies. When I was able to bring home a good report from my teacher, he was greatly pleased, and showed it in his eyes and voice, but he always insisted that I should get the 'maximum' that he would never be satisfied with less. That I did sometimes win it, deservedly, I know was due to his judicious and wise method of exciting my ambition and perseverance..."

"Curly"

In May of 1852, Lee received orders to report to West Point as the ninth Superintendent of that institution. He respectfully protested stating that there were abler men (as he would later state during the war) but it fell upon deaf ears. He and his family left Baltimore (he had been stationed there since 1848) on August 23 and became the superintendent of that prestigious military academy on September 1, 1852. He served in that capacity until March 31, 1855. As in all of his endeavors, he became quite active in making changes to better address the needs of the cadets both in the academic curriculum and discipline. To Lee discipline meant self-denial and obedience to the will of God and then man. Since he believed that he must lead by Christian example, one of the first things that he desired was to become confirmed within the Episcopal Church. He had grown up in the church and idealized the Reverend William Meade, his priest during his formative years. He rectified this on July 17, 1853, when he and two of his daughters sought and received confirmation.

Superintendent Lee was acutely aware of the need for discipline and order among his cadets. One of the stories that come to mind is of a young man that was known as "Curly". Although extremely talented in the field of art, he did not like the academics and soon began accumulating demerits. The superintendent patiently tried to guide the young boy but he continued down the path and had to be discharged from the academy. He later became internationally known for his artwork and when he reflected upon his days at West Point, he was always gracious in talking of the kindness of Lee. His name was McNeil Whistler, best known for his portrait entitled, "Whistler's Mother".

"If We Were All Like You"

Superintendent Lee believed that discipline had to be just, consistent but always fair. A rather large young man from New York by the name of Archibald Gracie Jr. had a tendency to use his size to bully smaller cadets. While on dress parade he began taunting Wharton Green, a smaller boy in stature but unbeknownst to Cadet Gracie possessed with a tenacity of spirit. Containing himself no longer, the smaller boy began fighting the larger Gracie and to Cadet Gracie's shock, was thoroughly whipped by the young cadet. When an adult came to intercede, Cadet Green slipped into the ranks and Gracie refused to tell with whom he had been brawling. Cadet Gracie was immediately arrested and when the superintendent was reviewing the charges, Cadet Green went to his office. Upon gaining an audience, he confessed to Lee that it had been he that had fought with Gracie.

"Colonel Lee, Mr. Gracie was yesterday reported for fighting on the parade ground, and the other fellow was not." "Yes sir, and I presume you are the other fellow?" Lee inquired. "I am sir and I wish to submit the case in full for your consideration. Don't you think it very hard on him, Colonel, after getting the worse of the fracas, to have to take all of the penalty?" "Admitted," Lee stated. "What Then?" "Simply this, sir. Whatever punishment is meted out to him, I insist on having the same given to me." Lee pondered for a moment then said, "The offense entails a heavy penalty." "I am well aware of the fact, Colonel, but Mr. Gracie is not entitled to a monopoly of it." With that Lee smiled and said, "No sir; you will get neither report nor penalty for this and neither will Mr. Gracie get the latter. I will cancel the report. Don't you think, Mr.

Green, that it is better for brothers to dwell together in peace and harmony?" "Yes Colonel," replied the young cadet, "and if we were all like you, it would be an easy thing to do."

While in the trenches of Petersburg the kindness of the just discipline that Colonel Lee had administered would come back to him in a surprising manner. While surveying the trenches, General Lee stepped upon one of the "firesteps" to get a better view, exposing himself to any sharpshooter anxiously awaiting a careless soldier to make such a fatal error. But before a shot could be born to flight, a man jumped up between the general and the enemy. "Why Gracie, you will certainly be killed," protested Lee. "It is better, general, that I should be killed than you. When you get down, I will." Lee complied with his former cadet's wisdom and went back to the safety of being a less conspicuous target.

"To Me He Seems a Hero"

Robert E. Lee loved his daughters very much and was very possessive of them. He desired his three sons to marry but did not encourage his four girls to do so. Mary, the oldest of the four was known as Daughter and somehow along her path had become distant in terms of not remaining around her mother and father as the younger girls did. She was known to have a sharp tongue and to speak her mind. Lee once wrote to Rooney about the status of the family making the following witted comment: "We are all as usual-the women of the family very fierce and the men very mild." She traveled constantly and enjoyed her stays abroad. Gentle Anna had passed on during the war but her memory was kept alive within the family circle. Agnes was considered the prettiest of the Lee

60

ladies. She was romantically involved with Colonel Orton William but broke off the romance due to his hardening of the heart while fighting. After losing her love (he was captured in a Union uniform and hung as a spy) she became despondent and lived with her parents. Their youngest daughter, Mildred, was a lover of cats and the child that held a special kinship with her father. She would sit, as he took his afternoon nap, and gently rub his hand. It was she that he called Life. It was to Mildred that her father wrote, "Experience will teach you that, notwithstanding all appearances to the contrary, you will never receive such a love as is felt for you by your father and mother. That lives through absence, difficulties, and time. Your own feelings will teach you how it should be returned and appreciated." It was she that wrote, "To me he seems a hero and all other men small in comparison!" After her father's death she wrote, "Most women when they lose such a father, replace it by husband and children-I have had nothing." Neither of his daughters married. (<u>Recollections of My Father's Death</u>; Lee, Mildred; deButts-Ely Collection; Library of Congress)

When I read the loving letter that was written by his daughter, I immediately recognized the love and devotion that this man had for his family. The institution of marriage was a sacred trust and the children were its crowning glory. Every letter to date from his children reveals a deep reverence for the man that gave them life. He was idolized even when he disciplined. He was adored when he scolded, as attempted to teach them the principles of self-denial and sacrifice. All those that had the privilege of calling him father loved him. His status of hero did not come from the legendary events of his life but in the simple devotions shown by a father to his family through unconditional love. The following poem is my attempt to honor his memory as a father, seen through his children's eyes. To me he seems a hero…

To Me He Seems a Hero

To me he seems a hero:
Taller than mortal man.
Much more than just a mural
Or canvas understands.

You see he was our father;
A man that made us proud.
A man who was not bothered
By praying in a crowd.

He filled our hearts with laughter
But disciplined our greed.
He'd toss us to the rafters
And filled our every need.

His feet, he loved them tickled.
Then stories he would tell.
He'd often run and giggled
Hiding from us as well.

He uttered not a curse word.
Stood tall while on his knees.
He showed love to even birds
That'd fallen from a tree.

To me he seems an idol:
Much taller than the rest.
The spirit of love unbridled
Beat deeply in his chest.

"As if He Spurned the Ground Which He Trod"

Even as a young cadet, Lee's physique, and the way he carried himself was graceful and quite pleasing to the observer. Many have attested to these characteristics. The following is a description of Lee while he was a cadet at West Point. (Robert E Lee; A Biography; Thomas, Emory M.; W. W. Norton & Company; New York/ London; 1995; page 55)

"His limbs, beautiful and symmetrical, looked as though they had come from the turning lathe, his step was elastic as if he spurned the ground upon which he trod."

"Knowing That His Father is Near"

One of the men that remembered Lee (and wrote Lee seeking his permission to write his saga regarding the War and Lee's role in it) served under him.   Here is another example of a first-hand source not only praising Lee but also honoring his character in print.   In his book entitled, A Life of General Robert E. Lee, John Eaten Cooke (1830-1886) stated that,

"The crowning grace of this man, who was thus not only great but good, was the humility and trust in God, which lay at the foundation of his character." He had lived, as he died, with this supreme trust in an overruling and merciful Providence; and this sentiment, pervading his whole being, was the origin of that august calmness with which he greeted the most crushing disasters of his military career. His faith and humble trust sustained him after the war, when the woes of the South well nigh broke his great spirit; and he calmly expired, as a weary child falls, asleep, knowing that its father is near." (<u>A life of General Robert E. Lee</u>; Cooke, John E.; Kessinger Publishing Company; New York; originally published in 1871; Project Gutenberg on line at http://www.gutenberg.org/etext/10692)

"The Noblest Looking Man I Have Ever Seen"

One of the best descriptions of Robert E. Lee comes from the Pulitzer Prize winning book by Douglas Freeman. In it he gives a detailed description of General Lee at the age of fifty-four as he took the command of the army that he would immortalize by their deeds. (<u>Lee</u>; Freeman Douglas Southall; An Abridgment by Richard Harwell of the Pulitzer Prize Winning four-volume Biography; New York; Touchstone; 1991; pages 113-116)

"He was then fifty-four years of age and stood five feet eleven inches in height, weighing slightly less than 170 pounds. In physique he was sound, without a blemish on his body. In the whole of his previous life he had suffered only one recorded illness and that had not been severe. Without having the bulging muscles of bovine strength, he was possessed of great powers of endurance. When he was past forty he had competed with his sons in high jumps at Arlington. He had skated and danced and had been an excellent swimmer. His vision and teeth were fine, his hearing was unimpaired, and his voice was rich and resonant. Few men were inheritors of a stronger nervous system.

"In appearance one fellow-traveller, who saw him that April day, considered Lee "the noblest-looking man I had ever seen." His fine large head was broadly rounded, with prominent brows and wide

64

temples, and was set on a short, strong neck. His hair was black, with a sprinkle of gray; his short mustache was wholly black. Brown eyes that seemed black in dim light and a slightly florid complexion gave warmth and color to his grave face. His mouth was wide and well-arched. His lips were thin. A massive torso rose above narrow hips, and his large hands were in contrast to very small feet. Sitting behind a desk, or on a horse, his shoulders, neck, and hands made him appear larger than he was. His finest appearance was when mounted, for he was an admirable rider, with the flat legs of the ideal cavalryman.

"His manners accorded with his person. In 1861, as always, he was the same in his bearing to men of every station, courteous, simple, and without pretense. Of objective mind, free of any suggestion of self-consciousness, he was considerate in his dealings with others, and of never-failing tact. He made friends readily and held them steadfastly. Close relations never lowered him in the esteem of his associates. He was clean-minded and frank with his friends, and confided in them more freely than has been supposed. Always he was unselfish, talked little of himself, and was in no sense egotistical. Although he was slow to take offense and was not quick to wrath, his temper was strong. Except when he was sick, he rarely broke the bounds of self-mastery for more than a moment. Then he was best left alone.

"The company of women, especially of pretty women, he preferred to that of men. In the presence of the other sex, he displayed a gracious, and sometimes a breezy gallantry; but no suggestion of a scandal, no hint of over-intimacy, was ever linked with his name. His conversation with his younger female friends was lively, with

65

many touches of teasing and with an occasional mild pun, but it was not witty. He had a good sense of humor, which his dignity rarely permitted him to exhibit in laughter. In dealing with children his manners were their finest. For them he always had a smile, no matter where he met them, and won their confidence almost invariably.

"His manners reflected his spiritual life. His was a simple soul, humble, transparent, and believing. Increasingly religion had become a part of his very being. Creeds meant little to him. Reading daily his Bible and his prayer book, spending much time on his knees, he believed in a God who, in His wisdom sent blessings beyond man's deserts, and visited him, on occasion, with hardships and disaster for the chastening of the rebellious heart of the ungrateful and the forgetful. In every disaster, he was to stand firm in the faith that it was sent by God for reasons that man could not see.

"Self-denial and self-control were the supreme rule of life. It was the basis of his code of conduct. He loved good food-but he was ready to eat thankfully the hardest fare of the field. In the confused councils he was doomed to share, he bore the contention of braggarts and swaggerers with self-control because it was his duty as a soldier to be patient and his obligation as a Christian to be humble. He had built up a dislike for tobacco, which he never used, and a hatred for whiskey. Wine he drank rarely and in small quantities.

"In intellect he was of an even higher order than had been demonstrated in thirty-two years of army service without a single failure to his discredit. His mind was mathematical and his imagination that of an engineer. The best of his results always were attained when originality and initiative could be employed. Routine office duties bored him. His culture was wider than most soldiers. Well-grounded in Greek and in Latin, he kept some of the spirit of the classics when he had forgotten the text. French he had mastered when he was in his first full vigor of mind. For Spanish he had an enthusiasm born of a belief in its utility. Of some phases of American history he had a measure of precise knowledge. Fiction he avoided, but poetry he enjoyed. He delighted to look at a sunset or at a garden. Birds were a particular care to him. His own contribution to physical beauty was through the promotion of orderliness and in the planting of trees. Outside his profession his chief interests were agricultural and social. The ideal life, had he been able to fashion it, would have been to entertain or to visit pleasant people while riding daily over a small plantation. As for society, he learned more from men than from books. All manner of acquaintances were his-generals, professors, planters, politicians, engineers, laborers.

"In those two unchanging fundamentals of military service, discipline and co-operation, Robert E. Lee had received the precise training of a professional soldier. Obedience to orders was part of his religion. Adverse decisions he had schooled himself to accept in the same spirit as approval. He could elicit the support of his superiors without flatter, and in the few instances where he had ever had subordinates, he had won their allegiance without threats. He was a diplomat among engineers. Fully qualified to deal with the politician in executive office, he was suspicious of him in the field or in the forum, though he was meticulous in subordinating himself to civil authority. His dealings with his brother officers had never been darkened by scheming or marred by jealously.

67

"Familiarity with the history was his in limited measure. The American Revolutionary campaigns he had surveyed carefully. Napoleon was the great captain whose battles he had carefully followed. To the Crimean War he had devoted at least casual study. With Hannibal and with Julius Caesar he was not wholly unacquainted. From these masters of war, and most of all from General Winfield Scott, he had learned the theory of strategy and had learned it well. He had participated, too, in nearly all the strategical preparation of the most successful series of battles ever fought prior to 1861 by an American army. The strategical function of high command he had learned from those battles in Mexico. That function, as he saw it, was to develop the lines of communication to direct the reconnaissance, to ascertain the precise position of the enemy, and then to bring all the combatant units into position at the proper time and to the best advantage. Thanks to Scott he had far more than the staff officer's approach to the duties that awaited him. In reconnaissance his experience had been sufficient to develop great aptitude. He was an excellent topographer and not without training as an intelligence officer. He had seen something of what sea power meant. Fortification he knew thoroughly.

"Such was the positive equipment of Robert E. Lee. It was the best equipment with which any soldier entered the struggle."

"Embodiment of a Line of Heroic and Patriotic Fathers"

Alexander H. Stephens, Vice President of the Confederate States of America, described his first contact with Robert E. Lee. His demeanor, his

68

eloquence, his mannerisms stayed fresh in the mind of Stephens long after the initial first contact. Such was his persona but more importantly, such was his lifestyle.

"As he stood there, fresh and ruddy as a David from the sheepfold, in the prime of his manly beauty, and the embodiment of a line of heroic and patriotic fathers and worthy mother, it was thus I first saw Robert E. Lee. I did not know then that he used no stimulants, was free from even the use of tobacco, and that he was absolutely stainless in his private life. I did not know then, as I do now, that he had been a model youth and young man; but I had before me the most manly and entire gentleman I ever saw."

"A Tower of Strength"

As war loomed in the minds of all, a Southern military leader that the nation would rally around was sought. The editor of the Alexandria newspaper sung the laurels of Lee and called upon the fledgling nation to offer him the command of the Southern forces: Grey Fox: Robert E. Lee and the Civil War; Davis, Burke; Wings Books, an imprint of Random House Value Publishing; New York; 1956; page 17)

"There is no man who could command more of the confidence of the people of Virginia…and no one under whom the volunteers and militia would more gladly rally. His reputation, his acknowledged ability, his chivalric character, his probity, honor- and, may we add, to his eternal praise-his Christian life and conduct-make his name 'a tower of strength.' It is a name surrounded by revolutionary and patriotic associations and reminiscences."

"He is Ineffable"

Lee had a manner about him that made men and women recall his presence. One such man was James Nisbet. Upon meeting Robert E. Lee James C. Nisbet wrote, "He was the only man I ever met who measured up to my concept of Washington. The grandeur of his appearance is beyond my power of portraiture. He is ineffable."

"The Soldiers Would Unconditionally Trust"

General Clement Evans was impressed with Lee and compared him to President Washington. He described the total devotion of his men towards the general's leadership abilities. His main impression was of Lee's character as seen in the following extract:

"...nearest approaching the character of the great and good George Washington than any living man. He is the only man living in whom the soldiers would unconditionally trust all their power for the preservation of their independence."

"The First Gentleman of Virginia"

In her diary, Mrs. Mary B. Chesnutt offered her first impression of Lee. She had heard of him, but she had not actually met the man. Her husband was well aware of him. During the prelude to the war in that first April of the four to follow, he served as an aide to General Beauregard and had been summoned to a meeting by Jefferson Davis. Included in the meeting were General Cooper, the Adjutant General and General Lee. The meeting lasted well into the day. She recalled her husbands unwillingness to share with her the details of that meeting but recorded in her diary that, "The news does not seem pleasant. At least he (her husband) is not inclined to tell me any of it. He satisfied himself with telling me how sensible and soldierly this handsome General Lee is. General Lee's military sagacity was his theme."

But at first, she was not that impressed with Lee nor shared her husband's optimism. She stated that, "He sat on his horse very gracefully, and he was so distinguished.... As he left us I said eagerly, 'Who is he?' 'You did not know? Why, that was Robert E. Lee, the first gentleman of Virginia.'" "All the same, I like Smith Lee better, and I like his looks, too. Besides, I know him well. Can anybody say they know his brother? I doubt it! He looks so cold, quiet and grand." (A Diary From Dixie; Chesnutt, Mary Boykin; Edited by Williams, Ben Ames; New York; 1906, 1949)

"Seeing Himself to be a Sinner"

Reverend J. William Jones offers keen insight into the Christian nature of Lee, the man. He had served with General Lee as a Pastor of Lee's flock and became a close friend of the family. He was the author of two books that helped establish Lee as more than just a man: a famed myth in which legends become known. He wrote, "If I have ever come in contact with a sincere, devout Christian, one who, seeing himself to be a sinner, trusted alone in the merits of Christ, who humbly tried to walk the path of duty, looking unto Jesus the author and finisher of our faith, and whose piety was constantly exemplified in his daily life, that man, was the world's great soldier, and modern man, Robert Edward Lee."

"Lee's Greatness Lies in His Response to God"

Bishop Robert R. Brown spoke of Lee and the way Lee sought doing God's will while denying himself. Bishop Brown stated that, "The beauty of God can be seen in his endless pursuit of righteousness...In short, Lee's greatness lies in his response to the initiative of a loving God and to the faith it supplied."

"Humility, Simplicity, and Gentleness"

J.W. Jones in his book entitled <u>Christ in the Camp</u> offers insight into the character and demeanor of Lee. One of his observations best sums up the man of legend.

"Modest humility, simplicity, and gentleness, were most conspicuous in his daily life."

"Unconscious Dignity"

While stationed in South Carolina, Lee was inspecting several coastal forts and fortifying the riverbanks around the Savannah area. The poet Paul Hamilton Hayne spotted him when he was at Fort Sumter. His encounter left an impression. (<u>Grey Fox: Robert E. Lee and the Civil War;</u> Davis, Burke; Wings Books, an imprint of Random House Value Publishing; New York; 1956; page 58)

"During the group, topping the tallest by half a head was, perhaps, the most striking figure we had ever encountered, the figure of a man seemingly about 56 or 58 years of age, erect as a poplar, yet lithe and graceful, with broad shoulders well thrown back...unconscious dignity, clear, deep thoughtful eyes, and the quiet, dauntless step of one ever the gentlemen and soldier."

"In the Atmosphere of Lee and Jackson"

One black leader was quite taken with both Lee and Jackson. When talking with Senator George Tucker, Booker T. Washington made the following observation:

"No people could live in the atmosphere of Lee and Jackson and not be the best."

"First Appeared before Us in Citizen's Dress"

After the wounding of General Joseph Johnston, General Robert E. Lee was given command of the men that would later be known as the Army of Northern Virginia. He immediately went to work rebuilding the army and at first was not well received. A young gunner captured the first impressions of Lee as commander of the Virginia forces. (Grey Fox: Robert E. Lee and the Civil War; Davis, Burke; Wings Books, an imprint of Random House Value Publishing; New York; 1956; page 79)

"General Lee first appeared before us in citizen's dress, in white duck with a bob tail coat; jogging along without our suspecting who he was. We thought at first he was a jolly easy going miller or distiller on a visit as a civilian to the front, and perhaps carrying out a canteen of whisky for the boys. He showed himself good-natured…stopping once to reprove, though very gently, the drivers for unmercifully beating their horses when they stalled; and walking about and laughing at one of Artemus Ward's stories; and kept in a good humor about it the rest of the day."

"The Meeting Finally Took a Playful Turn"

At first, Lee's leadership did not impress even General Longstreet, the man that later Lee would call his Old War Horse. But once he saw that Lee was a man of action and listened to his troops, he became receptive to the leadership style that made Lee famous. After a meeting of approximately forty general officers at a place called The Chimneys (close to the Nine Mile Road), it became increasingly clear that this man would lead and would fight.   One of the decisive conclusions reached by those in attendance was that their commanding general would listen and they left feeling that they were an integral part of the leadership and a valued component of the decision-making process. General Longstreet commented upon the meeting in his memoirs.

"As he disclosed nothing, those of serious thought became hopeful, and followed his wise example. The brigadiers talked freely, but only of the parts of the line occupied by their brigades; and the meeting finally took a playful turn."

"Has Gen. Lee that Audacity?"

In his personal recollections of the war, Edward Alexander recalls a meeting with Colonel Joseph Christmas Ives around Richmond. They were talking and the topic came up regarding the attack on Lee's character being made by John M. Daniel. He was screaming for the removal of Lee and that he was not the leader needed to win the war. Colonel Ives asked Edward if he felt these attacks had weakened the confidence of the officers under Lee. He replied that to his knowledge that they had not but then he asks a question those results in a prophecy regarding the boldness of Lee. (Fighting for the Confederacy: The Personal Recollections of General Edward Porter Alexander; Alexander,

Edward Porter; The University of North Carolina Press; Chapel Hill; 1989; page 91)

"Has Gen. Lee that audacity which is going to be required in the command of this army to meet the odds which will be brought against it? Our only hope is to bounce him & whip him somewhere before he is ready for us, and that needs audacity in our commander. Has Gen. Lee that audacity?"

Ives heard me through fully, & then stopped his horse in the road, to make his reply more impressive, & turning to me he said, "Alexander, if there is one man in either army, Federal or Confederate, who is, head & shoulders, far above every other one in either army in audacity that man is Gen. Lee, and you will very soon have lived to see it. Lee is audacity personified. His name is audacity, and you need not be afraid of not seeing all of it that you will want to see."

"Only a King Could Have Possessed Such Courage"

General Lee no doubt possessed the very essence of nobility. His pedigree reflects his noble ancestry and his demeanor attests to that fact. Probably more than any other Southerner (and possibly Northerner) Lee did more to mend the heart of a war-torn nation simply by setting the standards on how to be a good American. He could have been a king; he could have continued the strife simply by speaking and his boys would have followed him to the grave. Most assuredly he could have been but instead he chose the path of peacemaker that his Creator had traveled and because he chose not to be a king; he became one within the minds of Christians needing a mortal man to be an example of the teachings of Christ. The Christian General became a king.

"But there was only one Lee, and to him the South knew must her safety and hopes be committed. He failed to realize these hopes, but he gained, if not for his cause, at least for his country and himself, a glory imperishable and unclouded by his defeat...only a king of men could have possessed such courage and endurance, and his whole life is a proof that among the brotherhood of men Lee was indeed a king. When the last chance was gone, and all hope was at an end, the old hero bowed to a higher will than his own, and accepted the fate of the South with calm grandeur. But he was done with all his wars. He could never take the field again; he knew that it was not for him to see the act of secession upheld by the South and recognized by the North, and after the failure of his own countrymen he was too old and war-worn to draw his sword in a foreign quarrel. He passed from the fever of the camp into the quiet of the cloister, and as the president of Washington College, in Virginia, spent the remaining portion of his sixty-three years in working for the good of his native State. We cannot express all the truth that could be told about Lee, nor can we do justice to his worth and fame, but perhaps the few words of Sir Ector are the best after all. He is a good knight, a true gentleman; knowing this, let us leave him with fame and posterity; with the rest, the light, the Resurrection and the Life." (Personal Reminiscences, Anecdotes, and Letters of General Robert E. Lee; Jones, J. William; Appleton; New York; 1875; pages 68-69)

"Every Inch a King"

The following is a description of General Lee and the horse he named Traveller, as recorded by W. H. Tayloe. His presence and persona was such that men marveled and attempted to be like him in manner. But Lee's doctrine was that all men should follow Christ and therefore would be Christ like in spirit. For that was the path he had chosen and through all of life's adversity he attempted to maintain those sacred principles with honor and dignity of purpose. (<u>Lee, The Last Years</u>; Flood, Charles Bracelen; Houghton Mifflin Company; New York; 1981)

"He was passing just as I came out of the gate at the Episcopal Church. I saw him but a moment; the picture is with me yet. Traveller moved as if proud of the burden he bore. To me the horse was beautiful and majestic. It was the only time I was impressed with the greatness and beauty and power and glory of the man. He sat erect in the saddle. The gloved hand held the bridle, the other hung gracefully at his side. He was every inch a king."

Every Inch A King

Though born of noble blood lines
And every inch a king.
His men were foremost in his mind:
His boys meant everything.

A man of peace and morals
Surrounded by the war.
A man of constant sorrows;
The bloodshed he deplored.

He rode his Confederate Grey
And moved among the troops.
When he was riding their way
They would shout and whoop.

His heart always turned to God
In victory and defeat.
Greeted the boys with a nod;
They threw flowers at his feet.

He saw sunshine in the storm;
Prayed for all 'those people'.
And when the boys became forlorn
He took them to God's steeple.

Tho' some have tried to erase
His footsteps in the sand.
No one dares to take his place,
This marble of man.

On Christmas Eve, I had just completed reading
most of Lees' letters to his family on that same
occasion, but over one hundred forty plus years
ago. Somehow I felt as if I had intruded upon their
personal space. I had previously read about Lee's
love for his fellow man and his genuine regard for
all. I had read where he referred to the Northerners

as "Those people" and that he always turned to God in everything. The rare spark of inspiration moved me. A greater force than myself compelled me to sit at my desk and write a tribute to one of the men that I feel walked in harmony with his testimony to God. The gift that was so freely given to me, I offer to you in hopes that your spirit is touched by the wings of revelation in the realization that no matter what trials and tribulations await us in the future, we must celebrate our daily victories to the One that will never place upon us more than we can bear. God gracious God, a giving and loving God that will walk beside us through whatever perils that we must face. By faith we are conquerors of all things and hold within our hearts a promise of tomorrow.

"A Man Born to Command"

A staff officer later recalled seeing Lee during his arrival at Richmond to accept command of the forces of the Old Dominion. He stated that Lee was "Admirably proportioned, of graceful and dignified carriage, with strikingly handsome features, bright and penetrating eyes, his iron-gray hair closely cut, his face cleanly shaved except for a mustache, he appeared every inch a soldier and a man born to command."

"Let It Be Robert E. Lee!"

General Winfield Scott saw the merits of Lee's leadership years prior to the War Between the States. He wrote several official memos to Washington commending his gallantry and celebrating his bravery during the Mexican War. The following statement by ole Fuss and Feathers gives insight into the high esteem held by his former captain.

"If I were on my deathbed tomorrow, and the president of the Unites States should tell me that a great battle was to be fought for the liberty or slavery of the country, and asked my judgment as to the ability of a commander, I would say with my dying breath, 'Let it be Robert E. Lee!'"

"Rare Purity of the Ideal Christian Knight"

Colonel Charles Cornwallis Chesney had the following observation of Lee's demeanor:

"In strategy mighty, in battle terrible, in adversity as in prosperity a hero indeed, with the simple devotion to duty and the rare purity of the ideal Christian knight, he joined all the kingly qualities of a leader of men."

"The Beau Idea of a Christian Man"

In 1837 General M. C. Meigs served with Lee during the time that Lee and a handful of men changed the course of the Mississippi River. This was when the river was a looming threat to the city of St. Louis, Missouri and Lee was chosen to do whatever he could to save the city. This he did in grand fashion and his works still hold to this day. General Meigs wrote that Lee was

"A man then in the vigor of youthful strength, with a noble and commanding presence and an admirable, graceful and athletic figure. He was one with whom nobody ever wished or ventured to take a liberty, though kind and generous to all his subordinates, admired by all women and respected by all men. He was the model of a soldier and the beau ideal of a Christian man." (The Robert E. Lee Reader; edited by Stanley f. Horn; Smithmark

Publishing Company; New York, New York; 1995; page 42)

"No Commander was Ever More Careful"

Colonel A. L. Long speaking about Lee's stewardship toward his men:

"No commander was ever more careful and never had care for the comfort of an army given rise to greater devotions."

"The Impersonation of Every Manly Virtue"

From the writings of Major General John B. Gordon comes one of the best descriptions of the most famous general ever to serve an army. It offers insight into the level of respect held by those who knew and served under him. (Reminiscences of the Civil War; Gordon, Major General John B.; C. Scribner's Sons; New York; 1904)

"Unless it be Washington, there is no military chieftain of the past to whom Lee can be justly likened, either in attributes of character or in the impression for good made upon the age in which he lived. Those who knew him best and studied him most have agreed that he was unlike any of the great captains of history. In his entire public career there was a singular absence of self-seeking. Otherwise he would have listened to the woo-ings of ambition when debating the course he should take at the beginning of our sectional conflict. He knew that he could hold any position he might wish in the armies of the Union. Not only by General Scott, the commander-in-chief, but by his brother officers and the civil authorities, Lee was recognized as the foremost soldier in the United States army. He knew, for he so declared, that the

South's chances for success, except through foreign intervention, were far from encouraging. What would Caesar or Fredrick or Napoleon have done? Deaf to every suggestion of a duty whose only promised reward was an approving conscience in ultimate defeat, allured by the prospect of leading armies with overwhelming numbers and backed by limitless resources, any one of these great captains would have eagerly grasped the tendered power. It was not so with Lee. Trained soldier that he was, he stood on the mountain-top of temptation, while before his imagination there passed the splendid pageant of conquering armies swayed by his word of command; and he was unmoved by it. Graduated at West Point, where he subsequently served as command; and he was unmoved by it. Graduated at West Point, where he subsequently served as perhaps its most honored superintendent; proud of his profession, near the head of which he stood; devoted to the Union and its emblematic flag, which he long had followed; revered by the army, to the command of which he would have been invited—he calmly abandoned them all to lead the forlorn hope of his people, impelled by his conviction that their cause was just. Turning his back upon ambition, putting selfish considerations behind him, like George Washington in the old Revolution, he threw himself and all his interests into an unequal struggle for separate government. When John Adams of Massachusetts declared that, sink or swim, survive or perish, he gave his heart and hand to the Declaration of Independence, he stood on precisely the same moral plane on which Robert E. Lee stood from the beginning to the end of the war. As the North Star to the sailor, so was duty to this self-denying soldier. Having decided that in the impending and to him unwelcome conflict his place was with his people, he did not stop to consider the cost. He resolved to do his best; and in estimating now the relative resources and numbers, it cannot be denied that he did more than any leader has ever accomplished under similar conditions. And when the end came and he realized that Appomattox was the grave of his people's hopes, he regretted that Providence had not willed that his own life should end there also. He not only said in substance, to Colonel Venable of his staff and to others, that he would rather die than surrender the cause, but he said to me on that fatal morning that he was sorry he had not fallen in one of the last battles. Yet no man who saw him at Appomattox could detect the slightest wavering in his marvellous self-poise or any lowering of his lofty bearing. Only for a fleeting moment did he lose complete self-control. As he rode back from the McLean house to his bivouac, his weeping men crowded around him; and as they assured him in broken voices of their confidence and love, his emotions momentarily overmastered him, and his wet cheeks told of the sorrow which his words could not express. Throughout that crucial test at Appomattox he was the impersonation of every manly virtue, of all that is great and true and brave—the fittest representative of his own sublimely beautiful adage that human virtue should always equal human calamity."

"In Christ-Like Resignation"

The Reverend Randolph H. McKim was very impressed with the general's persona. But the Christ like way he carried himself made the greatest impression. It is the manner in which we handle tragedy that makes us above the average mold of humans. Lee's character captured a nation's heart; both blue and gray and another American hero was born.

"His countrymen boldly challenge the world to produce from the annals of time another supreme soldier who was also such a supreme examplar of Christian virtue, of spotless manhood, of high chivalry, of unselfish devotion to duty, as the commander of the Army of Northern Virginia. Few among the great captains of history have surpassed or even equaled his achievements in the field of war; but is there one among them all that can compare with this hero of the Southern Confederacy in purity of life, in steadfast lifelong devotion to high ideal, in modest self-effacement, in freedom from selfish ambition, in sublime patience under adversity, in moderation in victory, in composure in defeat, in Christ like resignation?"

"With No Thought of Tomorrow"

One of the impressions that General Lee made was on a Sergeant from Georgia. He recalled how Lee evoked confidence within the ordinary people and how they thought he could not fail. Just simply by riding by he offered hope and was a source of pride. Once when he was riding by the men paying homage with his hat in hand he uttered not a word. One observer by the name of Heros von Borcke noted the reverence and high esteem that both Lee and his men held for one another. The German born aide to J. E. B. Stuart commented that it was "the most eloquent address ever delivered." Such was the level of respect that each possessed for one another and his men, would follow his lead wherever it may take them.

"General Lee has won the confidence of his men. They trust him with the same faith that a child does while in its parent's arms, with no thought of tomorrow. We have been victorious under his

84

leadership in every battle, and expect to still win victory wherever he directs."

"He Was Approachable by All"

Moxley Sorrel, a well-known staff officer under General Longstreet reflected upon his impressions of General Lee. It is obvious that Lee won the hearts of all that he encountered simply by his humble nature and lack of airs. He was a gentleman that all could relate and I do believe there was something about his eyes that bore the essence of southern determination, southern pride while revealing a glimpse of a broken heart for his beloved country.

"When General Lee took command it was my first sight of him. Up to a short time before Seven Pines he had worn for a beard only a well-kept mustache, soon turned from black to grizzled. When he took us in hand his full gray beard was growing, cropped close, and always well tended…withal graceful and easy, he was approachable by all; gave attention to all in the simplest manner. His eyes-sad eyes! The saddest it seems to me of all men. The General was always dressed well in gray sack coat of Confederate cloth, matching trousers tucked into well-fitting riding boots-the simplest emblems of his rank appearing, and a good, large black felt army hat…He rarely wore his sword, but his binoculars were always at hand. Fond of the company of ladies, he had a good memory for pretty girls. His white teeth and winning smile irresistible." (Reflections of a Confederate Staff Officer; Sorrel, G. Moxley; Neale Publishing Co.; New York; 1905; page 315)

"His Heart Turned to God"

General Lee was a man who placed his faith in God and that God worked for those that sought His will. General Gordon was aware of the virtues that his commander possessed. General Gordon wrote on his observation of General Lee's faith in his book. Lee's character was his testimony. (<u>Lee: The Last Years</u>; Flood, Charles B.; Houghton Mifflin Company; Boston; 1981; pg. 56)

The sunshine and in storm, in victory and in defeat, his heart turned to God"

"Child-like in Simplicity and Unselfish in His Character"

Alexander H. Stephens, Vice President of the Confederacy complimented Lee's character through the following statement: "What I had seen General Lee to be at first--child-like in simplicity and unselfish in his character—he remained, unspoiled by praise and by success." (<u>Recollections and Letter of Robert E. Lee</u>; Lee, Robert E. Jr. Captain; Doubleday, Doran, and Company; 1904, 1924)

"A Monarch Still in the Hearts of His Countrymen"

Colonel Walter Herron Taylor was twenty-two years old upon the onset of the war. He cast his fate with the gray side of things. He had the distinct privilege of being on General Lee's staff throughout the war; first as aide-de-camp (ADC) and then as assistant adjutant general (AAG) of the Army of Northern Virginia. The bond of affection between him and his commanding officer was evident. The famous picture of Lee sitting with his son, Robert E. Lee Jr. on one side and his faithful adjutant on the other speaks volumes to the high esteem the young man held in the old general's eyes. The family members of Lee also honored him when he was asked to sit with the family during the funeral of his former commander. His writing on the subject of Lee and the Southern Cause is a first-hand reflection and is still considered to be a valuable appraisal of that struggle. The following extracts are examples of his devotion and position within Lee's heart. They offer even deeper insights into the mystic of the legendary Lee. (<u>Lee's Adjutant: The Wartime Letters of Colonel Walter Herron Taylor</u>; Taylor, Walter H.; Edited by Tower, R. Lockwood; University of South Carolina Press; 1995; pages 1-34)

"It was my particular privilege to occupy the position of a confidential staff-officer with General Lee during the entire period of the War for Southern Independence."

Lee's relationships with his subordinates were legendary. Colonel Taylor made the following observation regarding the camaraderie between Lee and his men. "There was between General Lee and his military family a degree of camaraderie that was perfectly delightful. Our conversation, especially at table, was free from restraint, unreserved as between equals, and often a bright and jocular vein."

There is one noted exception. Apparently on one occasion when Major Taylor felt that his work was not getting the credit worthy of his work became frustrated at General Lee's comment and "petulantly threw down his papers at his side. At which time General Lee in a calm tone stated, "Major Taylor, when I lose my temper, don't let it make you angry."

Speaking of General Lee after his surrender, Colonel Taylor commented that Lee was, "A monarch still in the hearts of his countrymen."

Lord Wolseley of England had visited Lee and his staff during the war. In 1907 he reflected on Lee to Taylor stating that he (General Lee) was, "One of the very few truly great men I was ever privileged to be personally acquainted with."

"He is a Perfect Gentleman in Every Respect."

Lieutenant Colonel James Fremantle was a British Officer that was on a three-month leave from his Majesty's service. Being a soldier, he decided to become an observer of the American civil strife that was occurring across the ocean. Arriving via Texas because of the Union blockade, he made his way through the South recording the events of the day. From the Rio Grande to his departure from New York, Colonel Fremantle was privileged to become an eyewitness to the vast destruction and yet record the dignity of those involved in the fight. In his diary, he records his first encounter with General Robert E. Lee. This transpired at a little-known place called Gettysburg. (The Fremantle Diary, A Journal of the Confederacy; Fremantle, James, Lt. Col.; edited by Walter Lord; Bufford Books; 1954; pages 197-198)

"30th June (Tuesday)-This morning, before marching from Chambersburg, General Longstreet introduced me to the Commander in Chief. General Lee is, almost without exception, the handsomest man of his age I ever saw. He is fifty-six years old, tall, broad-shouldered, very well made, well set up-a thorough soldier in appearance; and his manners are most courteous and full of dignity. He is a perfect gentleman in every respect. I imagine no man has so few enemies, or is so universally esteemed. Throughout the South, all agree in pronouncing him to be as near as perfection as a man can be. He has none of the small vices, such as smoking, drinking, chewing, or swearing, and his bitterest enemy never accused him of any of the greater ones.

"He generally wears a well-worn long gray jacket, a high black felt hat, and blue trousers tucked into his Wellington boots. I never saw him carry arms*, and the only mark of his military rank are the three stars on his collar. He rides a handsome horse, which is extremely well groomed. He himself is very neat in his dress and person and in the most arduous marches he always looks smart and clean.

"In the old army he was always considered one if its best officers, and at the outbreak of these troubles, he was lieutenant colonel of the 2nd cavalry. He was a rich man, but his fine estate was one of the first to fall into the enemy's hands. I believe he has never slept in a house since he had commanded the Virginian army, and he invariably declines all offers of hospitality, for the fear the person offering it may afterwards get into trouble for having sheltered the Rebel General."

"The relations between him and Longstreet are quite touching-they are almost always together. Longstreet's corps complain of this sometimes, as they say that they seldom get a chance of detached service, which falls to the lot of Ewell. It is impossible to please Longstreet more than by praising Lee. I believe these two generals to be as little ambitious and as thoroughly unselfish as any men in the world. Both long for a successful termination of the war, in order that they may retire into obscurity."

*According to the writings of General Fitzhugh Lee, his uncle carried a pistol in a holster on the left side of his saddle. This would make it easier for him to reach once he had dismounted. After the war, the same pistol hung over Lee's bedpost and was fired after his death. (General Lee; Lee, Fitzhugh; Premier Civil War Classics; Fawcett Publications, Inc.; Greenwich, Conn., 1961; page 300)

"We Listened With Reverence to His Voice"

Colonel Charles Marshall was Lee's military secretary and maintained a close relationship with the general. Colonel Marshall's comments note that General Lee always gave God the glory and that all things were of "God's will." (Personal Reminiscences, Anecdotes, and Letters of General Robert E. Lee; Jones, J. William; Appleton; New York; 1875; page 149) In a tribute to Lee's character, Colonel Marshall writes:

"We recall him as he appeared in the hour of victory, grand, imposing, awe-inspiring, yet self forgetful and humble. We recall the great scenes of his triumph, when we hailed him victor on many a bloody field, and when above the paeans of victory we listened with reverence to his voice as he ascribed, 'All glory to the Lord of hosts, from whom all glories are.' We remember that grand magnanimity that never stooped to pluck the meaner things that grow nearest the earth upon the tree of victory, but which, with eyes turned to the stars, and hands raised toward heaven, gathered golden fruits of mercy, pity, and holy charity, that ripen on its topmost bough beneath the approving smile of the great God of battles."

"I Cried Myself to Sleep There Upon the Bloody Ground"

One of the most insightful glimpses into the character of the great general came from Gamaliel Bradford, Jr., a Union soldier wounded at Gettysburg. It demonstrates the compassion General Lee felt for his fellow man. As Lee left the battlefield in a downpour, realizing that he had just lost probably the most important battle of the war, a lesser man would have yielded to the temptation of the passions of moment at that juncture. But not the old general. After being taunted by a wounded enemy soldier, It would have been so easy to end his defiance by a single motion of his hand. But not Lee. His Christian character would not even allow him to weigh that option or contemplate such an act. Gamaliel remembered that as he lay there bleeding, General Robert E. Lee and some of his staff passed by. He recalled that, "I had been a most bitter anti-South man, and fought and cursed the Confederates desperately. I could see nothing good in any of them. A ball shattered my left leg. I lay on the ground not far from Cemetery Ridge, and as General Lee ordered his retreat, he and his officers rode near me. As they came along I recognized him, and, though faint from exposure and loss of blood, I raised up my hands, looked Lee in the face, and shouted as loud as I could, 'Hurrah for the Union'. The General heard me, looked, stopped his horse, dismounted and came toward me. I must confess I at first thought he meant to kill me. But as he came up he looked down at me with such a sad expression upon his face that all fear left me, and I wondered what he was about. He extended his hand to me, grasping mine firmly, and looking right into my eyes, said: 'My son, I hope you will soon be well.' If I live to be a thousand years I shall never forget the expression on General Lee's face. There he was defeated, retiring from a field that had cost him and his cause almost their last hope, and yet he stopped to say words like those to a wounded soldier of the opposition who had taunted him as he passed by! As soon as the General had left me, I cried myself to sleep there upon the bloody ground." Such was the Christian character of Lee.

The Samaritan

As I laid there wounded,
I saw him passing by.
"Hurrah for the Union!"
Was my battle cry.

His boys were filled with anger,
"Let's put him in his place!"
I know there was no danger,
By the look on his face.

His eyes were lined with sadness.
He asked me how I felt.
His voice was filled with kindness.
My hate began to melt.

"I pray this day you're better"
And sent me to his tent.
He called his boys together
And down the road he went.

He left me his physician
And nursed me back to health.
He asked of my condition,
Not thinking of himself.

I raise my hand in salute;
He set my sprit free.
I offer him this tribute,
To the man, Bobby Lee!

Upon reading the statement of Gamaliel Bradford I was immediately struck by the aura of a man called Lee. He exhibited an almost Christ-like care and concern for his fellow man. And through the General's unconditional love and act of Samaritan's kindness, Gamaliel lost his bitterness. This author feels that he found himself again through his remorseful repentance. He later wrote of Lee as if he was one that followed his example. "If ever a man made his life a true poem it was Lee." He went on to say, "Lee had one intimate friend--God." Gamaliel also stated that, "His utterances were accepted as holy writ. No other earthly power could have produced such prompt acceptance of the final and irreversible judgment." But his love for Lee's Biblical kindness upon the battlefield and his admiration for the example that Lee set forth are most evident in the following passage. "It is an advantage to have a subject like Lee that one can not help loving...I have loved him, and I may say that his influence upon my own life, though I came to him late, has been as deep and as inspiring as any I have ever known." May we all attempt to follow his example.

I offered the preceding poem in hopes of capturing a portion of that moment when a Christian General was able to follow the commandments of his heart. The lesson of loving our enemies was demonstrated on that day. Both parties drank from the cup of forgiveness during that brief encounter on those sacred crimson-stained fields of Gettysburg.

While on the battlefield tour of Gettysburg, the preceding poem that I have entitled, "The Samaritan" was constantly in the forefront of my mind. Wherever I went along Cemetery Ridge, I noted all markers, signs and monuments. When I stood upon the very ground in which the immortal campaign occurred, I became almost obsessed with locating the area in which this Samaritan incident had transpired. After an exhaustive search, it dawned upon my persona that though I may never find a marker indicating the exact spot of the Samaritan story, it is for that very reason why such hallowed grounds must be preserved. It is for the minds sacred spark to chose the location of certain mysteries, and not be so dogmatic as to where it happened but rather why it happened and be satisfied in the serenity of an altruistic act in a time of devastation.

"From These Early Relations First Sprang My Affection"

John Bell Hood (the famous Kentuckian that would become the general over the Texans and later the Army of Tennessee) recalled the kindness afforded to him by Lee while a cadet at West Point. He also carried Lee's advice on marriage with him and relished Lee's fatherly approach towards him. "Never marry unless you can be so into a family which will enable your children to feel proud of both sides of the house."

"His uniform kindness to me whilst I was a cadet, inclined me the more willingly to receive and remember this fatherly advice; and from these early relations first sprang my affection and veneration which grew in strength to the end of his career." (Advance and Retreat: Personal Experiences in the United States and Confederate States Armies; Hood, John Bell; Hood Orphan Memorial Fund; New Orleans, Louisiana; 1880; 358 page)

94

"And My Heart Went With Him"

In his book, Private Sam Watkins writes his perspective of the General. The admiration and genuine love for his leader is quite evident in his passages referring to Lee. (Co. Aytch a Side Show of the Big Show; Watkins, Sam R.; Touchstone, Rockefeller Center, 1230 Ave. of the Americas, N.Y.; copyright 1962)

"One evening, General Robert E. Lee came to our camp. He was a fine looking gentleman, and wore a moustache. He dressed in blue cottonade and looked like some good boy's grandpa. I felt like going up to him and saying, good evening, Uncle Bob: I am certain at this late day that I did not do so. I remember going up mighty close and sitting there and listening to his conversation with the officers of our regiment. He had a calm and collected air about him, his voice was kind and tender, and his eye was as gentle as a dove's. His whole make-up of form and person, looks and manner had a kind of gentle and soothing magnetism about it that drew every one to him and made them love, respect, and honor him. I fell in love with the old gentlemen and felt like going home with him. I know I have never seen a finer looking man, nor one with more kind and gentle features and manners. His horse was standing nipping the grass, and when I saw that he was getting ready to start I ran and caught his horse and led him up to him. He took the reins of the bridle in his hand and said, "Thank you, my son," rode off, and my heart went with him. There was none of his staff with him; he had on no sword or pistol, or anything to show his rank. The only thing that I remember he had was an opera glass hung over his shoulder by a strap."

"He Could Not Help From Breaking Down"

A South Carolinian Private (<u>Reminiscences of a Private</u> by Mixson) tells of the unique bond between the old commander and his boys. He was so loved by his boys. They were willing to do his bidding no matter the personal cost. And the price was costly! The private's statement demonstrates the complete unadulterated regard that was reciprocated between general and his soldiers. (<u>Grey Fox: Robert E. Lee and the Civil War;</u> Davis, Burke; Wings Books, an imprint of Random House Value Publishing; New York; 1956; page 279)

"The men hung around him and seemed satisfied to lay their hands on his gray horse or to touch the bridle, or the stirrup, or the old general's leg-anything that Lee had was sacred to us fellows who had just come back. And the General-he could not help from breaking down…tears traced down his cheeks, and he felt that we were again to do his bidding."

"It Awes Him"

General Alexander wrote of a conversation that he overheard between Reverend Boggs (chaplain from South Carolina) and Colonel Venable. The Reverend stated how proud Lee must be of the open affection the soldiers displayed towards him. The reply sums up the persona of the man.

"Doesn't it make the General proud to see how these men love him?" Boggs asked.

"Not proud," Venable said. "It awes him."

The legend and legacy of Lee was based in part on the acts of kindness this man of morals bestowed upon his boys. One incident involved a soldier marching towards Gettysburg. He was sweating profusely and as the General rode by, he broke rank approached his commander and stated, "Please General, I came aside to this old hill to get a rag or something to wipe the sweat out of my eyes." The knightly old General immediately reached into his pocket and gave his handkerchief to the soldier. (Recollections of a Confederate Staff Officer; Sorrel, Moxley; McCowat-Mercer Press; Jackson, Tennessee; 1958; page 173)

"He Covered the Soldier with his Blanket"

In another incident, an exhausted soldier sought rest and refuge in the General's tent. Upon entering, Lee saw the man and realized that one of his boys was weary and worn. He walked over, and covered the soldier with his blanket. He then left the sleeping soldier in his personal space and allowed him to rest before the morning light. Such was the altruistic character of the man. (Unveiling of Valentine's Figure of Lee; Daniel, John W.; Southern Historical Society Papers11; page 377) Yet another tale of his kind heart is reflected in a story of one of his staff members, Major Charles Venable. After the defeat at Gettysburg, Major Venable was very loudly complaining about the deteriorating conditions that prevailed. Lee immediately rebuked him stating that he must not say such things in front of the men. The Major took exception to that and began to pout. Realizing that he had hurt the Major's feelings, the kindly old general invited him into his tent for a glass of buttermilk. But that did not suffice and the Major continued licking his wounds. Later he became sleepy and laid down to rest. A storm was developing and the old general quietly yielded his coat to the sleeping man. When Major Venable awoke, he realized that the great man had offered him a gift of appeasement and the issue was settled with Major Venable's pride still intact.

"The Handsomest Specimen of Manhood"

John H. Warsham of Company F (21st Virginia Infantry, Second Brigade of Jackson's Division) gives a candid interpretation of his first impression of the future general of the Confederacy in his book entitled One of Jackson's Foot Cavalry.   His description paints such a picture that this author felt compelled to include it in an attempt to demonstrate to the reader the level of respect, wonder and sense of awe that this man's persona captured. He possessed within his being the optima of manhood that is rarely privileged to mortals. (One of Jackson's Foot Cavalry, His Experience and What He Saw During the War 1861-1865; Worsham, John H.; New York; The Neale Publishing Company; 1912)

"I was standing in the door of our headquarters in Richmond about the middle of April, 1861, when my attention was attracted by a man approaching; he wore a uniform.   It was not the uniform that attracted my attention but the man himself. He was tall and straight, and I thought the handsomest specimen of manhood I had ever seen, both in face and figure. He made such an impression that as he came opposite me I could not keep from looking at him, and when he had passed my eyes still followed him, until I actually stepped outside of the door in order to keep him in sight. About an hour later he returned up the street and went into the Spottswood Hotel. I followed and asked some friend if he could tell me who that splendid looking man was. He informed me that it was Colonel Robert E. Lee.

"The next time I saw him was on Valley Mountain in Pocahontas Co., Va. (now West Va.). He was a general in the Confederate army and in command of our department. I saw him daily before he was ordered to another command. In our advance to attack McClellan at Cold Harbor in 1862, after passing through the woods and reaching a field, the first man we saw was our beloved old general on his gray horse, and although he was some distance, we recognized him at once. He was then in command of the army of Northern Virginia, and we joined him to remain till the end came at Appomattox. I saw him several times after this around Richmond. The next time I saw him he was sitting on a stump on the battlefleld of Second Manassas observing Longstreet's men taking position in line of battle, as they came on the field to join Jackson. I saw him often from that time till Grant's campaign of 1864. The last time I saw him he was at Spotsylvania Court House, the day our corps left to head Grant off at Hanover Junction. He appeared to me the same ideal man, except that his hair had become almost white and the dark mustache of my first acquaintance was exchanged for a full beard of gray. As our column approached him, an old private stepped out of ranks and advanced to Gen. Lee. They shook hands like acquaintances and entered into a lively conversation. As I moved on I looked back and the old man had his gun in one hand and the other hand on Traveler's neck, still talking.

"It was such scenes as that, that made Gen. Lee so popular. He believed in his men and thought they could do anything that mortals could do. His men worshiped him, and I think the greatest man the world ever saw was Robert E. Lee."

"

He is Particular in Setting an Example Himself"

Field Marshal Lord Wolseley (the man who became Commander-in-Chief of the British Army) expressed his impression of Lee in a statement written and published in 1863. In the article, Lord Wolseley discussed the simplicity of General Lee's camp, his lack of staff compared to other generals and the aura of respect shown by the men who followed the man in gray. To set an example for all officers and enlisted men Lee insisted upon living under the same conditions as his boys. (A Month's Visit to the Confederate Headquarters; Wolseley, Colonel; Blackwood's; January 1863 as quoted in Lee's Aid-De-Camp; Marshall, Charles; University of Nebraska Press; Lincoln and London; @1927; First Bison Books printing: 2000; xxxii-xxxiii)

"In visiting the headquarters of the Confederate generals, and particularly those of General Lee, anyone accustomed to seeing European armies in the field cannot fail to be struck with the great absence of all the pomp and circumstance of war in and around their encampments. Lee's headquarters consisted of about seven or eight pole tents, pitched with their backs to a stake fence, upon a piece of ground so rocky that it was unpleasant to ride over it, its only recommendation being a little stream of good water which flowed close by the General's tent. In front of the tents were some three or four wagons, drawn up without any regularity, and several horses roamed loose about the field. The servants-who were, of course, slaves-and the mounted soldiers called couriers, who always accompany each general of division in the field, were unprovided with tents, and slept in or under the wagons.

"Wagons, tents, and some of the horses were marked U.S., showing that part of the huge debt in the North had gone to furnishing even the Confederate generals with camp equipment. No guards or sentries were to be seen in the vicinity, no crowd of aides-de-camp loitering about, making themselves agreeable to visitors and endeavoring to save their generals from those who had no particular business. A large farmhouse stands close by, which in any other army would have been the General's residence pro tem, but as no liberties are allowed to be taken with personal property in Lee's army, he is particular in setting an example himself. His staff are crowded together two or three in a tent, none are allowed to carry more baggage than a small box each, and his own kit is but very little larger. Everyone who approaches him does so with marked respect, although there is none of that bowing and scraping and flourishing of forage caps which occurs in the presence of European general; and whilst all honour him and place implicit faith in his courage and ability, those with whom he is most intimate feel for him the affection of sons for a father."

"This Army Will Respect Your Choice"

Upon his first move into Maryland, Lee addressed the people through a proclamation. In it, one can readily see the intent of respect for the decision that the people of Maryland made. It was given on September 8, 1862, after Second Manassas and just prior to Antietam.

"No constraint upon your free will is intended; no intimidation will be allowed within the limits of this army, at least. Marylanders shall once more enjoy their ancient freedom of thought and speech. We know no enemies among you, and will protect all, of

101

every opinion. It is for you to decide your destiny freely and without constraint. This army will respect your choice, whatever it may be; and while the Southern people will rejoice to welcome you to your natural position among them, they will only welcome you when you come of your own free will." (Lee; Freeman, Douglas Southall; Touchstone Book; Simon & Schuster; New York; 1961, 1991; pages 247-248)

"Won't You Sit and Eat With Me?"

While at Sharpsburg, a distant relative by the name of Colonel Stephen D. Lee (he would later rise to become a general and is noted as the first commander of the Sons of Confederate Veterans) ordered that the apples in an orchard be gathered and presented to General Lee. A sixteen-year-old private was given the task of gathering them and to take them to Lee. He ripped out the pocket of his coat and filled it with apples. He then proceeded to General Lee's headquarters. Upon arrival, he offered them to the commanding general. Lee thanked the young man and then stated, "Now, sir, won't you sit down and eat one of these apples with me?" One can only imagine the delight and pride that this young man felt as he sat beside the Hero of the South and partook of the gift intended only for the general. Such was the aura of the man that loved his men, especially the privates that were willing to offer all upon the altar of freedom's cause. It has been noted that he would spend hours upon hours of time writing to those who had lost a loved one and offering his condolences. He was noted as being a soldier's general, full of compassion and love of all. He demonstrated this throughout his life. Even when he accompanied the President, his feelings for his men were ever present. On one occasion as Lee escorted President Davis via train, a wounded veteran climbed aboard and was trying to put on his overcoat with no success due to his injury. General Lee immediately went to the man's assistance and then returned to the side of the President. From private to president, Lee only saw the man not the station in life. In fact, Freeman states that when he addressed his subordinates, privates and especially the couriers, he would, "proffer it in the same tones he would have employed in addressing the President." (Robert E. Lee Man and Soldier; Page, Thomas Nelson; Charles Scribner's sons; New York; 1926; 2:324)

"None Less Than God Could Have Made Such A Man"

One night while sitting around the campfire, the topic of Charles Darwin's evolutionary theory was mentioned regarding man being directly descended from apes and monkeys. Several took exception to such thoughts as the concept was contemplated and postulated among the audience. Finally one man could not contain himself no longer. "Well boys," he stated quite earnestly, "The rest of us may have developed from monkeys; but I tell you none less than God could have made such a man as Marse Robert."

"All That Soldiers Dream"

The following narrative is the reflections of Colonel Marshall (an aid to General Lee) regarding the aftermath of the brilliant victory at Chancellorsville, Lee's presence, and stature among his boys. The scene of such carnage as the smoke rising from the burning buildings and woods, the sound of death howling on the wind and yet men rejoicing at the sight of their general brings to mind such a contrast that the concept eludes the present generations.

The lure of this mortal man was such that men would do extraordinary feats in the name of honor.

"General Lee accompanied the troops in person, and as they emerged from the fierce combat they had waged in the depths of that tangled wilderness, driving the superior forces of the enemy before them across the open ground, he rode into their midst. The scene is one that can never be effaced from the minds of those who witnessed it. The troops were pressing forward with all the ardor and enthusiasm of combat. The white smoke of musketry fringed the front of the line of battle, while the artillery on the hills in the rear of the infantry shook the earth with its thunder and filled the air with the wild shrieks of the shells that plunged into the masses of the retreating foe. To add greater horror to the sublimity of the scene, the Chancellorsville house and the woods surrounding it were wrapped in flames.

"In the midst of this awful scene General Lee, mounted upon that horse which we all remember so well, rode to the front of his advancing battalions. His presence was the signal for one of those uncontrollable outbursts of enthusiasm which none can appreciate who have not witnessed them. The fierce soldiers, with their faces blackened by the smoke of battle; the wounded, crawling with feeble limbs from the fury of the devouring flames; all seemed possessed with a common impulse. One long, unbroken cheer, in which the feeble cry of those who lay helpless on the earth blended with the strong voices of those who still fought, rose high above the roar of battle and hailed the presence of the victorious chief.

"He sat in the full realization of all that soldiers dream of-triumph; and as I looked on him in the complete fruition of the success which his genius, courage and confidence in his army had won, I thought that it must have been from some such scene that men in ancient days ascended to the dignity of gods."

"The Greatest Man Now Living"

Reverend William Jones offers an inspirational story of the self-denial and true altruistic spirit that the man possessed. In his writings, he tells of the memorial service held for the Legend called Lee by the Reverend Doctor T. V. Moore of Richmond's First Presbyterian Church. During the time of his son's (W. F. Lee) incarceration after being severely wounded a Union officer of the same rank wrote General Lee requesting that based on the circumstances, a special exchange could possibly be made. This was also during the time that his son's wife was laying on her deathbed and did expire prior to his release. The threat of hanging loomed over his head for alleged cruelties committed on Northern prisoners by some Confederate guards. The pressure of a father's love for his son and the families' desire for his safe return must have weighed heavily upon his shoulders. As tempting as the offer must have been, never the less, General Lee, "Firmly declined to ask any favor for his own son that could not be asked for the humblest soldier in the army." Upon receiving word of not making an exchange, (disappointed yet overwhelmed by the nobleness of the act) the Union general asked to keep the letter adding, "Sir, I regard him as the greatest man now living." (Personal Reminiscences, Anecdotes, and Letters of General Robert E. Lee; Jones, J. William; Appleton; New York; 1875; page 184)

A Chance Reunion

During the Fredericksburg engagement, concerned about his boys, the Confederate Commander was riding through the ranks when a young private approached him. The boy was dirty, blackened by powder and dressed in ragged and tattered clothing. The great general asked the young man what he could do for him. "Why, General," the boy exclaimed, "Don't you recognize me?" It was his own son, Robert E. Lee Jr., a member of the 1st Rock Bridge Artillery!

"The Personification of Dignity and Grace"

Pvt. George F. Peterkin of the 21st Virginia Infantry offers this insightful observation of the reverence his men held for Lee.

"General Lee was...the very personification of dignity and grace and I can never forget the impression he made on us all." (One of Jackson's Foot Cavalry; Worsham, John H.; Neale Publishing Company; New York; 1912; pg. 299)

"The Grandest Specimen of Manhood I Ever Beheld"

During the 3rd year of the war Colonel Oats had occasion to see Lee pass by. Colonel Oates had been the famous commander of the 15th Alabama that was made immortal by the charge at Little Round Top at Gettysburg against Joshua Chamberlain. While engaged close to Wilderness Tavern, William C. Oates recalls his encounter with the general. These are the words of a warrior upon viewing his commander.

"To reach our position we had to pass within a few feet of General Lee. He sat his fine gray horse 'Traveler' (sic) with the cape of his black cloak around his shoulders, his face flushed and full of animation. The balls were flying around him from two directions. His eyes were on the fight then going on south of the Plank Road between Kershaw's division and the flanking column of the enemy…He turned in his saddle and called to his chief of staff in a most vigorous tone, while pointing with his finger across the road, and said" 'Send an active young officer down there.' I thought him at that moment the grandest specimen of manhood I ever beheld." (The War Between the Union and the Confederacy; Oates, William C.; Neale Publishing Company; 1905; page 808)

"As Long as I Have Rations I Shall Divide Them with My Prisoners"

While brilliantly fighting off the Federal Army from such locations as the Wilderness, The Angle and Spotsylvania, a question was raised by one of Lee's generals regarding the prisoners. The general stated that if he, "Were in command of this army, I would notify General Grant that, inasmuch as he had sent his cavalry to the rear and destroyed our rations, I should not give his prisoners whom we hold a morsel of food; and if he wanted to save them from starvation, he would have to send rations here to them!" Upon hearing the rhetoric of the general, Lee replied, "The prisoners that we have here, General are my prisoners; they are not General Grant's prisoners and as long as I have any rations at all I shall divide them with my prisoners." The issue was immediately dropped and nothing else was said in front of Lee about the matter. (Lee; Freeman, Douglas S.; Touchstone Book; Simon & Schuster; New York; 1961, 1991; 3: pages 238-239)

"A Fearless Look of Self-Possession"

Captain Robert Graham from North Carolina described his encounter with General Lee and the impression that he took away with him. The month was November of 64 within the perimeters of the city under siege; Petersburg. "He is neatly attired in regulation gray, but without the general's white buff coat collar and cuffs...there is no gold wreath, nor a particle of gold lace...He might have been mistaken for a colonel in his best fatigue suit...His hat is a soft black felt...Hair and full beard are both short. Complexion is a healthy, ruddy hue, indicating a temperate life. There is a fearless look of self-possession, without a trace of arrogance." (Grey Fox: Robert E. Lee and the Civil War; Davis, Burke; Wings Books, an imprint of Random House Value Publishing; New York; 1956; page 351)

"An Unquestioning Trust in the Decrees of an All-Wise Creator"

While entrenched in the quagmires of Petersburg, all eyes were upon their general. To the soldiers under siege he offered hope and confidence. To the people entrapped and living in hand dug tunnels referred to as "gopher town" he was a point

108

of inspiration and determination. During the dark hours of the beginning of the end when the gallant Army of Northern Virginia began retreating from the city, one of his staff officers noted his charisma and eloquently penned his impressions and preserved it for prosperity. (<u>Lee of Virginia</u>; Freeman, Douglas Southall; Charles Scribner's & Sons; New York; 1958; page 190)

"Self-contained and serene, he acted as one who was conscious of having accomplished all that was possible in the line of duty, and who was undisturbed by the adverse conditions in which he found himself. There was no apparent excitement and no sign of apprehension as he issued his orders for the retreat of his sadly reduced army and the relinquishment of the position so long and successfully held against the greatly superior force opposed to him...It was a striking illustration of Christian fortitude, the result of an habitual endeavor to faithfully perform the duties of one's station, and of unquestioning trust in the decrees of an all-wise Creator..."

"The Legend Walked Amongst Them"

Another example of the admiration held by this man was during the low point of his life. After the surrender at Appomattox, General Lee came into Richmond alone, riding his faithful stead. His boys immediately recognized him and word spread like a wildfire that the legend walked among them. One by one the vanquished soldiers dropped in behind their hero and with uncovered heads they reverently followed him to his home. "Then they silently dispersed." (<u>One of Jackson's Foot Cavalry, His Experience and What He Saw During the War 1861-1865</u>; Worsham, John H.; New York; The Neale Publishing Company; 1912; pg. 88)

"I Sat Immovable, With a Certain Awe and Admiration"

One of my favorite writers that fought on the side of 'Those People' was Joshua Chamberlain. General Chamberlain became immortal at Gettysburg when he held Little Round Top with the 20th Maine and gave a final charge down the mountain pushing the remnants of the 15th Alabama under the command of Colonel Oaks down the mountain, capturing many and turning the tide of the battle. But to this offer his greatest moment was at Gettysburg where he offered the last salute to his former adversaries and gave the Confederate soldiers' one last hurrah. He wrote of his first glance of Lee.

"`I turned about, and there behind me, riding between my two lines, appeared a commanding form, superbly mounted, richly accoutered, of imposing bearing, noble countenance, with expression of deep sadness overmastered by deeper strength. It was none other than Robert E. Lee! I sat immovable, with a certain awe and admiration."

"Goodbye, Colonel! God Bless Ye!"

Lee's son wrote a couple of stories that caught the attention of this fielder. It pertained to an incident after the war in which a former soldier came to their house and knocked. When his cousin Dan Lee and the General's youngest son answered the door, a man stood there with a black man holding a basket filled with a variety of commodities that he wanted to present to the general. The man was "Irish all over" and had heard that Lee's family was in need of provisions. He frankly stated that as long as he had breath the Lee family would not go without

110

food. Upon hearing voices, General Lee stepped out of the room and immediately the soldier snapped to attention and saluted. The gesture of respect was returned and then the man as he cried explained his mission of mercy. General Lee was very moved by the offer but declined to take the food. The man persisted until he agreed to take it and give it to the local hospital. This seemed to pacify the man and as he departed, he threw his arms around the General and attempted to kiss him. As he left he said, "Goodbye, Colonel! God bless ye! If I could have got over in time I would have been with ye!"

In another incident, a man dressed in very ragged apparel came to the house. He was chosen to represent several other poor men that had served under General Lee. He asked to speak to the general and when he met with him he explained that they were offering him and his family a home in which to live. They also offered their lives in protecting him and his loved ones, for they had heard that Lee would soon be charged with treason. The old general was moved to tears but graciously declined their kind act of love and undying commitment to him and his loved ones. (Recollections and Letters of Robert E. Lee; Lee, Robert E. Jr. Captain; Doubleday, Doran, and Company; 1904,1924)

"Not a Single Word Was Spoken"

Another story of the love and admiration between Lee and his Texans is evident in the writing of Charles Flood. Shortly after the end of the war, a Texan visited Lee's home at his 707 Franklin Street address in Richmond. He stated that he was a former member of the Texas Brigade and his heart's desire was to look upon General Lee's face

111

one more time before his return to Texas. While the Texan waited, Custis went upstairs to see his father. Colonel Clement Sullivane, a former aide of Custis, monitored the door while waiting to see if General Lee was available. The following account is from the words of Colonel Sullivane. It describes the emotion of the moment and the deep mutual respect held by both. <u>(Lee, The Last Years; Flood, Charles Bracelen;</u> Houghton Mifflin Company; New York; 1981; pages 54-55)

"I offered the old soldier a seat and entered into a friendly conversation with him about his wounds, etc. Presently I heard the stately step of General Robert E. Lee descending the stairway. As we both arose on his entrance into the room, he bowed gravely to me and then advanced to the Texan, with his hand extended. The poor fellow grasped it, looked General Lee straight in the eyes, struggled to say something, but choked and could not, and, wringing Lee's hand, he dropped it as he burst into tears; then, covering his face with his arm, he turned away and walked out of the room and the house.

"General Lee gazed after him for a few moments motionless, his fine, deep dark eyes suffused with emotion, and then, again gravely bowing to me, he left the room and returned upstairs. Not a single word was spoken."

"They Snapped to Attention"

Another insightful glimpse into the legend of Lee comes from the writing of Charles Flood. As Lee took one of his daily rides, which was his custom, one can only imagine the manner in which he was perceived and received by his former boys in gray. The man and horse were one; synonymous with each other. The pride of Dixie rode down the streets of Lexington and all that witness to the two must have been in awe of their good fortune to have the legends in gray riding amongst them. Rarely in the chronicles of history has one man and one horse represented such awe-inspiring victory in the sweet refrain of defeat. (<u>Lee: the last Years</u>; Flood, Charles Bracelen; Houghton Mifflin Company; 1981)

"At one o'clock in the afternoon Lee crossed the North River and entered the town of Lexington...Coming up the main street, riding slowly, Lee raised his hat to those who recognized him. Several out-of-work veterans of the Army of Northern Virginia were aimlessly talking in front of the Lexington Hotel when their former commander reined up on Traveller. They snapped to attention. One of them saluted before placing a hand upon Traveller's bridle and another on the stirrup, waiting for Lee to dismount...A small crowd had gathered; unseen by Lee, a youth acquired a souvenir by slipping behind Traveller and plucking some hairs from his tail."

"I Try Every Day to Pray for Them"

After the war, one of the chaplains that had served the Confederate States of America planned to make a tour of the states that had been loyal to the South in hopes of a revival. He stopped by to see General Lee. Upon hearing his mission, he asked the chaplain to carry a message to his beloved men. "You will meet many of my old soldiers during your trip, and I wish you to tell them that I often think of them, try everyday to pray for them and am always gratified to hear of their prosperity."

"In the Presence of a Man Cast in a Grander Mould"

Sir Garnet Joseph Wolseley (1833-1913), an English officer (he later became Commander-in-chief of the British Army) serving in the capacity of observer, reflected in writing upon his meetings with General Lee during the Civil War. He offered the following tribute to the Southern Commander. A remarkable footnote would be to remember that this man met the king and queen of England in his day and still felt that all paled in significance to the gray headed chieftain.

"I never felt my own individual insignificance more keenly than I did in his presence. I have met many of the great men of my time, but Lee alone impressed me with the feeling that I was in the presence of a man who was cast in a grander mould, and made of different and of finer metal than all other men."

"His Bearing Was That of a Friend"

Another officer recounted the presence of Lee by stating that Lee, "Assumed no airs of superior authority…His bearing was that of a friend having a common interest in a common venture with the person addressed…He was less of an actor than any man I ever saw."

"Every Motion is Instinct with Natural Grace"

A faithful soldier from Virginia wrote a letter home telling his loved ones of his first encounter with the general. "It is impossible for me to describe the impression made upon me by his bearing and manners. I felt myself in the presence of a great man…every motion is instinct with natural grace

114

which…makes one feel a sense of confidence and trust that is delightful."

"A Child Would Run to Claim His Protection"

A reporter from the London Times wrote of Lee stating that his manner was, "calm and stately," his presence, "impressive and imposing," and that, "The general was so kind and courteous that a child thrown among a knot of strangers would inevitably be drawn to him…and would run to claim his protection." (Jackson & Lee; Legends in Gray; Kunstler, Mort, paintings of; Text by Robertson, James I., Jr.; Rutledge Hill Press; Nashville, Tennessee; 1995; pages 6-30)

"He was Likely to Make an Impression upon the Old Fogy Schools"

During his presidential tenure at Washington College, Lee's vision was starting to be realized. Under his leadership, the school flourished. His legacy of building a university that would lead the Southern States back into harmony economically was being realized. His law school, press scholarships, the study of law (international law as well), his school of engineering, the farm project and a school for business were all well ahead of their time. President Lee not only saw the need but he made the dream a reality. Sometimes compliments and recognition comes from the unlikeliest of places. The New York Herald applauded his innovations and stated that Lee, "Was likely to make as great an impression upon our old fogy schools and colleges as…in military tactics upon our old fogy commanders in the palmy days of the rebellion." The prophecy of yesteryear became true and now the prestige of being a student or graduate from Washington Lee College is equal to the major universities around the world.

"Designed by God to Teach"

Edward Clifford Gordon was President Lee's aide for over three years. He was privileged to spend countless hours with the old general and had real insight into his character. During Gordon's tenure as Lee's aide he established a trust and bond that only true friendship and admiration can create. He listed that among Lee's many virtues that his modesty, his kindness with animals and love for children were possibly his greatest. But there was also the infamous temper. Gordon stated that, "But these characteristics were combined with what I may call a fierce and violent temper, prone to intense expression." Edward Gordon's best overview of Lee was stated in the following manner, "Intellectually he was cast in a gigantic mold. Naturally he was possessed of strong passions. He loved excitement, particularly the excitement of war. He loved grandeur. But all these appetites and powers were brought under the control of his judgment and made subservient to his Christian faith. This made him habitually unselfish and ever willing to sacrifice himself on the altar of duty and in the service of his fellows...He is an epistle, written of God and designed by God to teach the people of this country that earthly success is not the criterion of merit, not the measure of true greatness." During the fall semester of 1868 Edward Clifford Gordon followed his calling to become a preacher. He left Washington College and attended the Virginia Theological Seminary. (<u>Lee, The Last Years</u>; Flood, Charles Bracelen; Houghton Mifflin Company; New York; 1981; pages 213-214)

"He is an Epistle, Written of God"

Edward Clifford Gordon was Robert E. Lee's aide for three years during his tenure as president of Washington College. The man and his Christian outlook on life profoundly impressed Mr. Gordon. The following summates his impression of the character of Lee. (Lee, The Last Years; Flood, Charles Bracelen; Houghton Mifflin Company; New York; 1981; page 83)

"Intellectually he was cast in a gigantic mold. Naturally he was possessed of strong passions. He loved excitement, particularly the excitement of war. He loved grandeur. But all these appetites and powers were brought under the control of his judgments and made subservient to his Christian faith. This made him habitually unselfish and ever willing to sacrifice himself on the altar of duty and in the service of his fellows...He is an epistle, written of God and designed by God to teach the people of this country that earthly success is not the criterion of merit nor the measure of true greatness."

"They Retained Their Seat in Solemn Silence"

A classic example that demonstrates Lee's true Christianity and leadership was when he had returned from the war and was living in Richmond. He was a devoted Episcopalian and attended service regularly at St. Paul's Episcopal Church. During the invitation to accept communion, a black parishioner went forward to surrender and partake in the sacrament. The effect was immediately electrifying. "Upon the communicants was startling, and for several moments they retained their seat in solemn silence and did not move." With reverenced silence the gallant old general rose from the pew and walked forward in submission to his Creator. He knelt beside his brother, seeing no color but a man worshiping his God and partook of the body and blood of Christ.   Calmness and reason prevailed as the worshipers went forward to accept the communion.   Without words, without a speech, armed with only his actions, Lee led the wayward flock back to the truths of the teaching of Christ as love overcame and reason prevailed on that day.

The General's Values

A personal glimpse into the character of Robert E. Lee was presented in the film series called The Civil War by Ken Burns. Mr. Burns states that after the war, General Lee was left without any means of support. An insurance company offered him fifty thousand dollars (a sizeable sum considering the times) for the use of his signature. The old gentleman of character declined stating that he couldn't accept money for services that he didn't render.   He later accepted the presidency of Washington College at a salary of fifteen hundred dollars a year.

"Whatever Happens, Know This"

One of the great values that he possessed was his high esteem for his men that fought in the Confederacy. He was quick to their defense and allowed no man to offer ill tidings of them. Whenever questioned about his men he stood firm and proud on the laurels of their loyalties and their commitment to duty.   His love and devotion to those that had served followed him to his grave and was a key component as to why all so revered him.

"Whatever happens, know this-that no men ever fought better than those who have stood by me."

"Miss Josie, Has Your Father a Good Hat?"

A delightful story has been preserved for us to cherish by Major Robert Stiles. The major tells of the generosity of General Lee and his piety. He referred to a particular incident when his sister Josephine, a close friend of the Lee family, was assisting in packing for a trip in which the general was about to embark. It enlightens the reader into the nature of Lee. I took the liberty of quoting Major Stiles words for authenticity. (<u>Four Years Under Marse Robert</u>; Stiles, Robert; The Neale Publishing Company; New York and Washington; 1904; page 357)

"My sister had been spending the morning at the General's residence, 707 East Franklin Street, Richmond, Va., sitting most of the time with the ladies of the family in Mrs. Lee's room. The General was preparing for a trip somewhere, and was leisurely packing his trunk, that is, after the ladies had done what they could to aid him--and every now and then he would enter the room where they were bringing in his hand something which he thought would interest them. In one of these incursions he brought a wide-brimmed drab or gray-brown felt hat, saying: 'Miss Josie, has your father a good hat?' My sister replied that she really did not know, as we had not seen him for some time. 'Well,' said the General, 'I have two good hats, and I don't think a good rebel ought to have two good articles of one kind in these hard times. This was my dress-parade hat. Take it, please, and if your father has not a good hat give him this one from me.' Father would not wear the hat, deeming it too sacred a thing for common use; but after the General's death, by permission of his daughters, who were present, I wore it at two of our great Confederate reunions, with my dear old Confederate jacket, and I need scarcely say was

119

the object of more intense interest than ever in my life, before or since. I made bold, too, to have my photograph taken with the hat on--of course, the jacket, also,--as a sort of heirloom for my family."

"They Could Not Do a Deed of Lawless Violence"

In an incident occurring off campus, General Lee's level of regard by his former soldiers and fellow citizens is evident. It was towards the end of his first year as President of Washington College. A rash of horse thefts had occurred and a man by the name of Jonathan Hughes was notorious for his ability to walk in and ride out on a horse borrowed from a farmer or citizen. He had been captured and was housed in the Lexington jail. That warm May afternoon saw the disposition of the towns people turn ugly and soon they were talking of taking justice into their own hands. A witness to the scene by the name of Charles Graves stated that, "At the top of the jail steps in front of the locked door, stood the old jailor, Thomas L. Perry, holding the jail keys high above his head, and facing, with grim and resolute aspect, the would-be lynchers who surrounded him. For some reason, perhaps respect to the old man's gray hairs, the men next to him had forborne to seize him and snatch from him the jail keys, as they could easily have done." But the momentum to break the man out of jail and to pronounce sentence via the hanging was escalating.

Suddenly, the crowd quietly parted as a gray-haired gentleman walked silently amongst them. He stopped and spoke cordially to a few of his fellow citizens, many of whom were his former soldiers. The tide of hatred subsided and reason regained the thoughts of men. "The end was there. Those stern Scotch-Irishmen, whose tenacity of purpose is proverbial, remounted their horses and rode out of town. They could not do a deed of lawless violence in the presence of Mares Robert." (Lee, The Last Years; Flood, Charles Bracelen; Houghton Mifflin Company; New York; 1981; pages 131-132)

"Remember General Lee!"

In one of Charles B. Flood's marvelous books he tells of an incident involving the students of Washington College that threatened it to be shut down permanently except for the quick thinking of Givens B. Strickler and General Lee. Givens was the captain of the Liberty Hall Volunteers and had seen his share of action. He participated in the battle of Gettysburg and had been captured there after leading an attack.

The incident occurred only nine days after the state of Virginia was stripped of its statehood. Rumors had spread of a meeting to be held by Northerners speaking to local blacks. This upset some of the students at Washington College. Five of them (three from Texas, one from Alabama and one from Georgia) decided to go see for themselves the exact nature of the meeting. The young man from Alabama brought along a pistol. Upon arriving at the schoolhouse, they attempted to look into the window. The Freedman's Bureau held classes for blacks at this location and it was well known to be an area in which blacks frequented in an effort to better themselves via education. As the boys looked through the window, a black man approached them and a scuffle broke out between the man and the Alabama youth. In the heat of the moment, the Alabama lad hit the black man with the pistol. All five boys fled the scene but all were apprehended except for the one from Alabama who had hit the man.

Although Lee was unaware of what was transpiring on his campus, word spread and many of the students became alarmed and wanted to rescue their comrades and fellow students. As the mob mentality grew, those rallying their support and courage began snaking their way towards the jail. Givens stepped up to the moment and stated, "Steady men! Steady men! Remember General Lee! No violence! Remember General Lee! Let the law take its course. You must do what General Lee would wish."

The silent crowd immediately went back to being students and left the area for the confines of their campus. The four jailed students were found guilty of disturbing the peace and released. President Lee sent for the boys. When they entered his office, they found the boy from Alabama already in Lee's presence. He shouldered the blame for the incident and stated that it was his fault for the assault of the man. President Lee concurred and immediately expelled him from the college. He placed the others on probation but the worst part must have been the disappointment seen in the eyes of the old general turned gentleman as he expressed his dismay and distaste for this type of behavior. Both General Lee's action and the quick thinking of Givens probably averted sanctions (if not the closing) against the floundering college. (<u>Lee, The Last Years</u>; Flood, Charles Bracelen; Houghton Mifflin Company; New York; 1981; pages 150-151)

"We Must Live for Our Afflicted Country"

One of the few authors privileged to have permission from the Lee family and wholeheartedly endorsed by Mrs. Mary Custis Lee (also was sanctioned by Washington and Lee College) to write a book on the general was the Reverend John William Jones. He not only followed his banner during the war, he was privy to personal accounts during that time. After the war, he became one of the Chaplains at the college and became intimately acquainted with the family, having dinner at his home and visiting him at the office. His book is a must for those seeking knowledge of the great commander. In it he discusses an interview held with a writer discussing the results of the war. Lee in typical fashion stated, "Yes: all that is very sad, and might be a cause of self-reproach, but that we are conscious that we have humbly tried to do our duty. We may, therefore, with calm satisfaction, trust in God, and leave results to him."

General John Gordon stated that during that time of confronting the inevitable, the commander was in "agony of spirit" because of the suffering of his boys due to the surrender. General Gordon states that at one point Lee exclaimed, "I could wish that I were numbered among the slain of the last battle," but that he at once recalled his wish, and said, "No! We must live for our afflicted country." When questioned regarding the surrender by a staff officer, Lee stated, "How easily I could get rid of this and be at rest! I have only to ride along the lines, and all will be over. But it is our duty to live, for what will become of the women and children of the South if we are not here to support and protect them." (<u>Personal Reminiscences, Anecdotes and Letters of General Robert E. Lee</u>; Jones, J. William; Appleton; New York; 1875)

"The Hero of Our Dreams"

During the summer of 1867, the Lee family made a pilgrimage to the White Sulphur Springs (Greenbrier) some fifty miles west of Lexington. At a roadside tavern where the Lees were staying, a group of young ladies from Maryland stopped. One of the ladies was Christiana Bond who later wrote of their first impression of Lee. A friendship resulted from that chance encounter that lasted until Lee's passing.

"We were aware of some one standing at the turn of the steep stairway above us. Looking up, at the sound of a rich, beautifully modulated voice, we knew that we were in the presence of General Robert E. Lee, the hero of our dreams. The man who stood before us, the embodiment of a Lost Cause, was the realized King Arthur. The soul that looked out of his eyes was as honest and fearless as when it first looked on life. One saw the character, as clear as crystal, without complications or seals, and the heart, as tender as that of ideal womanhood. The years which have passed since that time have dimmed many enthusiasms and destroyed many illusions, but have caused no blush at the memory of the swift thrill of recognition and reverence which ran like an electric flash through one's whole body. General Lee stood above us on the stairway, clad in Confederate grey, his wide, soft hat in his hand, which still wore his riding gauntlet. He looked very tall and majestic standing

124

there, beaming down upon us with his kindly, humorous smile and the wonderful beauty of his dark eyes. When we recovered our wits we found a courteous invitation was being extended to refresh ourselves in the room which had been reserved for Mrs. Lee's party."

As word spread that General Lee was staying at the White Sulphur Springs, several of his former men became concerned because of the high delegation of former Union men also relaxing there. The former rebels hastily held a meeting to discuss how they should recognize and honor Lee at the dinner that evening without creating tension between the two former enemies. But when the time arrived, they had not reached an agreement. Anxiously worried and concerned they watched their former Commander in Chief walk in with his family. In unison, as if by design, all five hundred guest rose in tribute and homage to the Grey Knight.

"I Only Wanted to See Him"

A story shared by his son on the high esteem held by his old soldiers occurred during a retreat at Ole Sweet Springs during the late summer of 1867. The trip was to help in the healing of his wife who was in a wheelchair. While staying at that location, he became quite sick, to the point that he could take his daily constitutional ride on his faithful horse. He was on the first floor with a window opening on the end of the building that possessed shutters. "One morning, when he was very unwell and it was important that he should not be disturbed, Miss Pendleton found a countryman cautiously opening the shutters from the outside. She quickly interfered, saying, "Go away: that is

General Lee's room." The man dropped back, saying mournfully, "I only wanted to see him."

"On another occasion some country people came to the Springs with plums and berries for sale. Catching sight of him on the piazza, they put down their baskets, took off their hats, and hurrahed most lustily for Marse Bob. They were his old soldiers. When he acknowledged their loyalty by shaking hands with them, they insisted on presenting him with their fruit." (Recollections and Letters of Robert E. Lee; Lee, Robert E. Jr. Captain; Doubleday, Doran, and Company; 1904,1924)

"The One of Lee is the Perfect Picture"

The Swiss commissioned a well-known Swiss painter by the name of Frank Buchser who came to America with the intent of painting Grant. His idea was to paint both Lee and Grant at Appomattox. Upon meeting the old general he was smitten by his charisma. He was soon taken under the general's care and found himself privy to Lee's candor. He soon was a devoted admirer of Lee and on October 3, he wrote, "What a gentle noble soul, how kind and charming the ole white-haired warrior is! One cannot see and know this great soldier without loving him." As he painted, he came upon the realization that Lee embodied what he sought. Busher claimed that Lee "Is furthermore the ideal of American democracy. Therefore, of all my American portraits, the one of Lee is the perfect picture to hang in the democratic Swiss parliament." His supporters refused to pay him stating that he was sent to capture the Union victory but "All agreed he (Lee) is the greater character." His portrait is on display in the Swiss national Museum. (Lee, The Last Years; Flood,

Charles Bracelen; Houghton Mifflin Company; New York; 1981; pages 217-222)

"The Best Promise of Any Soldier of Beating Him Again"

During the Presidential election of 1868 the New York Herald, Northern newspaper with democratic ties, came out and surprised the country by stating that Robert E. Lee would make a viable candidate for this office! Only a few months earlier, due to a statement made by the congress, a fund raiser in New York and an incident involving a Union soldier and a twelve-year-old boy, not only was Lee getting blasted in the papers but also the college. How time changes things! Even if Lee was inclined to do so (nor would the Party entertain such boldness), he could not have been a candidate due to not having citizenship and still being under the auspices of the court. Nor would he have done so because of his character and realization that the wound that he sought to heal may be reopened. He did not fancy the thought of "military statesmen and political generals" and would never allow himself to be put into such an arena that he felt he was unqualified to fill and was not ordained by the will of God. In the advertisement, the editorial stated:

"We will recommend a candidate for its favors. Let it nominate General R. E. Lee. Let it boldly take over the best of all its soldiers, making no palaver or apology. He is a better soldier than any of those they thought upon and a greater man...For this soldier, with a handful of men whom he had molded into an army, baffled our greater Northern armies for four years; and when opposed by Grant was only worn down by that solid strategy of stupidity that accomplishes its object by mere weight."

"With one quarter the men Grant had this soldier fought magnificently across the territory of his native state, and fought his army to a stump. There never was such an army or such a campaign, or such a General for illustrating the military genius and possibilities of our people, and this General is the best of all for a Democratic candidate. It is certain that with half as many men as Grant he would have beaten him from the field in Virginia, and he affords the best promise of any soldier for beating him again." (R. E. Lee, a Biography; Freeman Douglas South all; four-volume; New York; Scribner; 1934-35)

"But We Must Not Remember That against Him"

There are several qualities that have endeared Lee to both sides of the conflict over the generations. One of the best examples is personified by an account in William J. Jones's book. It demonstrates the genuine concern that Lee held in his heart for his fellow man. In Jones's reminiscences, he relates a story as told by a neighbor of Marse Robert. This incident happened during the autumn of 1869. General Lee was standing by his gate and had just concluded talking to a rather poorly dressed man when the neighbor arrived. After talking of usual pleasantries, the image of the poor man leaving just as the neighbor arrived entered into the conversation. The kindly old general simply stated in a matter of fact fashion, "That is one of our old soldiers who is in necessitous circumstances." With his curiosity aroused, the neighbor questioned President Lee as to what command the gentleman was from and much to the neighbor's surprise General Lee replied, "He fought on the other side, but we must not remember that against him now."

On another occasion, General Lee's neighbor happened upon the man that had been talking to Lee on that autumn day. Eventually the topic of the much-admired General entered Into the conversation. Remembering what the general had said, Lee's neighbor inquired further as to their communication topic. The man respectfully stated, "Sir, he…not only had a kind word for an old soldier who fought against him, but he gave me some money to help me on my way." This demonstration of love and fulfillment of Jesus' commandments to serve one another struck me with reverence and awe for the man. "For I was hungry and you fed me, I was naked and you clothed me." It humbled me with shame as I reflected on the times that I have neglected to serve my fellow man. With this act he personified a true Christian. The following poem is my attempt to honor this act of compassion and is my interpretation of the events. (Personal Reminiscences, Antidotes, and Letters of General Robert E. Lee; Jones, J. William; D. Appleton; New York; 1875)

We Must Not Remember It against Him

He was talking to a stranger
While standing by his gate.
But there seemed to be no danger

As each recalled his fate.

Lee handed him some money
As he bid him adieu.
It struck me kind of funny:
The man was wearin' blue.

When asked he simply listened
With silence for a while.
"We must not hold that against him;
We're all united now."

I later saw the soldier
Dressed in faded blue.
I asked him, getting bolder
Who he'd been talking to.

"It was a kindly old man.
His name I can't recall.
But with his out stretched hand
He has given me his all."

"For I was broke and all alone
He asked me in to eat.
I'm a soldier going home
Now with shoes on my feet."

I could not come to tell him
Our general he had met.
Lee's love for God compelled him:
For that I love him yet.

"He was Full of Sympathy and Kindness"

After General Lee's death, many tributes were paid. Among them was an old classmate by the name of General Joseph E. Johnston. In a correspondence, General Johnston paid homage to Lee's character. (Life & Letters of Gen. Robert Edward Lee; Jones, W.J.; Sprinkle Publications; Harrisonburg, Virginia; 1986; @ by Neale Publishing Company in 1906; pages 36-37)

"No one among men but his own brothers had better opportunity to know General Lee than me. We entered the Military Academy together as classmates, and formed then a friendship never impaired. It was formed very soon after we met, from the fact that my father served under his in the celebrated Lee's Legion. We had the same intimate associates, who thought, as I did, that no other youth or man so united the qualities that win warm friendship and command high respect. For he was full of sympathy and kindness, genial and fond of gay conversations, while his correctness of demeanor of language and attention to all duties, personal and official, and a dignity as much a part of himself as the elegance of his person, gave him a superiority that every one acknowledged in his heart. He was the only one of all the men I have known who could laugh at the faults and follies of his friends in such a manner as to make them ashamed without touching their affection for him, and to confirm their respect and sense of superiority.

"I saw strong evidence of the sympathy of his nature the morning after the first engagements of our troops in the Valley of Mexico. I had lost a cherished young relative in that action, known to General Lee only as my relative. Meeting me, he suddenly saw in my face the effect of that loss, burst into tears, and expressed his deep sympathy as tenderly in words as his lovely wife would have done."

"The Students Should All Become a Sincere Christian"

As was his wish during the war, Lee's greatest desire was that his students (former soldiers and sons/daughters of the country) would drink from the cup of salvation. He prayed about it constantly and put his words into action by being that model that youth so desperately need to have in order to emulate their actions in that direction. That was his goal and it should be ours. In order to save our great heritage, in order to retrieve the greatest of our country, we must return to the old paths and follow the captain as he heads us to Christ.

"He was always solicitous for the promotion of religion in the college, and warmly encouraged the work of the Young Men's Christian Association. He allowed more emotion than on almost any other occasion in expressing his fervent wish that the students should all become sincere Christians. Rev. Randolph H. McKim

"Looking Unto Jesus the Author and Finisher of Our Faith"

The Reverend J. William Jones walked with Lee and knew of his walk with God. His interpretation of Lee's Christian nature best sums up the many accolades that were laid at Lee's feet because of his walk with Christ. He was a true disciple and was humbled by the thought that he was but a sinner saved by the intercession of Christ. The values of past generations need to be rekindled for this generation.

"If I have ever come in contact with a sincere, devout Christian—and one who, seeing himself to be a sinner, trusted alone in the merits of Christ,-- who humbly tried to walk the path of duty, 'looking unto Jesus the author and finisher of our faith' and whose piety was constantly exemplified in his daily life, that man was the world's great soldier, and model man, Robert Edward Lee."

"The Undulating Plain of Humanity"

One of the greatest tributes to Lee came from a speech presented to the Southern Historical Society by Benjamin Harvey Hill. He captured the Christian persona of the late general. The presentation was given on February 18, 1874.

"When the future historian shall come to survey the character of Lee, he will find it rising like a huge mountain above the undulating plain of humanity, and he must lift his eyes high toward heaven to catch its summit. He was a foe without hate, a friend without treachery, a soldier without cruelty, a victor without oppression, and a victim without murmuring. He was a public officer without vices, a private citizen without wrong, a neighbor without reproach, a Christian without hypocrisy, and a man without guile. He was a Caesar without his ambition, a Frederick without his tyranny, a Napoleon without his selfishness, and a Washington without his reward."

LEE'S LOVE OF ANIMALS

Not only did General Lee show his humanity for others during a time of devastation but he also possessed a deep commitment to the creatures that existed around him throughout his life. General Lee was a great lover of animals. Several stories still permeate the minds of men and have been recorded regarding his kindness and heart felt appreciation for the creatures around him. One such story comes to the mind of this dramatist regarding an incident involving Lucy Long, one of Lee's long time steeds. While residing in Lexington he purchased a buggy (little carriage) in which he could take his invalid wife on excursions around the town. On one such occasion, he was attempting to ascend a steep incline when Lucy Long fell and was choked unconscious by the collar. The old general jumped from the carriage and loosened the collar from around the neck of his mare. Once his beloved horse was in total possession of her senses, Lee became very vigorous towards the careless manner in which he had harnessed his mare. He patted and talked soothingly to her, asking her for forgiveness. He was upset with himself that he had caused injury to a true companion.

The Mounts of Lee

Much has been written about Traveller but General Lee also had other horses that he rode during the war. He was deeply attached to all of them and regarded them as partners. The following is a brief description of his other mounts:

Richmond was a bay stallion, purchased in 1861. He rode Richmond during his inspection of the defenses of the city that the horse was named. Richmond died in 1862, after the battle of Malvern Hill.

Brown Roan was bought in West Virginia at the onset of the Civil War. In 1862, the Roan went blind and was left with a farmer.

Ajax was a sorrel. He was killed in the mid sixties when he accidentally ran into an Iron Gate latch prong. General Lee did not ride him frequently due to the horse being so large, making him uncomfortable and awkward to ride.

Lucy Long was a mare that was used as the primary backup for Traveller. She was seen often in the presence of general Lee or being ridden by the Lee ladies. She died when she was thirty-three years old. A newspaper article in the Abingdon Virginian, dated February 13, 1891, described Lucy Long and made obvious the high standing that this little warhorse held in the general's heart.

"There have appeared from time to time during the past year announcements in Southern newspapers of war-horses ridden during the war by some Confederate soldier, with the caption, 'The Last War-horse of the Confederacy;' or something similar. It will be learned, doubtless with surprise by some, that there is yet living and in good health, save for the infirmities common to old age, a horse ridden in battle during the war by General Robert E. Lee. It is 'Lucy Long,' a little sorrel mare, which many will recall having seen ladies ride through the streets of Lexington alongside of General Lee astride of his more famous war-horse 'Traveller.'

"Lucy Long was a present to General Lee from General J. E. B. Stuart in 1862, when the former was conducting the Sharpsburg campaign. That summer General Lee was standing in a skirmish line holding Traveller. The horse was high-spirited, impatient and hard to hold and pulled the General down a steep bank and broke his hands. For a time he found it necessary to travel in an ambulance. It was then that General Stuart found Lucy Long, bought her and gave her to him. "She was a low, easy moving, and quiet sorrel mare. General Stuart purchased her from Mr. Stephen Dandridge, the owner of 'The Bower,' a country place in Jefferson County, famous in that day for its hospitality and a famous resort of Stuart with his staff when in that locality. General Lee rode Lucy Long for two years until, when in the lines around Petersburg, she got with foal, and he sent her to the rear, and once more mounted Traveller. She was stolen just before the close of the war and after the surrender was found in the eastern part of the State, and Captain R. E. Lee brought her to Lexington to his father.

"Several years after General Lee's death, and possibly thirteen years ago, while running at large in the grounds in the rear of the University, by some unknown means Lucy Long got the leaders of her hind legs cut. She was henceforth of no service, and General Custis Lee got the late John Riplogle, the greatest horse lover in Rockbridge in his day, to take charge of her on his farm on Buffalo. On Mr. Riplogle's death, a few years ago, she was turned over to the care of Mr. John R. Mackay, who lives in the same neighborhood, and there she is at this time.

"When purchased by General Stuart she was said to be five years old. She is probably now in her thirty-fourth year. She is thin in flesh, though her eye has not lost its wonted brightness and her health apparently is good. She eats dry food with difficulty, hence her present condition. During the grazing season she fattens on the soft grasses of the pasture."

During the Mexican War, he wrote about a horse that he owned by the name of Creole. He stated that she, "Stepped over the dead men with such care as if she feared to hurt them, but when I started with the dragoons in the pursuit, she was as fierce as possible, and I could barely hold her." On a return trip from the Mexican War, he brought his son Robert Jr. a fine young pony that was appropriately named <u>Santa Anna</u>. Young Robert vividly recalls in his memoirs the first time he laid eyes upon the little pony. While stationed in Texas, he had a particular horse that he was quite attached to by the name of Grace Darling. The chestnut colored steed had caught his eye. Reportedly, it had been shot seven times. He brought Grace Darling back with him and owned it until the spring of 1862 when Federal troops confiscated it. (<u>Recollections and Letters of General Robert E. Lee</u>; Lee, Robert E. Lee Jr.; Garden City Publishing Company; Garden City, New York; 1904; pages 10-11)

Lee also possessed dogs. Lee had a black and tan terrier by the name of Spec and another by the name of Dart (mother of Spec). He thought so much of the animals that he referred to them during his correspondences home. He had a Maltese cat (Tom Nipper) that was considered to be a member of the family. It was reported by the family that it was always underfoot and would even attend church, much to the delight of the Lee children. (Traveller; Adams, Richard; Alfred A. Knopf; New York; 1988)

One of the more enduring stories revolves around a little squirrel (chipmunk) that Agnes held dear. She had named It Custls Morgan (the flrst name for the Custis family and the last for the infamous General John Hunt Morgan that was idealized for the persona of being a gallant cavalier). Her father would always joke with her that the squirrel would best serve the cause of freedom in a stew rather than scurrying around the home. The daughter's will prevailed and little Custis Morgan became a family treasure as another legend of Lee was born.

General Lee held a deep reverence, respect and affection all for animals. One story in particular comes to mind. While on an active battlefield, General Lee was assessing the day's events when he spotted what appeared to be a bird that had fallen from a tree. Not thinking of the danger in which he was placing himself, he went to the creature's rescue. He carefully took the bird into his grasp and placed it back among the branches. The man who witnessed the death of hundreds of thousands was showing concern for the death of a bird. Even in death he had a reverence for life.

General Lee and the Little Hen

My favorite story regarding Lee's natural love for animals is that of Lee and his little hen. While at Hamilton's Crossing, just after the victory at Fredericksburg, a little hen became the proud property of the general. A local farmer had given several chickens in gratitude for the general and his men. A particular little hen won favor in the eyes of General Lee by laying an egg under his bed. It was said that the little hen faithfully laid an egg within the confines of its master's tent on a daily basis. It quickly became his pet and was seen in the front of his tent, within the confines of her refuge, safe from the cook's glaring eye. All around the camp the hen was seen scratching, clucking, and cackling to its heart's content. Whenever the camp moved to a new location, the hen followed or would procure a ride in one of the wagons. Lee was quite attached to the hen. A story that has been preserved relates that after the carnage of Gettysburg, General Lee refused to move the camp for over an hour until the hen was located. Everyone was looking for the little hen so that the army could move forward. It was found perched upon its usual traveling roost awaiting the command to strike the tents.

As the war took its toll upon the resources of the Southern Army, food and commodities became scarce. General Lee was hosting a staffing and the food supplies had dwindled to barely having anything edible. While encamped at Orange Court House in 1864, the cook decided that mouths must be fed and he captured the hen and made a meal of her. After the supper, Lee began inquiring as to the whereabouts of his little hen. A hush came upon the mouths of those in close proximity to the general. Finally the cook confessed with an explanation. General Lee softly scolded him and went to his tent to mourn his loss and the state of affairs of his men. (In the Footsteps of Robert E. Lee; Johnson, Clint; John H. Blair Publisher; Winston-Salem, North Carolina; 2001; pages 12-13)

The Little Hen and Lee

The first time I saw them,
It was a sight to see
She fell in right behind him;
The little hen and Lee.

She strutted through the campground.
She sang so merrlly.
In her nest was always found
An egg for General Lee.

She traveled in cook's wagon;
Escort the company.
And if the cook was nagging,
Refuge with Robert E.

One day the ole cook caught her
And put her in his pot.
And when the general sought her,
He could find her not.

Ole Perry finally told him
That he had mouths to feed
The general softly scolds him;
Went to his tent and grieves.

Their time together ended.
A note that was forlorn.
The hen the Lee befriended.
Another legend borne.

The first time that I encountered this wonderful little sidebar story, I reflected upon my own similar experience. I felt, as he must have, the love and loss of a pet. As I traveled to a conference in Louisville, the little hen rode beside me and I must confess that I was mystified as to the reason or its purpose. I kept wondering as I drove, what color was the hen; did it have a name, would it come when called? I was led to a rest area and within five minutes I was able to express my thoughts on paper. The catharsis worked and I was able to continue on my journey thinking of other thoughts. The little hen (for some reason I perceive it to be a little red hen but according to the writings of William Mack Lee, the hen was black in color and named Nell) went back to its master within the confines of the pages of history.

"He is a Confederate Grey"

But when it was all said and done, the love of his life was Traveller. Both were famous and could be recognized anywhere. They seemed to be one with the wind when they rode the valleys, hills, and hollows of the Lexington mountainside. Though two separate beings, they were perceived as one.

Lee had first encountered Traveller (known as Jeff Davis and later Greenbrier) when a Major by the name of Thomas L. Broun (3rd Virginia) rode through the encampment past Lee's quarters. One of the soldiers described him as a steed of, "No pedigreed, wide nostrilled, round-barrelled, healthy, comfortable, gentleman's saddle horse. Gray, with black points, he was sound in eye, wind and limb…ready to go…without a single fancy trick, or the pretentious bearing of the typical charger." Upon seeing the horse, General Lee asked the Major if he would sell him "my colt" but for some reason, he did not ride away with the horse that he would soon after journey into history upon that broad back. Later he was loaned the horse and around Christmas he bought the horse that he had affectionately called 'my colt". The original price was $175 but Lee gave Major Broun $200 to allow for inflation. (<u>Grey Fox: Robert E. Lee and the Civil War;</u> Davis, Burke; Wings Books, an imprint of Random House Value Publishing; New York; 1956; pages 51-60)

"He Needed neither Whip nor Spur"

The following account regarding the wonder horse called Traveller was reported by Major Thomas L. Broun. He was living in Charleston, West Virginia (Kanawha County) when this article was published on August 10, 1886, in the Richmond Dispatch.

"In view of the fact that great interest is felt in the monument about to be erected to General Lee, and that many are desirous that his war-horse should be represented in the monument, and as I once owned this horse, I herewith give you some items respecting this now famous war-horse, Traveller.

"He was raised by Mr. Johnston, near the Blue Sulphur Springs, in Greenbrier County, Virginia (now West Virginia); was of the 'Gray Eagle,' stock, and, as a colt, took the first premium under the name of 'Jeff Davis' at the Lewisburg fairs for each of the years 1859 and 1860. He was four years old in the spring of 1861. When the Wise legion was encamped on Sewell Mountain, opposing the advance of the Federal Army under Rosecranz, in the fall of 1861, I was major to the Third regiment of infantry in that legion, and my brother, Captain Joseph M. Broun, was quartermaster to the same regiment.

"I authorized my brother to purchase a good serviceable horse of the best Greenbrier stock for our use during the war. After much inquiry and search he came across the horse above mentioned, and I purchased him for $175 (gold value), in the fall of 1861, from Captain James W. Johnston, son of the Mr. Johnston first above mentioned. When the Wise legion was encamped about Meadow Bluff and Big Sewell mountains, I rode this horse, which was then greatly admired in camp for his rapid, springy walk, his high spirit, bold carriage, and muscular strength.

"He needed neither whip nor spur, and would walk his five or six miles an hour over the rough mountain road of Western Virginia with his rider sitting firmly in the saddle and holding him in check by a tight rein, such vim and eagerness did he manifest to go right ahead so soon as he was mounted.

"When General Lee took command of the Wise legion and Floyd brigade that were encamped at and near Big Sewell Mountains, in the fall of 1861, he first saw this horse, and took a great fancy to it. He called it his colt, and said that he would use it before the war was over. Whenever the general saw my brother on this horse he had something pleasant to say to him about 'my colt,' as he designated this horse. As the winter approached, the climate in the West Virginia Mountains caused Rosecranz's army to abandon its position on Big Sewell and retreat westward. General Lee was thereupon ordered to South Carolina. The Third regiment of the Wise legion was subsequently detached from the army in Western Virginia and ordered to the South Carolina coast, where it was known as the sixtieth Virginia regiment, under Colonel Starke.   Upon seeing my brother on this horse near Pocotalipo, in South Carolina, General Lee at once recognized the horse, and again inquired of him pleasantly about 'his colt.'

"My brother then offered him the horse as a gift, which the General promptly declined, and at the same time remarked: 'If you will willingly sell me the horse, I will gladly use it for a week or so to learn its qualities.'   Thereupon my brother had the horse sent to General Lee's stable. In about a week the horse was returned to my brother, with a note from General Lee stating that the animal suited him, but that he could not longer use so valuable a horse in such times, unless it was his own; that if he (my brother) would not sell, please to keep the horse, with many thanks.

"This was in February, 1862. At that time I was in Virginia, on the sick list from a long and severe attack of camp fever, contracted in the campaign on Big Sewell Mountains. My brother wrote me of General Lee's desire to have the horse, and asked me what he should do. I replied at once: 'If he will not accept it, then sell it to him at what it cost me.' He then sold the horse to General Lee for $200 in currency, the sum of $25 having been added by General Lee to the price I paid for the horse in September, in 1861, to make up the depreciation in our currency from September, 1861, to February, 1862.

"In 1868 General Lee wrote to my brother, stating that this horse had survived the war--was known as 'Traveller' (spelling the word with a doubled in good English style), and asking for its pedigree, which was obtained, as above mentioned, and sent by my brother to General Lee."

Lee wrote to his wife's cousin, Markie Williams, describing Traveller. Markie was interested in painting a portrait of the famous Confederate grey mount. In the letter Robert E. Lee eloquently describes Traveller in the following fashion:

"If I Was an Artist like You"

"If I was an artist like you, I would draw a true picture of Traveller, representing his fine proportions, muscular figure, deep chest, short back, strong haunches, flat legs, small head, broad forehead, delicate ears, quick eye, small feet, and black mane and tail. Such a picture would inspire a poet, whose genius could then depict his worth, and describe his endurance of toil, hunger, thirst, heat and cold; and the dangers and suffering through which he has passed. He could dilate upon his sagacity and affection, and his invariable response to every wish of his rider. He might even imagine his thoughts through the long night marches and days of the battle through which he has passed. But I am no artist Markie, and can therefore only say he is a Confederate grey. I purchased him in the mountains of Virginia in the autumn of 1861, and he has been my patient follower ever since-to Georgia, the Carolinas and back to Virginia. He carried me through the Seven Days' battle around Richmond, the Second Manassas, at Sharpsburg, Fredericksburg, the last day of Chancellorsville, to Pennsylvania, at Gettysburg, and back to the Rappahannock. From the commencement of the campaign in 1864 at Orange till its close around Petersburg the saddle was scarcely off his back, as he passed through the fire of the Wilderness, Spotsylvania, Cold Harbor and across the James River. He was in almost daily requisition in the winter of 1864-1865 on the long line of defenses from the Chickahominy north Richmond to Hatcher's Run south of the Appomattox. In the campaign of 1865 he bore me from Petersburg to the final days at Appomattox Court-house."

First Impressions of Confederate Grey

As I walked toward Lee's Chapel during my fifth summer visit to Lexington, Virginia, I noticed a young father with his family. They were about twenty paces in front of me and the father was giving a history lesson to his three children. He was explaining the saga of Lee and the history of the college named for Washington and Lee, when he abruptly stopped at the entrance to the lower level in which the Lee family is enshrined. His youngest had noticed a plaque and, being a nonreader due to his young age, asked his daddy what it meant. As his father read the inscription and explained that this was the final resting-place of Traveller, I heard his voice crack with emotion. I gazed upon the scene as unobtrusively as possible. I witnessed a young man full of emotion, pride, and love for a horse of mythical proportions that even after one hundred thirty-one years, the essence of his spirit could still be captured on that hallowed ground. He reached into his pocket and gave each child a coin. As only the innocent can do with such reverence, they each in turn placed their treasure upon the plaque. A tribute not only to what was being taught but the love being shared.

As he walked in reverence with his loved ones through the Chapel, I was privileged to witness the knowledge of a present generation regarding past events being passed on to the future. This fine young man whose name I will never know, unknowingly gave me inspiration. The gift he unwittingly gave allowed me to sit upon that campus of honor and pay tribute. The tribute is not only to the animal that came to be one with his master but the actual feeling of the spirit of the time and the realization that our true history will be forever passed from father to child. As I feebly wrote the rough draft while sitting beneath a magnificent oak, for a brief instance, I heard a voice on the wind and the sound of a horse gently replying to its master. (<u>Fading of the Grey</u>; Chaltas, David; Copyrighted Material; 2001)

Confederate Grey
David Chaltas

Black mane and tail, with hair of grey
Glistens when I run.
Retired now in fields of hay,
I'm every Confederate's son.

I stood sixteen hands; eyes of fire.
First named for old Davis.
I was later called Greenbrier
But Traveller made me famous.

I carried my burden proudly.
Given sugar lump treats.
The Southern boys yelled loudly,
Throwing flowers at my feet.

I stood my ground with General Lee
Fighting until sixty-five.
Returning home, he set me free
But I stayed until he died.

The boys of ole Lexington town
Took me under their wing.

148

I was free to roam around.
I was treated like a king.

While in my prime, I stepped on a nail
The poison did set in.
At thirteen years, I stumbled and fell
I now ride with Lee again.

My iron-grey bones were displayed
For all the world to see.
Nineteen-seventy-one I was laid
Close by my Bobby Lee.

United again, family and friends
We roam the streets so free.
When you feel the wind, we're riding again
OLE Trav' and Bobby Lee.

"Tell Him I Miss Him Dreadfully"

His heart truly belonged to Traveller. Oh, how the
old man loved his faithful charger! Even when his
grand steed was spooked and bolted resulting in
both of Lee's wrists being sprained, not once did he

blame his iron-clad grey. The horse and rider were one. During a trip in which he did not take Traveller, Lee wrote to Gordon, "How is Traveller? Tell him I miss him dreadfully and have repented of our separation but once, and that is the whole time since we parted." (Lee, The Last Years; Flood, Charles Bracelen; Houghton Mifflin Company; New York; 1981; page 194)

"Opportunity for Quiet Thought"

His delight was in riding his steed. At times they seemed to be one. One particular statement by the General illustrates how comfortable he felt whenever he was riding his mount and that he used this special time for reflective thought. "My only pleasure is in my solitary evening rides which give me abundant opportunity for quiet thought."

"You Must Make Haste and Get Well"

Even on his death bed the Doctors used Traveller as an incentive for Lee to get better, "You must make haste and get well; Traveller has been standing so long in the stable that he needs exercise." He made no reply, but slowly shook his head and closed his eyes. (Recollections and Letters of General Robert E. Lee; Lee, Robert E. Lee Jr.; Garden City Publishing Company; Garden City, New York; 1904)

The Grey Ghost Horse

I can vividly remember the very first time I saw a picture of Traveller. I was a young lad in a bookstore and happened to turn to a page in which this magnificent gentleman was mounted upon the most striking horse. I remember its mane and tail and how long they seemed to be. The off white or as Lee described him "Confederate Grey" was the most beautiful color I had ever been privileged to have seen within the confines of a book. I dreamed of owning such a fine steed. I also thought what an easy target that unique animal offered. Easily recognized and the old gentleman representing the cause of Southern Independence seemed like a beacon on a lighthouse. Later in my life I found a reference to a term called "ghost". It referred to a white horse and how easy they were to spot among the smoke and mist of the battlefield, making the rider a prime target for a sharpshooter. I incubated my idea and one day it dawned upon my psyche that General Lee not only rode one of the finest animals in existence but also possessed an enchanted "ghost horse". The accretion of my thinking reached its zenith in the following poem that I call <u>The Grey Ghost Horse</u>. It was written to pay tribute to the horses of that color and honor those men that were audacious enough to ride them knowing the high risk of being shot because he stood out among the haze.

"Ghost Horse"

The sight of gray powdered smoke
Upon the morning mist
Brings to the poor common folk
The baby waker's kiss.

The haze upon the meadows
Brings darkness to the land.
And as the cannons bellows
Fear grips the heart of man.

But cast within the image
A rider and its host
The cavalier's one blemish?
He rides upon a ghost!

He rides passed others hidden;
As he plots his own course.
For very few have ridden
A ghost colored white horse.

He makes himself a martyr.
He is an easy mark.
He rides out like King Arthur
A candle in the dark.

Above the cannon's rattle
All wonder, "Who this be?"
The wind removes the shadows:
It's Trav' and General Lee!

The Counterfeit Saddle

An interesting incident occurred in 1861. Lee had just returned from Texas and had sent his belongings, including his saddle by boat. When it finally reached New York, Lee had resigned his commission and had taken on the grey color of valor. The authorities confiscated it (as they did his Arlington Estate) and Lee was forced to have another one made from the original saddle maker located in St. Louis. He sent notice that, "If he were willing to risk receiving his pay," he would forward the money to him as soon as he could. He possessed it for the remainder of his life and the second saddle was the one that became famous, serving both rider and horse well. The question unanswered by the fielder is what happened to the original saddle that was made for his stature and dimensions? Does it still exist and if so who possesses it? (The Boys' Life of Robert E. Lee; Horn, Stanley F.; Harper Brothers Publishers; New York and London; 1935; pages 99-100)

GENERAL ORDERS

The following are general orders that were issued by General Lee. They were taken from Official Records (OR's), Harper's Ferry, the writing of Robert E. Lee Jr. (Recollections and Letter of Robert E. Lee; Lee, Robert E. Jr. Captain; Doubleday, Doran and Company; 1904,1924), and the Wartime Papers of Robert E. Lee. (The Wartime Papers of Robert E. Lee; Dowdey, Clifford, Editor; Manarin, Louis H., Associate Editor; Da Capo Press; an unabridged reproduction of the edition published in Boston in 1961; Commonwealth of Virginia) and other selected materials as referenced in the bibliography. The purpose is to provide a brief glance into the many commands that General Lee enacted during his period of command. The intent is to demonstrate through his own words the heart of his thinking and the mastery of executing those mandates. Please note that these are only a few of the orders that he penned while serving as a Confederate American.

General Orders, No. 1
(Robert E. Lee Assumes Command)

Headquarters, Richmond, Virginia
April 23, 1861

In obedience to orders from his excellency John Letcher, governor of the State, Maj. Gen. Robert E. Lee assumes command of the military and naval forces of Virginia. R. E. Lee Major-General

Special Orders, No. 16
(The eyes of the Country are upon you)

The excerpt from this order vividly demonstrates the passion that the general had for the cause. In his heart, he believed that his beloved country, his Virginia, and sister states were being invaded. His plea exemplifies the desperateness of the situation and his call to arms resounded across a nation ready to defend to the death their rights as they saw them. On page 3 of his book entitled The Maxims of Robert E. Lee for Young Gentlemen, Richard G. Williams, Jr. expresses the order in the following manner:

"The eyes of your countrymen are turned upon you, and again do wives and sisters, fathers, and mothers, and helpless children, lean for defense on your strong arms and brave hearts." Note the similarities of the following order issued by Lee while at Valley Mountain.

Headquarters of the forces
Valley Mountain, Virginia
September 9, 1861

"The forward movement announced to the Army of the Northwest in Special Orders No. 28, from its headquarters, of this date, gives the general commanding the opportunity of exhorting the troops to keep steadily in view the great principles for which they contend and to manifest to the world their determination to maintain them. The eyes of the country are upon you. The safety of your homes and the lives of all you hold dear depend upon your courage and exertions. Let each man resolve to be victorious, and that the right of self-government, liberty, and peace shall in him find a defender. The progress of this army must be forward." R. E. Lee, General Commanding

Special Orders Number 191
(The Lost Orders)

One of the tragedies for the Confederacy involved an envelope, three cigars, and a piece of paper lying in a mile southeast of Frederick, Maryland. While bivouacked on September 13, 1862, a Private Barton W. Mitchell of the 27th Indiana, accompanied by a Sergeant John. M. Bloss, discovered a document wrapped in an envelope and three cigars. Upon examination, the document turned out to be a copy of General Lee's orders for the invasion of Maryland. Known as Special Orders, No. 191, this offered General McClellan an opportunity to gaze into the mind of his enemy. McClellan stated, "Here is a paper with which, if I cannot whip Bobby Lee, I will be willing to go home."

HDQRS. ARMY OF NORTHERN VIRGINIA, September 9, 1862

I. The citizens of Fredericktown being unwilling, while overrun by members of his army, to open

155

their stores, in order to give them confidence, and to secure to officers and men purchasing supplies for benefit of this command, all officers and men of this army are strictly prohibited from visiting Fredericktown except on business, in which case they will bear evidence of this in writing from division commanders. The provost-marshal in Fredericktown will see that his guard rigidly enforces this order.

II. Major Taylor will proceed to Leesburg, Va., and arrange for transportation of the sick and those unable to walk to Winchester, securing the transportation of the country for this purpose. The route between this and Culpeper Court-House east of the mountains being unsafe will no longer be traveled. Those on the way to this army already across the river will move up promptly; all others will proceed to Winchester collectively and under command of officers, at which point, being the general depot of this army, its movements will be known and instructions given by commanding officer regulating further movements.

III. The army will resume its march to-morrow, taking the Hagerstown road. General Jackson's command will form the advance, and, after passing Middletown, with such portion as he may select, take the route toward Sharpsburg, cross the Potomac at the most convenient point, and by Friday morning take possession of the Baltimore and Ohio Railroad, capture such of them as may be at Martinsburg, and intercept such as may attempt to escape from Harper's Ferry.

IV. General Longstreet's command will pursue the main road as far as Boonsborough, where it will halt, with reserve, supply, and baggage trains of the army.

V. General McLaws, with his own division and that of General R. H. Anderson, will follow General Longstreet. On reaching Middletown will take the route to Harper's Ferry, and by Friday morning possess himself of the Maryland Heights and endeavor to capture the enemy at Harper's Ferry and vicinity.

VI. General Walker, with his division, after accomplishing the object in which he is now engaged, will cross the Potomac at Cheek's Ford, ascend its right bank to Lovettsville, take possession of Loudoun Heights, if practicable, by Friday morning, Keys' Ford on his left, and the road between the end of the mountain and the Potomac on his right. He will, as far as practicable, co-operate with Generals McLaws and Jackson, and intercept retreat of the enemy.

VII. General D. H. Hill's division will form the rear guard of the army, pursuing the road taken by the main body. The reserve artillery, ordnance, and supply trains, & c., will precede General Hill.

VIII. General Stuart will detach a squadron of cavalry to accompany the commands of Generals Longstreet, Jackson, and McLaws, and, with the main body of the cavalry, will cover the route of the army, bringing up all stragglers that may have been left behind.

IX. The commands of Generals Jackson, McLaws, and Walker, after accomplishing the objects for which they have been detached, will join the main body of the army at Boonsborough or Hagerstown.

X. Each regiment on the march will habitually carry its axes in the regimental ordnance wagons, for use of the men at their encampments, to procure wood, & c.

By command of General R. E. Lee: R. H. CHILTON, Assistant Adjutant-General.

General Order No. 127
(General Lee Pained to Learn the Vice of Gambling Exists)

Penned in 1862, General Lee addresses the gambling problem to the Army of Northern Virginia: (Taken from <u>Official Records</u>; Volume 19; series 1; part 2; page722)

"The general commanding is pained to learn that the vice of gambling exists, and is becoming common in this army...He regards it as wholly inconsistent with the character of a Southern soldier and subversive of good order and discipline in the army. All officers are earnestly enjoined to use every effort to suppress this vice, and the assistance of every soldier having the true interests of the army and of the country at heart is evoked to put an end to a practice which cannot fail to produce those deplorable results which have ever attended its indulgence in any society."
R.E. Lee General Commanding

General Orders, No. 61
(The Death of General Jackson)

Headquarters, Army of Northern Virginia
May 11, 1863

"With deep grief the commanding general announces to the army the death of Lieut Genl T. J. Jackson, who expired on the 10th instant, at 3:25 p.m. The daring, skill, and energy of this great and good soldier, by the decree of an all wise Providence, are now lost to us. But while we mourn his death, we feel that his spirit still lives, and will inspire the whole army with his indomitable courage and unshaken confidence in God as our hope and our strength. Let his name be a watchword to his corps who have followed him to victory on so many fields. Let officers and soldiers emulate his invincible determination to do everything in the defense of our beloved country." R. E. Lee General

General Order No. 16
(Win from Him Honor worthy of Your Right Cause)

While bivouacked at Hagerstown General Lee composed the following order to his beloved army. It was written on Saturday and found when General Kilpatrick entered the town the next day.

General Order-No. 16
Headquarters, Army of Northern Virginia
July 11, 1863

"After the long and trying marches endured with the fortitude that has ever characterized the soldiers of the Army of Northern Virginia, you have penetrated to the country of our enemies, and recalled to the defenses of their own soil those who were engaged in the invasion of ours. You have fought a fierce and sanguinary battle, which, if not attended with the success that was hitherto crowned your efforts, was marked by the same heroic spirit that has commanded the respect of your enemies, the gratitude of your country, and the admiration of mankind.

"Once more you are called upon to meet the enemy from whom you have won on so many fields a name that will never die. Once more the eyes of your countrymen are turned upon you, and again do wives and sisters, fathers and mothers, and helpless children, lean for defense on your strong arms and brave hearts. Let every soldier remember that on his courage and fidelity depends all that makes life worth having-the freedom of his country, the honor of his people, and the security of his home. Let each heart grow strong in the remembrance of our glorious past, and in the thought of the inestimable blessings for which we contend; and, invoking the assistance of that benign Power which has so signally blessed our former efforts, let us go forth in confidence to secure the peace and safety of our county. Soldiers, your old enemy is behind you. Win from him honor worthy of your right cause, worthy of your comrades dead on so many illustrious fields."

R. E. Lee, General Commanding
(The Harper's Weekly: Journal of Civilization; New York, Saturday, July 25, 1863; Vol. VII; No. 343)

General Order No. 72
(We Make War Only on Armed Men)

General John Brown Gordon adored the old commanding officer and spoke highly of him throughout his memoirs. During the invasion of Pennsylvania, General Lee made it clear directly that his army would not pillage or no "straggling into private homes". According to General Gordon, Colonel Freemantle (attached to the Army of Northern Virginia as a correspondent/eye witness for the Royal British Army) attested to that fact by stating, "Nor were the inhabitants disturbed or annoyed by the soldiers. I went into Chambersburg and witnessed the singular good behavior of the troops towards the citizens. To one who has seen the ravages of the Northern troops in southern towns, this forbearance seems most commendable and surprising."

General Gordon followed the wishes and mandates of General Lee. In a speech given to the inhabitants of York, Pennsylvania, General Gordon made it clear that the war was between men and not made of women and children nor did they take vengeance or require a "natural revenge" upon the innocent citizens living in the north. Such were the Christian warriors of the southern cause. They believed that this war was just and followed the will of God. Total war was an enigma to them and they could not phantom such concepts or actions. (Personal Reminiscences, Anecdotes, and Letters of General Robert E. Lee; Jones, J. William; Appleton; New York; 1875; pages189-190)

"Our Southern homes have been pillaged, sacked, and burned; our mothers, wives, and little ones, driven forth amid the brutal insults of your soldiers. Is it any wonder that we fight with desperation? A natural revenge would prompt us to retaliate in kind, but we scorn to war on women and children. We are fighting for the God-given rights of liberty and independence, as handed down to us in the Constitution by our fathers. So, fear not: if a torch is applied to a single dwelling, or an insult offered to a female of your town by a soldier of this command, point me out the man, and you shall have his life."

General Lee despised the actions of Generals like Pope, Sherman and others that believed in total warfare resulting in the disintegration of a way of livelihood as well as life. He stated that, "No civilized nation with my knowledge has ever carried on wars as the United States government has against us." He further denounced their actions in a letter to his wife stating that, "These people delight to destroy the weak and those who can make no defense, it just suits them!"

An example of his modeling and following his own orders that he mandated came when he was riding through the northern countryside. He noticed a fence rail had not been replaced after his men had passed by. The general got off his horse, placed the rail back in close proximity to its original location and then remounted, as he continued his journey. Lee believed that this war was ordained by Almighty Providence and that an individual's conduct as well as the army's must be conducted in a Christian manner. Once again, he reinforced his beliefs. Another illustration of Lee's belief in war being between men and not, women, children, or personal property was addressed in the following order.

To make this point abundantly clear, General Lee issued the following general order on June 27, 1863 at Chambersburg, to his boys pertaining to maintaining the dignity and integrity of his army: (Robert E. Lee Man and Soldier; Page, Thomas Nelson; Charles Scribner's sons; New York; 1926; page 633)

"The commanding general has observed with marked satisfaction the conduct of the troops on the march, and confidently anticipates results commensurate with the high spirit they have manifested. No troops could have displayed greater fortitude or better performed the arduous marches of the past ten days. Their conduct in other respects has, with few exceptions, been in keeping with their character as soldiers and entitles them to approbation and praise.

"There have, however, been instances of forgetfulness on the part of some that they have in keeping the yet unsullied reputation of the army, and that the duties exacted of us by civilization and Christianity are not less obligatory in the country of the enemy than in our own. The commanding general considers that no greater disgrace could befall the army, and through it our whole people, than the perpetration of the barbarous outrages upon the innocent and defenseless and the wanton destruction of private property that have marked the course of the enemy in our own country. Such proceedings not only disgrace the perpetrators and all connected with them, but are subversive of the discipline and efficiency of the army and destructive of the ends of our present movements. It must be remembered that we make war only on armed men, and that we cannot take vengeance for the wrongs our people have suffered without lowering ourselves in the eyes of all whose abhorrence has been excited by the atrocities of our enemy, and offending against Him to whom vengeance belongeth, without whose favor and support our efforts must all prove in vain.

"The commanding general, therefore, earnestly exhorts the troops to abstain with most scrupulous care from unnecessary or wanton injury to private property, and he enjoins upon all officers to arrest and bring to summary punishment to all who shall in any way offend against the orders on this subject." R. E. Lee

General Orders No. 83
(Call for A Day of Fasting, Humiliation, and Prayer)

Headquarters, A. N. Va.,
August 13, 1863

"The President of the Confederate States has, in the name of the people, appointed the 21st day of August as a day of fasting, humiliation and prayer. A strict observance of the day is enjoined upon the officers and soldiers of this army. All military duties, except such are absolutely necessary will be suspended. The commanding officers of brigades and regiments are requested to cause divine service, suitable to the occasion, to be performed in their respective commands. Soldiers! We have sinned against Almighty God. We have forgotten His signal mercies, and have cultivated a revengeful, haughty, and boastful spirit. We have not remembered that the defenders of a just cause should be pure in His eyes; that 'our times are in His hands,' and we have relied too much on our own arms for the achievement of our independence. God is our only refuge and our strength. Let us humble ourselves before Him. Let us confess our many sins, and beseech Him to give us a higher courage, a purer patriotism and more determined will; that He will convert the hearts of our enemies; that He will hasten the time when war, with its sorrows and sufferings, shall cease, and that He will give us a name and place among the nations of the earth."

R. E. Lee, General

General Order No. 7
(Request for patience and sacrifice for the Cause)

Jan. 22, 1864

"The commanding general considers it due to the army to state that the temporary reduction of rations has been caused by circumstances beyond the control of those charged with its support. Its welfare and comfort are the objects of his constant and earnest solicitude, and no effort has been spared to provide for its wants. It is hoped that the exertions now being made will render the necessity of short duration, but the history of the army has shown that the country can require no sacrifice too great for its patriotic devotion.

"Soldiers! You tread with no unequal step the road by which your fathers marched through suffering, privations, and blood, to independence. Continue to imitate in the future, as you have in the past, their valor in arms, their patient endurance of hardships, their high resolve to be free, which no trial could shake, no bribe seduce, no danger appall; and be assured that the just God who rewarded their efforts with success will in His own good time, send down His blessings to you. R.E. Lee General"

General Orders, No. 15
(Assemble for the Purpose of Worship)

Headquarters, Army of Northern Virginia
February 7, 1864

"The attention of the army has already been called to the obligation of a proper observance of the Sabbath, but a sense of its importance, not only as a moral and religious duty, but as contributing to the personal health and well being of the troops, induces the commanding general to repeat the orders on that subject.

"He has learned with great pleasure that in many brigades convenient houses of worship have been erected, and earnestly desires that every facility consistent with the requirements of discipline shall be afforded the men to assemble themselves together for the purpose of devotion.

"To this end he directs that none but duties strictly necessary shall be required to be performed on Sunday, and that all labor, both men and animals, which it is practicable to anticipate or postpone, or immediate performance of which is not essential to the safety, health, or comfort of the army, shall be suspended on that day.

"Commanding officers will require the usual inspections on Sunday to be held at such time as not to interfere with the attendance of the men on divine service at the customary hour in the morning.

"They also will give their attention to the maintenance of order and quiet around the places of worship, and prohibit anything that may tend to disturb or interrupt religious exercises." R. E. Lee Genl

General Order No. 1
(Command of the Military Forces of the Confederate States)

Headquarters, Confederate Army
February 9, 1865

"In obedience to General Orders, No. 3, Adjutant and Inspector General's Office, February 6, 1865, I assume command of the military forces of the Confederate States. Deeply impressed with the difficulties and responsibility of the position, and humbly invoking the guidance of Almighty God, I rely for success upon the courage and fortitude of the army, sustained by the patriotism and firmness of the people, confident that their united efforts, under the blessing of Heaven, will secure peace and independence. The headquarters of the army, to which all special reports and communications will be addressed, will be, for the present, with the Army of Northern Virginia. The stated and regular returns and reports of each army and department will be forwarded, as heretofore, to the office of the Adjutant and Inspector General." R.E. Lee General

General Orders, No. 8
(Evil Habit Prevails in Proposing Desertion)

Headquarters, Army of Northern Virginia
March 17, 1865

"It having been reported that the evil habit prevails with some in this army of proposing to their comrades in jest to desert, and go home, the commanding general earnestly warns those guilty of this practice against the danger they incur. The penalty for advising or persuading a soldier to desert is death; and those indulging in such jests will find it difficult on a trial to rebut the presumption of guilt arising from their words.

"This order and the 23rd Article of War will be forthwith read to each company in the army once a day for three days, and to every regiment at dress parade once a week for a month; and at such other times hereafter, in addition to those prescribed for the Articles of War, as commanding officers may deem proper."

By command of General R.E. Lee
W. H. Taylor
Assistant Adjutant General

QUOTES

"Let it be Robert E. Lee"

General Scott, the supreme commander of the Union forces prior to the Civil war stated several times that he felt Lee was, "The greatest living soldier in America" and said to the governor of Kentucky, "I tell you that if I were on my death-bed tomorrow, and the President of the United States should tell me that a great battle was to be fought for the liberty or the slavery of the country, and asked my advice as to the ability of a commander, I would say with my dying breath: "Let it be Robert E. Lee.' " (The Boys' Life of Robert E. Lee; Horn, Stanley F.; Harpers Brothers Publishers; New York and London; 1935)

"The Very Greatest of All Captains"

Noted men of the 20th century admired Lee. President Theodore Roosevelt once stated that his impression of Lee was, "Without any exception the very greatest of all the great captains that the English-speaking peoples have brought forth."

"One of the Noblest Americans Who Ever Lived"

England's Prime Minister Winston Churchill was a long-time admirer of General Lee. He wrote that Lee was, "One of the noblest Americans who ever lived, and one of the greatest captains known to the annals of war." (<u>Robert E. Lee on Leadership;</u> <u>Executive Lessons in Character, Courage, and</u> <u>Vision</u>; Crocker III, H. W.; Forum, an Imprint of Prima Publishing; Rocklin, California; 1999)

"A Nation of Men of Lee's Caliber Would Be Unconquerable"

Another man of influence in the 20th Century also noted the importance of General Lee as a true American hero. This five-star general and hero of World War II had a picture of Lee hanging in his office. A Doctor Scott had occasion to visit him and noting the picture inquired about his reason for having in it in such a prestigious position as his office. The following letter summated his reason and offers absolution for Lee since he had not yet been reinstated as an American citizen. Note that the author of the letter later purchased land at Gettysburg next to Seminary Ridge, just below the location of the statue of Lee during the fabled Pickett's Charge. The following letter is submitted for your consideration:

"Dear Dr. Scott:

"Respecting your August 1 inquiry calling attention to my often expressed admiration for General Robert E. Lee, I would say, first, that we need to understand that at the time of the War Between the States the issue of Secession had remained unresolved for more than 70 years. Men of probity, character, public standing and unquestioned loyalty, both North and South, had disagreed over this issue as a matter of principle from the day our Constitution was adopted.

"General Robert E. Lee was, in my estimation, one of the supremely gifted men produced by our Nation. He believed unswervingly in the Constitutional validity of his cause which until 1865 was still an arguable question in America; he was thoughtful yet demanding of his officers and men, forbearing with captured enemies but ingenious, unrelenting and personally courageous in battle, and never disheartened by a reverse or obstacle. Through all his many trials, he remained selfless almost to a fault and unfailing in his belief In God. Taken altogether, he was noble as a leader and as a man and unsullied as I read the pages of our history.

"From deep conviction I simply say this: a nation of men of Lee's caliber would be unconquerable in spirit and soul. Indeed, to the degree that present-day American youth will strive to emulate his rare qualities, including his devotion to this land as revealed in his painstaking efforts to help heal the nation's wounds once the bitter struggle was over, we, in our own time of danger in a divided world, will be strengthened and our love of freedom sustained.

"Such are the reasons that I proudly display the picture of this great American on my office wall.

"Sincerely,
Dwight D. Eisenhower"

"In Whose Defence Alone will I Ever Again Draw My Sword"

Upon Virginia's succession from the Union, for a brief period of time, it remained an independent republic. A convention was held in Richmond in which a commander was elected. Robert E. Lee was the choice of the convention members. At that time, he was fifty-four years old, hair slightly peppered with gray and a black mustache. During the convention a series of speeches were presented in which each orator seemingly attempted to out do the other. Lee rose to the occasion with a simple but powerful acceptance speech that personifies the modesty of the man.

"Profoundly impressed with the solemnity of the occasion, I accept the position assigned me by your partiality. I would have much preferred had the choice fallen on an abler man. Trusting in Almighty God, an approving conscience, and the aid of my fellow-citizens, I devote myself to the service of my native state, in whose behalf alone will I ever again draw my sword."

"The better role is to judge our adversaries from their standpoint, not from ours."

"It is much more easy to make heroes on paper than in the field."

"He who gave freedom to our fathers will bless the efforts of their children to preserve it."

"Occupy yourself in helping those more helpless than yourself."

(Unveiling of Valentines's Recumbent Figure of Lee; Daniel, John W.; Southern Historical Society Papers 11; page 378)

"The Government Should Be Administered in Purity and Truth"

In the following statement our general sums up the sentiment of the Southern people. All that the South ever wanted was to be governed by the original intent of the Declaration of Independence and Constitution. Lee was against anything that would dissolve the Union with the exception of honorable duty.

"All the South has ever desired was that the Union, as established by our Forefathers, should be preserved, and that the government, as originally organized, should be administered in purity and truth."

"Do Your Duty in All Things"

In a letter to his son who was a cadet at West Point, Lee offers sound fatherly advice. He talks of honor, self-respect and duty. Within the confines of the following two hundred plus words, he captures the very essence of living a virtuous life based on honesty with oneself and honor while serving God. Therein lies the peace that passeth all understanding.

"You must study to be frank with the world: frankness is the child of honesty and courage. Say just what you mean to do on every occasion, and take it for granted that you mean to do right. If a friend asks a favour, you should grant it, if reasonable; if not, tell him plainly why you cannot: you will wrong him and yourself by equivocation of any kind. Never do a wrong thing to make a friend or keep one; the man who requires you to do so is dearly purchased at a sacrifice. Deal kindly, but firmly, with all your classmates; you will find it the policy which wears best. Above all, do not appear to others what you are not. If you have any fault to find with any one, tell him, not others, of what you complain; there is no more dangerous experiment than that of undertaking to be one thing before a man's face and another behind his back. We should live so as to say and do nothing to the injury of any one. It is not only best as a matter of principle, but it is the path to peace and honour…Duty, then, is the sublimest word in our language. Do your duty in all things. You cannot do more. You should never wish to do less."

"Hold Yourself above Every Mean Action"

The old general believed in honor, honesty, humility, duty, and teaching by example. He followed his convictions to the letter and remained humble throughout his life, serving his God and country in what he felt was the best manner to do so. The following quotes reflect kindly upon his lifestyle and philosophy. I pray that we all endeavor to follow the sound Biblical principles that he applied to his everyday life.

"I am willing to starve myself, but cannot bear my men or horses to be pinched."

"Hold yourself above every mean action. Be strictly honorable in every act, and be not ashamed to do right."

""No honest man can take long to deliberate which side he will choose."

174

"The teacher should be the example to the pupil."

The education of a man is never completed until he dies."

"The teacher should aim in the highest attainable proficiency and not at pleasing mediocrity."

"I think it better to do right, even if we suffer in so doing."

"As long as virtue was dominate in the republic, so long was the happiness of the people secure."

"We must not, however, yield to difficulties, but strive the harder to overcome them."

"The greater difficulties in our lives the harder must we strive for success."

"It is men of high integrity and commanding intellect that the country must look to give character to her councils."

"It is necessary we should be humbled and taught to be less boastful, less selfish, and more devoted to right..."

"Time brings a cure to all things."

"Lay nothing too much to heart."

"All my thoughts and strength are given to the cause to which my life, be it long or short, will be devoted."

"You must endeavor to enjoy the pleasure of doing good. That is all that makes life valuable."

"You must study hard, gain knowledge and learn your duty to God and your neighbor; this is the great object of life."

"There is no more dangerous experiment than that of undertaking to be one thing before a man's face and another behind his back."

"Abstinence from Spirituous Liquors is the Best Safeguard"

Lee believed that for a man to reach his full potential, he must deny himself certain pleasures of the world. He totally refused to smoke or drink and made the following comments regarding such:

"My experience through life has convinced me that, while moderation and temperance in all things are commendable and beneficial, abstinence from spirituous liquors is the best safeguard of morals and health."

"Whiskey-I liked it, I always did and that is the reason I never use it."

"The Old Book"

In all things, Robert Edward Lee sought the guidance of his Creator. He believed that the Bible was the divine revelation to man and that within the old ragged book that he always carried was all the answers to the questions of life. He was an avid reader of the Bible and believed in its truths. He had a practice of reading it in the morning, the evening and sharing its wisdom during family devotionals. But when did his conversion and complete submission to God's will occur? Some speculate that it was during the Mexican War (Somewhere between 1847-1848). On July 17,

1853, after hearing a sermon entitled, "Lord, to whom shall we go?" by Bishop John Johns of Christ Church in Alexandria, Virginia, Lee came forward with two of his daughters (Anne and Mary), kneeling at the altar and professed publicly his faith. But to this author this was simply an act of faith by a man that had committed his heart to Christ years earlier. His mother was devoutly faithful in following her God and there is no doubt that he was brought up in a Christian home. There is no doubt that his mother nurtured him and taught him the very morals and values that he later so eloquently modeled. His example at West Point offers insight into his example, as do the writings of General Winfield Scott. But in truth the evolution of his strong Christian character and conviction is only known of God. For is this not the essence of salvation? General Lee led by example and the Light that he chose to follow was one that made him the man of marble and a true Christian hero for all times. The following are a series of statements that demonstrate his love of the book of books.

"The Bible is the Book of Books"

"I Salute the Church of God!"

"There are many things in the old Book which I may never be able to explain, but I accept it as the infallible Word of God, and receive its teachings as inspired by the Holy Ghost."

"I prefer the Bible to any other book. There is enough in that to satisfy the most ardent thirst for knowledge; to open the way to true wisdom and to teach the only road to salvation and eternal happiness. It is not above human comprehension, and its sufficient to satisfy all its desires."

177

Upon discovery of a child that had been named after him, General Lee wrote the child stating what he believed was the key to life. They were all contained within the covers of the Bible.

"Above all things, learn at once to worship your Creator and to do His will as revealed in His Holy Book."

"There is no labor so beneficent, so elevated and so sublime, as the teaching of salvation to every man."

"My chief concern is to try to be a humble, earnest Christian."

"People must help themselves; or Providence will not help them."

"The object of this life is to prepare for a better and brighter world."

"How good God is to us! Oh that I could praise Him and thank Him as I ought."

"This morning the glorious sun is out, and will soon warm and dry us. How good is God!"

"No day should be lived unless it was begun with a prayer of thankfulness and an intercession for guidance."

"My whole trust is in God, and I am ready for whatever He may ordain."

"God does not always give the battle to the strong."

"God disposes. This ought to satisfy us."
(Found in a drawer at Lee's home after his death)

"God knows what is best for us."
(July 9, 1862, letter to his wife)

"I try to keep my eyes and thought fixed on those eternal shores to which I am fast hastening."
(Excerpt from a letter to Markie)

"God's will ought to be our aim, and I am quite contented that His designs should be accomplished and not mine."

"God alone can save us from our folly, selfishness and short sightedness."

"We poor sinners need to come back from our wanderings to seek pardon through the all-sufficient merits of our Redeemer. And we need to pray earnestly for the power of the Holy Spirit to give us a precious revival in our hearts and among the unconverted."

"We must rely for guidance and protection upon a kind Providence."

"Young men must not expect to escape contact with evil, but must learn not to be contaminated by it."

"Nothing will compensate us for the depression of the standard of our moral and intellectual culture."

"We must implore the forgiveness of God for our sins, and the continuance of His blessings. There is nothing but His almighty power that can restrain us."

"Leave the Results to Him"

In 1866 General Lee in a conversation with J.W. Jones stated one of the most profound statements about resolution and acceptance of the result of the war. Again one can feel his firm conviction in trusting God in all things.

"We have humbly tried to do our duty. We may, therefore, with calm satisfaction, trust in God, and leave results to Him."

"Joy Out of Your Present Misery"

Upon learning of the death of his granddaughter, General Lee acting in the capacity of a consoling father again revealed the true character of his Christian nature. He penned the following message to his beloved daughter-in-law, Charlotte in an effort to comfort her.

"May God give you strength to bear the affliction He has imposed, and produce future joy out of your present misery, is my earnest prayer."

"As soon as I order them forward into battle, I leave my army in the hands of God."

"I tremble for my country when I hear of confidence expressed in me. I know too well my weakness, and that our only hope is God."

"What a glorious world God Almighty has given us. How thankless and ungrateful we are, and how we labour to mar His gifts."

"Perfect and true are all His ways, whom heaven adores and earth obeys."

"With calm satisfaction, trust in God and leave results to Him."

"We must all try to be good Christians-that is the most important thing."

"You will meet many of my old soldiers during your trip, and I wish you to tell them that I often think of them, try everyday to pray for them and am always gratified to hear of their prosperity."

"Hold to your purity and virtue. They will sustain you in all trials and difficulties and cheer you in every calamity."

"Be true, kind and generous, and pray earnestly to God to enable you to keep His commandments and walk in the same all the days of your life."

"With all my devotion to the union and the feeling of loyalty and duty of an American citizen, I have not been able to make up my mind to raise my hand against my relatives, my children and my home. I have, therefore, resigned my commission in the army, and save in defense of my native state...I hope I may never be called on to draw my sword."

"The safety of your homes and the lives of all you hold dear depend upon your courage and exertions. Let each man resolve to be victorious, and that the right of self-government, liberty, and peace shall find him a defender."

"What a cruel thing is war: to separate and destroy families and friends, and mar the purest joys and happiness God has granted us in this world; to fill our hearts with hatred instead of love for our neighbors, and to devastate the fair face of this beautiful world."

"What a beautiful world God in His loving kindness to His creatures has given us! What a shame that men endowed with reason and knowledge of right should mar His gifts."

"My Whole Trust is in God"

General Lee's faith in providence was and still is an inspiration to all that have studied on his triumphs and ordeals. In all things he praised his God. He earnestly sought to do the bidding of Christ and attempted in all aspects of his life to live within the guidelines offered by the Bible. He felt that he was merely a sinner that held all his hopes in the saving grace of God. One of his sayings that best sums up his belief that it is all in God's hands was the following:

"My whole trust is in God, and I am ready for whatever He may ordain."

"Do You Think Your Remarks Were in the Spirit of That Teaching?"

General Lee's ability to remain calm during adverse times is legendary. After the course of the war he was indicted for treason and would later appear before Congress. Most men would be bitter but he retained his Christian nature. On one occasion a preacher was visiting him at his home and, complaining about the despicable acts that were being heaped upon the old general. As the man began to leave, Lee reminded him of the principles he was called to follow. The pastor must have gone away quite humbled from the mild admonishment. This profound truth in his own words says it all in summating the man called Lee.

"Doctor, there is a good old book which I read and you preach from, which say, 'Love your enemies, bless them that persecute you, do good to them that hatred for you, and pray for them which despitefully use you.' Do you think your remarks this evening were quite in the spirit of that teaching?"

"Those who oppose our purposes are not always to be regarded as our enemies."

"Every one should do all in his power to collect and disseminate the truth, in hope may find a place in history and descend to posterity, but that which shows the principles for which the South contended and which justified her struggle for those principles."

"I can anticipate no greater calamity for the country than a dissolution of the Union."

"To Feel Proud of Both Sides of the House"

General Lee was a very wise counselor in domestic affairs. Once while with the future General Hood, they were discussing the virtues of marriage. The old general made a stunning statement that holds merit even to this day. Again, it offers insight into not only how important marriage was to him but also the legacy to the family as inherited by the children. Such is the essence and spirit of the legend.

"Never marry unless you do so into a family that will enable your children to feel proud of both sides of the house."

"Surrendered but Never Defeated!"

"I Shall Not Prove Recreant to My Duty"

Upon hearing the news of the war and asked if he would fight, Lee made a gracious statement. It summates how Lee felt about the question.

"I shall never bear arms against the Union, but it may be necessary for me to carry a musket in defense of my native state, Virginia, in which case I shall not prove recreant to my duty."

General Lee comments about the many changes in command made by the Federal Government:

"I fear they may continue to make these changes till they find someone whom I don't understand."

"Those who oppose our purposes are not always to be regarded as our enemies."

"I believe all who can should vote for the most intelligent, honest and conscientious men eligible to office."

"I cannot trust a man to control others who cannot control himself."

"The real honest man is honest from conviction of what is right, not from policy."

"No man can be so important in the world that he need not the good-will and approval of others."

"I am unwilling to do what is wrong."

"I must say that I am one of those dull creatures that cannot see the good of secession."

"It is well that war is so terrible lest we should grow too fond of it."

"Human virtue should be equal to human calamity."

"Fame which does not result from good actions and achievements for the good of the whole people is not to be desired. Nero had fame…Who envies him?""

"Get correct views of life, and learn to see the world in its true light. It will enable you to live pleasantly, to do good, and, when summoned away, to leave without regret."

"The soldiers know their duties better than the generals officers do."

"We Made a Great Mistake in The Beginning"

The general was noted for his keen sense of humor. On several occasions, the newspapers would second-guess him and make critical comments about what should have been done. His reply was quite comical, sharp and to the point.

"We made a great mistake in the beginning of our struggle, and I fear, in spite of all we can do, it will prove to be a fatal mistake. We appointed all our worst generals to command our armies, and all our best generals to edit the newspapers."

"There is a true glory and a true honor: the glory of duty done-the honor of the integrity of principle." (Found in his personal notes)

"There never were such men in an army before, they will go anywhere and do anything if properly led."

"Without music, there would be no army."

"I did only what my duty demanded. I could have taken no other course without dishonor."

"Hold to your purity and virtue. They will sustain you in every calamity."

"You must make friends while you are young, that you may enjoy them when old. You will find when you become old, it will then be too late."

"For myself, I intend to die sword in hand rather than to yield."

"When love influences the parent the child will be activated by the same spirit." (From Lee's diary)

"My experience of men has neither disposed me to think worse of them nor indisposed me to serve them."

It is History That Teaches Us Hope

"The march of Providence is so slow and our desires so impatient; the work of progress is so immense and our means of aiding is so feeble; the life of humanity is long; that of the individual so brief, that we often see only the ebb of the advancing wave and are thus discouraged. It is history that teaches us to hope."

"I Am Rejoiced That Slavery is Abolished"

General Lee was not a supporter of slavery and on several occasions, spoke against it. In fact, he freed the last slave owned by his father-in-law one week before the Emancipation Proclamation (a decree freeing only slaves in the South) and he done so with an education for the former slaves. The works of William Mack Lee (a black body servant) gives testament to the kindness of Lee and his befriending him.   The following statement attributed to him demonstrates his commitment to seeing it abolished.

"So far from engaging in a war to perpetuate slavery, I am rejoiced that Slavery is abolished. I believe it will be greatly for the interest of the South. So fully am I satisfied of this that I would have cheerfully lost all that I have lost by the war, and have suffered all that I have suffered to have this object attained."

On one occasion as Lee overlooked the vista from Arlington's Heights he made a keen observation concerning the events that were transpiring in the valley below, the city known as Washington. (Call to Duty: The Sterling Nobility of Robert E. Lee; Wilkins, J. Steven; Cumberland House Publishing; 1997; page 94)

"That beautiful feature of our landscape has ceased to charm me as much as formerly. I fear the mischief that is brewing there."

"You Have Only Always to do what is Right"

Regarding the inevitable secession of his beloved state, the following comment was attributed to Lee. (Lee; Freeman Douglas Southall; An Abridgment by Richard Harwell of the Pulitzer Prize Winning four-volume Biography; New York; Touchstone; 1991; page 111)

"You have only always to do what is right. It will become easier by practice, and you will enjoy in the midst of your trials the pleasure of an approving conscience. That will be worth everything else."

"I Fear the Liberties of Our Country will be buried"

Lee wrote a letter to his friend A.G. Brackett. One statement in it is profound in that it offers a warning regarding the tragedy of commons that will befall the South if we are not vigilant.

"I fear the liberties of our country will be buried in the tomb of a great nation."

"Both Sides Forget That We Are All Americans"

General Lee was not only a brilliant military mind but also possessed a keen insight into the looming conflict. On one occasion, he stated that the war would not be a short event but literally be fought for years and would entail a great suffering for all the people. His predictions rang true.

"They do not know what they say. If it came to a conflict of arms, the war will last at least four years. Northern politicians will not appreciate the determination and pluck of the South, and Southern politicians do not appreciate the numbers, resources, and patient perseverance of the North. Both sides forget that we are all Americans. I foresee that our country will pass through a terrible ordeal, a necessary expiation, perhaps, for our national sins."

On April 20, 1861, one of the neighbors of the Lee household made a comment regarding the mood and emotion that permeated Arlington prior to their departure. (Grey Fox: Robert E. Lee and the Civil War; Davis, Burke; Wings Books, an imprint of

Random House Value Publishing; New York; 1956; page 17)

> "The house was as if there had been a death in it, for the army was to him home and country."

The following incident readily sees the quick wit and humor of Lee. During a parade, the famous Texas Brigade marched by in review. A foreign officer standing next to General Lee noted that the backs of their trousers and shirts had rips and tears in them. To which Lee immediately replied,

> "The enemy never sees the backs of my Texans."

"The Chickens Roost High!"

The humor of Lee is quite evident in a documented comment he made to General Hood regarding his Texans raiding local farmhouses for chickens. (<u>Advance and Retreat</u>; Hood, John Bell; Hood Orphan Memorial Fund; New Orleans; 1880)

> "Ah, General Hood, when you Texans come about, the chickens have to roost mighty high!"

"Straight as the Needle to the Pole"

General Lee held such a high regard for Stonewall Jackson's leadership abilities. It was said that the two seemed to be one in thinking when upon the battlefield. Lee once said of Jackson's character and abilities that, "Such an executive officer, the sun never shone on. I have but to show him my design, and I know that if it can be done, it will be done. No need for me to send or watch him. Straight as the needle to the pole he advanced to the execution of my purpose." (<u>Lee</u>; Freeman Douglas Southall; An Abridgment by Richard

Harwell of the Pulitzer Prize Winning four-volume Biography; New York; Touchstone; 1991; page 292)

When General Lee heard of the tragic news of Jackson's injury, he let out a heart-wrenching groan from his very soul. Attempts to contain his emotions failed as his eyes yielded to his grief. For a moment, Lee was unable to reply as he dealt with the emotions of his Christian nature. Finally rallying himself for a brief interlude, Lee replied to Captain Lilbourn who had brought the news that Stonewall Jackson had been wounded:

"Ah, captain, any victory is dearly bought which deprives us of the services of General Jackson, even for a short time!"

"Two Old Friends"

The rationale behind the writing of this poem was to pay tribute to a friendship that was forged during the greatest crisis that our nation has ever endured. It reflects upon that fateful day in May when Lee and Stonewall sat discussing their strategy at Chancellorsville. Neither of them could comprehend the great paradox of tragedy that was mixed with the greatest victory in military history up to that time. The cost was tremendous and Lee stated on several occasions that if General Stonewall Jackson had lived, he would have been victorious at Gettysburg and the course of history may have been written differently. But the main emphasis of the poem is to mourn the loss of a friend. Lee was seen many times in the late hours of evening and among the early morning dew at the gravesite of his friend. Two Old Friends remembers that friendship and embraces a time when the 'immortals reflected upon mortality.

190

Two Old Friends

Two old friends under the trees;
Both planning strategies.
They must whip the enemy
On a spring day of May.

One sat on a cracker box;
Drew a map near the rocks.
"Those people must be outfoxed
By the end of the day!"

His sword leaned against a tree.
It fell so suddenly.
A sign from the enemy?
As one friend rode away.

Horseless rider in the dark.
The cries of a meadowlark
Three bullets hit their mark.
A soldier fell in gray.

One old man sits all alone.
Chilled to the very bone.
Listens to his spirit groan.
His friend has gone away.

"He has Lost His Left Arm, But I Have Lost my Right"

Basking in the apex of his most remarkable victory at Chancellorsville, Lee found his mind preoccupied with concern for his fallen Lieutenant. General Lee sent Jackson a dispatch congratulating him on the brilliant victory. "Give {Jackson} my affectionate regards, and tell him to make haste and get well, and come back to me as soon as he can. He has lost his left arm, but I have lost my right."

"Oh, Sir, He Must Not Die"

Upon hearing that Jackson's condition had made a sudden turn for the worse, it was said that General Lee prayed continuously through the night for his executive officer. "Tell him that I am praying for him as I believe I have never prayed for myself." On May 10th, realizing his fate, General Jackson instructed the Reverend R. T. Lacy to go and hold his regularly scheduled services for the men. General Lee was in attendance and when the opportunity arose, he asked the Reverend about the status of his Christian warrior brother. When the Reverend told him that he probably had seen his last sunrise, General Lee was beside himself with grief. "Oh, sir, he must not die. Surely God will not visit us with such a calamity. If I have ever prayed in my life I have pleaded with the Lord that Jackson might be spared to us." He could say no more and immediately burst into tears that could not be comforted or consoled by those around him. (Christ in the Camp: Religion in the Confederate Army; Jones, J. William; Martin and Hoyt Company; Atlanta; 1904; pages 75-76)

"The Flight of the Sparrow"

Upon hearing the news that his friend and chief executive was gravely wounded, Lee was horrified. His greatest victory paled in his mind compared to the grief within his heart. He must have prayed constantly for his friend. If General Lee had written his thoughts of that event, what would he say? Would he not also herald the exploits of the Savior of Shenandoah? As I read, rehashed in my mind's eye, and rediscovered the agony of the loss, I envisioned a sparrow's flight against the forces of nature and the inevitable outcome of the sparrow's battle. I saw the sparrow fall and felt the pain of the wound, likened unto what General Lee must have been feeling upon hearing the news. They were two that acted as one and shared a kindred spirit. There is no doubt in this writer's mind that on numerous occasions in the twilight of the evening or during the mist of the dawn, Lee could be spotted at the cemetery where his friend lay. This meager effort is an attempt to pay tribute in writing as only Marsh Robert could do. An offering of honor from one soldier to another through the medium of a devote follower.

The Sparrow

Twas the flight of the sparrow
Riding against the wind.
Going straight as an arrow
To where his life would end.

Victory on the morrow;
Then comes the setting sun.
While riding on Ole Sorrel
He's got'em on the run.

Three bullets pierce his left wing.
Two aides fall at his side.
His body feels the sharp sting
"The sparrow can not fly!"

They take him to a friend's house,
McGuire's by his bed.
The fever he cannot roust;
By morning he'll be dead.

He called for Hill's division.
The sparrow left his nest.
He made his last decision
To cross over and rest.

He bowed and prayed to the Lord.
Too weak to bend his knees.
The sparrow has his reward,
He rests among the trees.

Let's remember the sparrow
And how his blue eyes shined
His wind song will be heralded
Until the end of time.

Lee was beside himself because of the loss of Jackson. How could he replace such a leader? Who would step up and be as bold as his executive officer? Who would fight with such a tenacity of spirit? In a letter to his son Custis Lee he exclaimed, "It is a terrible loss."

"I Know Not How to Replace Him"

After the tragic death of General Jackson, General Lee was at a loss on how to replace his executive officer. His following comment demonstrates his belief that Jackson was irreplaceable.

"I know not how to replace him. God's will be done. I trust He will raise up someone in his place."

"The Enemy is here"

After an anguishing soul search, Lee made the decision to replace Stonewall with General Ewell. Although a capable general in his own right, he was not a Jackson. Jackson was bold and daring while General Ewell planned engagements with caution. His caution would soon be noted at a place called Gettysburg.

A few weeks after the great victory at Chancellorsville, the Army of Northern Virginia accidentally ran headlong into the Army of the Potomac. A skirmish over shoes ensued that resulted in the greatest battle to ever occur on American soil. General Longstreet did not want to fight on that ground but wished to find an area between Washington and the Union Army. The Confederates would have the high ground and the battle would be brought to them. General Lee's blood was up and he was determined to make a stand at that location. Victory had been so close the first day, surely more resistance would repel 'those people'. He was determined to fight. General Lee speaking to General Longstreet at Gettysburg:

"The enemy is here, and if we don't whip him he will whip us."

"General Lee, I Have No Division"

After the immortal charge of Pickett's men on that fateful day in July 1863, General Lee rode astride Traveller offering his remorse and taking full blame for the day's failure. He saw General Pickett coming in the distance and he rode to him and stated, "General Pickett place your division in rear of this hill, and be ready to repel the advance of the enemy should they follow up their advantage." To which Pickett mournfully replied, "General Lee, I have no division now, Armisted is down, Garnett is down, and Kemper is mortally wounded." "Come, General Pickett," stated the shaken General Lee, "This has been my fight and upon my shoulders rests the blame. The men and officers of your command have written the name of Virginia as high today as it has ever been written before." Later that night after returning exhausted to his camp in the late hours of night, Lee spoke to General Imboden about his brave Virginians. "I never saw troops behave more magnificently than Pickett's division of Virginians did today in that grand charge upon the enemy. And if they had been supported as they were to have been-but for some reason not yet fully explained to me, were not-we would have held the position and the day would have been ours." Too bad! Too bad! Oh, too bad!" (<u>Lee</u>; Freeman Douglas Southall; An Abridgment by Richard Harwell of the Pulitzer Prize Winning four-volume Biography; New York; Touchstone; 1991; pages 340-341)

"Too Bad! Too Bad! Oh, Too Bad!"

The following excerpt lengthens the previous passage but it sets the stage and the demeanor of a saddened Lee. It is taken from the writings of Brigadier General John D. Imbolden. His first-hand account paints a graphic picture of the retreat from Gettysburg.

"About 11 o'clock a horseman came to summon me to General Lee. I promptly mounted and accompanied by Lieutenant George W. McPhail, an aide on my staff, and guided by the courier who brought me the message, rode about 2 miles towards Gettysburg to where a half a dozen small tents were pointed out, a little way from the roadside to our left, as General Lee's headquarters for the night. On inquiry I found that he was not there, but had gone to the headquarters of General A. P. Hill, about half a mile nearer to Gettysburg. When we reached the place indicated, a single flickering candle, visible from the road through the open front of a common wall-tent, exposed to view Generals Lee and Hill seated on camp-stools with a map spread upon their knees. Dismounting, I approached on foot. After exchanging the ordinary salutations General Lee directed me to go back to his headquarters and wait for him. I did so, but he did not make his appearance until about 1 o'clock, when he came riding alone, at a slow walk, and evidently wrapped in profound thought.

"When he arrived there was not even a sentinel on duty at his tent, and no one of his staff was awake. The moon was high in the clear sky and the silent scene was unusually vivid. As he approached and saw us lying on the grass under a tree, he spoke, reined in his jaded horse, and essayed to dismount. The effort to do so betrayed so much physical exhaustion that I hurriedly rose and stepped forward to assist him, but before I reached his side he had succeeded in alighting, and threw his arm across the saddle to rest, and fixing his eyes upon the ground leaned in silence and almost motionless upon his equally tired horse, the two forming a striking and never-to-be forgotten group. The moon shone full upon his massive features and awed by his appearance I waited for him to speak until the silence became embarrassing, when, to break it and change the silent current of his thoughts, I ventured to remark, in a sympathetic tone, and in allusion to his great fatigue:

"General, this has been a hard day on you." He looked up, and replied mournfully: "Yes, it has been a sad, sad day to us," and immediately relapsed into his thoughtful mood and attitude.

Being unwilling again to intrude upon his reflections, I said no more. After perhaps a minute or two, he suddenly straightened up to his full height, and turning to me with more animation and excitement of a manner than I had ever seen in him before, for he was a man of wonderful equanimity, he said in a voice tremulous with emotion: "I never saw troops behave more magnificently than Pickett's division of Virginians did today in that grand charge upon the enemy. And if they fully explained to me, were not, we would have held the position and the day would have been ours." After a moment pause he added in a loud voice, in a tone of almost agony, "Too bad! Too bad! Oh! Too bad!"

I shall never forget his language, his manner, and his appearance of mental suffering. In a few moments all emotion was suppressed and he spoke feelingly of several of his fallen and trusted officers; among others of Brigadier Generals Armistead, Garnett, and Kemper of Pickett's division. He invited me into his tent, and as soon as we were seated he remarked: "We must now return to Virginia. As many of our poor wounded as possible must be taken home. I have sent for you, because your men and horses are fresh and in good condition, to guard and conduct our train back to Virginia. The duty will be arduous, responsible, and dangerous, for I am afraid you will be harassed by the enemy's cavalry. How many men have you?" (Battles and Leaders of the Civil War; edited by Johnson, Robert Underwood and Buel, Clarence Clough; editorial staff of The Centruy Magazine; Castle N. J; Volume III; pages 420-423

A note dated December 9, 1863, from General Lee to his 30-year-old champion cavalier, General Stuart

"My heart and thoughts will always be with this army."

General Lee loved General Stuart as a son. He was distant kin, had admired Mary Custis as a cadet, and JEB had always served the general gallantly. He was with Lee at Harpers Ferry and served until his death at Yellow Tavern. Robert E. Lee speaking about the death of J.E.B. Stuart

"I can scarcely think of him without weeping."

"A Humble Earnest Christian"

The General was a high profile public figure but a very private man. He was also a deeply committed man to his beliefs and his God. By example he demonstrated how to conduct oneself regarding religion and faith. The Reverend J. W. Jones in his book Christ in the Camp reflected upon a meeting held with General Lee in the month of February 1864 while encamped upon the Rapidan. He was an army chaplain and was a member of the Chaplain's Association. They had asked for an audience to discuss the revival sweeping the soldiers and how to increase the attendance of services on Sunday. Reverend B.T. Lacy and he were given an appointment. Both were worried as to how to address the General but within a few minutes, the kindly old gentleman had put all their fears aside. Reverend Jones states, "…But as we presently began to answer his questions concerning the spiritual interests of the army and to tell of that great revival which was then extending through the camps and bringing thousands of our noble men to Christ, we saw his eyes brighten and his whole countenance glow with pleasure; and as, in his simple, feeling words, he expressed his delight, we forgot the great warrior, and only remembered that we were communing with a humble, earnest Christian." (<u>Christ in the Camp:</u> <u>Religion in the Confederate Army</u>; Jones, J. William; Martin and Hoyt Company; Atlanta; 1904)

"While Christ Is in the Camp"

In his delightfully refreshing book, the Reverend J. William Jones talked about the religious revival that swept over the armies during the time of their conflict. He was an actual witness to that great event and his documented accounts of faith and testimonies are uplifting to the spirit. He talks of General Lee as being a man of extreme religious convictions and strongly supported his boys getting right with God prior to facing death on the field of battle. The following poem was inspired from a combination of his book, my Saturday afternoon with my children, and Easter Sunday. Also, I reflected on the numerous times it was said that it was in God's hands or His will be done. I felt the keen presence of Lee's religious convictions whenever I read his personal letters and heard him talk of God in such manner to offer assurances of a close walk with the Almighty. I attempted to capture the charismatic feeling of the person experiencing his or her own personal deliverance during the chaotic times of war. When that great roll call is given, I pray that all our names are listed for the greatest camp meeting of all, as Christ walks through the camp....

While Christ Is in the Camp

I knelt beside Bobby Lee
While Christ was in our camp.
There I prayed on bended knee
When Christ was in our camp.

Death can't keep me in the ground
While Christ is in the camp.
Within my heart love abounds
When Christ is in the camp.

All my fears are washed away
While Christ is in the camp.
When I'm scared, I start to pray
Then Christ is in the camp.

Feel the love replace the hate
When Christ is in the camp.
Long to see them golden gates
Where Christ is in the camp.

With His blood, He cleansed my sins
When Christ was in the camp.
Open arms he took me in
When Christ was in the camp.

From now on I have no fears
For Christ is in my camp.
He'll wipe away all your tears
When Christ is in your camp.

"You are Always Getting Wounded"

In May of 1864, after the death of General Stuart, Colonel Mosby* tells in his memoirs about being directed to report to the commanding general. On his third visit, after being wounded on two occasions prior to each visit, Mosby stated that General Lee introduced him to General Longstreet and said with a twinkle in his eye, "Colonel, the only fault I have ever had to find with you is that you are always getting wounded." (The Memoirs of Colonel John S. Mosby; Mosby, John Singleton; Edited by Russell, Charles W.; Little, Brown, and Company; Boston; 1917; page 374) *General Lee wrote more about Mosby than any officer under his command.

"I Grieve for You, My Poor Fellow"

One of the stories that personifies the essence of the level of respect each held for the other is offered in the works of William J. Jones. As General Lee rode Traveller, a wounded soldier was walking toward the rear to obtain medical assistance for a shattered arm. Upon seeing the wounded man, Lee had compassion and stated, "I grieve for you, my poor fellow. Can I do anything for you?" The wounded soldier looked admiringly at his idol and simply stated, "Yes sir, you can shake hands with me, General, if you will consent to take my left hand." Such was the reverence and respect held by his boys for their leader. (Personal Reminiscences, Anecdotes, and Letters of General Robert E. Lee; Jones, J. William; Appleton; New York; 1875)

"The Air Was Made of Lead"

On my first visit to the Mule Shoe or Bloody Angle, the concentrated area of close quarter fighting that occurred at that location, filled me with awe and reverence for those that argued upon that plain. Such ferocious hand-to-hand mortal combat that transpired upon the hallowed acres stuns the thoughts of man. One of the officers stated that, "We not only shot down an army, we shot down a forest." This sums up the intensity of the fighting better than anything that I could add. I looked at the grand oaks that bordered the field and wondered if their ancestors gave their lives on that field of battle. Were they the saplings that had viewed the carnage first hand? The fighting was so desperate that General Lee again started to lead the charge but was repulsed by the love of his men who refused him that responsibility. In my imaginings as I walked the field listening to the guide, I could see the men contesting each inch of hallowed ground and stubbornly advancing and withdrawing. The retreating little Army of Northern Virginia was again noted on that day as one inspired by the love of God and the leadership of Lee but the cost of freedom and the momentary victory was again stained with blood of countless lives.

The Air Was Made of Lead

At a place called the Angle
Where the lead rode the wind.
The Blue and Gray entangled
As death began to grin.

The Mule Shoe was encircled!
The air was made of lead.
Each overcoming hurdles
In piles of living dead.

Lee said that they must stop them
"So give it to 'em boys!"
"You know that you must drop them!"
He yelled above the noise.

They held on to positions
That was paid for in blood.
They played a sad rendition
Of dying in the mud.

The Wilderness was burning
As lead cut down the trees.
The battle tide was turning
A nation on her knees.

But the boys in gray rallied
They fought among the dead.
The final cost was tallied
The price was paid with lead.

No one foresaw the slaughter
Or the cost of blood shed.
The Angle's was the alter
When air was made of lead.

"General Lee to the Rear"

One of my favorite stories of General Lee pertains to the time when he was engaged in a battle that was going poorly for his boys. Apparently, he was vexed and overwhelmed by the losses. He turned to his staff and made the comment of how easy it would be for him to go closer to those people and it would all be over for him. He then recanted his thoughts and stated that it would not be fair for his country if he should do so. He decided that he would personally lead a rally of his men by going to the front. Once his intentions were made known by his actions, his boys' love overwhelmed him by pleads and demands for hlm to return to the rear. In one version of the story, an older soldier came to him and stated with tears running down his cheeks that if he must do so, he would carry him and Traveller back to safety of the trees. On three occasions during a two-week period the General demonstrated his intent to lead his boys into battle. His boys always denied him that honor and insisted they would give all if he would go to the rear. He finally stated with humorous frustration that, "I wish I knew where my place was on the battlefield. Where ever I go someone tells me that is not the place for me to be." The will of his boys prevailed on those last days and another piece of the legacy was added to the great puzzle. (In the Footsteps of Robert E. Lee; Johnson, Clint; John H. Blair Publisher; Winston-Salem, North Carolina; 2001; page 22). William T. Poague documented yet another incident of General Lee being reminded of his place in the rear of the army. He remembered seeing his commander during a battle on May 6, as; "Gregg's Texans came in line of battle at a swinging gait from the rear of our position. They passed through our guns, their right near the road, General Lee was riding close behind them. Of course our firing to the front had to cease now and only two pieces continued across the road. Soon the Texans began to call to General Lee to go back, and as he seemed not to heed they became clamorous, insisting that if he did not go back they would not go forward...then, turning Traveller about, he rode quietly to the rear of our line of guns, amid the cheers of the artillerymen." (<u>Gunner with Stonewall: Reminiscences of William Thomas Poague, a Memoir, Written for His Children in 1903</u>; Poague, William Thomas; ed. Cockrell, Monroe F.; McCowat-Mercer Press; Jackson, Tennessee; page 181)

"General Lee to the Rear"
By David Chaltas

He had a look of sorrow
As tears ran down his face.
For some, no more tomorrow:
This was their dying place.

The Wilderness was calling,
His boys must go and fight.
The battle was a mauling;
It was a bloody sight.

He said it would be easy
To end it all right here.
We cried as hearts turned queasy,
"General Lee to the rear!"

His boys crowded around him,
Reached out and grabbed his reins.
Their love all but astounds him;
Intentions were quite plain.

"Old Trav and you we'll carry
Your loss, our greatest fear.

In front you cannot tarry
General Lee to the rear!"

Reluctantly he yielded.
They made their plan quite clear.
His life his boys had shielded,
"General Lee's to the rear!"

"Is This Any of You-r-r Mule?"

In his book, General Alexander gives a vivid account of not only camp life but also rare insight into the level of respect Lee had for animals even in a time of planning for the next engagement. The passage also demonstrates the mannerisms of the general when he became upset. The setting is Monday May 23, 1864 near Hanover Junction. The battle of Mule Shoe (Bloody Angle) had just occurred and the enemy was advancing steadily, even with their staggering losses. The following excerpt portrays the event as only a witness to the scene could express. (Fighting for the Confederacy: The Personal Recollections of General Edward Porter Alexander; Alexander, Edward P.; Edited by Gary W. Gallagher; University of North Carolina Press; Chapel Hill/London; 1989; pages 389-390)

"All around us troops were going into bivouac for the night. Men loaded with bunches of canteens, which rattled as they walked, were wandering about inquiring for wells & springs & streams. Company cooks were kindling their fires & impatient mules were braying for their suppers. The air was still & it was far-reaching. Gen. Lee sat on a big root, back against the tree, with some of his own staff around & some three or four engineers, among whom I remember Sam Johnston & Proctor Smith. Those who wanted the line in front of the swamp were invited to explain why & then those who preferred to have the swamp in front. Gen. Lee heard the arguments, which were all brief & to the point, for all night would be needed to distribute troops & artillery, & prepare for the assault at day break, which we fully expected. Then Gen. Lee decided that the line should have the swamp in front, & began giving details about the location of troops.

"Just then a teamster began to remonstrate with a mule, some hundred yards or more across the clearing. His remarks were as audible as if he had been under the tree with us....Gen. Lee could stand anything better than having an animal mistreated. He hesitated a moment in his speech & gave that peculiar little shake of his head which he used when we was worried, & which we used to call snapping at his ear. But the misunderstanding between the man & mule only seemed to widen. I won't try to repeat his lurid language, for I could not do it justice, & only a pile driver could describe the whacks which accompanied his volley of oaths. Gen. Lee stopped his discourse, snapped at his ear a time or two, & and then shouted out in a tone which I thought would scare anybody, "What are you beating that mule for?" But the teamster evidently thought only that some one was guying him, for assuming a sort of Georgia cracker whine in his voice, he sung out, "Is this any of you-r-r mule?" It was an awful moment. Not one of us dared to crack a smile. The general snapped at his ear again a time or two & then apparently determined to finish with us first, before making good his claim to the mule. I have no doubt that he did this as soon as we were gone and to the teamster's entire satisfaction, but I never heard any particulars."

"The Line has been stretched Until it had to Break"

Upon the imminent fall of Petersburg resulting from his line being stretched too thin, Lee stated, "It is as I feared it would be. The line has been stretched until it had to break."

"He is now at Rest"

Another one of Lee's favorite generals was A. P. Hill. Lee even called for him to come up prior to saying 'Strike the Tent.' Upon hearing that his gallant General A. P. Hill had been shot while attempting to capture two Union soldiers, General Lee, with tears trickling down his face said, "He is now at rest, and we who are left are the ones to suffer."

"What Are You Doing With All That Grey?"

Even in the most distressful of times, humor can be found. One such incident occurred a day or two after Lee's surrender at Appomattox. Several soldiers that had chosen to fight for the northern cause called upon General Lee. One of the visitors was General George Gordon Meade that Lee had befriended prior to the war. Meade had given Lee stout resistance at Gettysburg. Lee received him cordially and jovially remarked to him, "But what are you doing with all that grey in your beard?" At which General Meade quickly responded, "You have to answer for most of it!" (Lee, The Last Years; Flood, Charles Bracelen; Houghton Mifflin Company; New York; 1981; page 23)

"The Same Self-Possessed, Dignified Gentleman"

On April 10, 1865, General Henry J. Hunt had an opportunity to visit his friend General Lee at his headquarters. General Hunt was a Union artillery officer who had known Lee prior to the war. They conversed politely for approximately half an hour. Sometime after taking his leave from his former adversary, General Hunt stated that he found Lee, "Weary and care-worn, but in this supreme hour the same self-possessed, dignified gentleman that I had always known him." Note that this was the date in which Lee presented to his army General Order 9, bidding his beloved boys an affectionate farewell. (Lee; Freeman Douglas Southall; An Abridgment by Richard Harwell of the Pulitzer Prize Winning four-volume Biography; New York; Touchstone; 1991; page 496)

"Even if We Perished in the Endeavor"

During the last year of the war, General Lee spoke regarding his determination to continue the struggle. Note that he was still steadfast in his faith in the cause and believed that duty, honor, and sacrifice was worth offering up his life, if necessary. His sacred principles are those that we must also embrace; that of honor, duty, and Christian values.

"I have never believed we could, against the gigantic combination for our subjugation, make good in the long run our independence, unless foreign powers should, directly or indirectly, assist us. But such considerations really made with me no difference. We had, I was satisfied, sacred principles to maintain and rights to defend, for which we were in duty bound to do our best, even if we perished in the endeavor."

"I Would Rather Die a Thousand Deaths"

Lee's reply to General Gordon at Appomattox after being told of how exhausted the boys were:

"There is nothing left for me to do but to go and see General Grant, and I would rather die a thousand deaths."

"I Have Done the Best That I Could Do for You"

General Lee while riding by his weeping troops after signing the surrender terms at Appomattox:

"Men, we have fought through the war together. I have done the best that I could do for you."

In the year 1866, Lee was approached to ascertain his views upon the removal of the Confederate war dead from the hallowed fields of Gettysburg. Lee's comment was brief but concise and firmly established his thinking on the matter.

"I know of no fitter resting place for a soldier than the field on which he has nobly laid down his life."

"It is a Crime Previously Unknown"

General Lee's words upon hearing of the assassination of President Lincoln:

"It is a crime previously unknown to this Country, and one that must be deprecated by every American."

"As a Crime it was Unexampled"

A reporter by the name of Thomas Cook interviewed Lee regarding matters of the South. Lee saw an opportunity to assist in the healing of the nation. When asked about his thoughts on the assassination of Lincoln, he made the following paraphrased reply:

"The General considered this an event in itself one of the most deplorable that could have occurred. As a crime it was unexampled and beyond execration. It was a crime that no good man could approve from any conceivable motive. Undoubtedly the effort would be made to fasten the responsibility of it upon the South; but from his intimate acquaintance with the leading men of the South, he was confident there was not one of them who would sanction or approve of it."

"Restoration of Peace and Harmony"

General Lee a few months after his surrender:

"I think it the duty of every citizen, in the present condition of the Country, to do all in his power to aid in the restoration of peace and harmony, and in no way to oppose the policy of the State or General Government directed to that object."

"I Have Never Known One Moment of Bitterness"

General Lee speaking on the feelings he had towards the North:

"I believe I may say, looking into my own heart, and speaking as in the presence of God, that I have never known one moment of bitterness or resentment."

"I have fought against the people of the North because I believed they were seeking to wrest from the South its dearest right. But I have never cherished toward them bitter or vindictive feelings, and I have never seen the day when I did not pray for them."

212

The General's wisdom was beyond his years. He saw into the future and fought for what he believed was a righteous cause but in the end he placed the outcome into the hands of a kind providence and worked towards the healing of our land. Such was the character of the man.

"We failed, but in the good providence of God apparent failure often proves a blessing."

"The Duty of its Citizens Appears to Me too Plain to Admit Without Doubt"

Prior to his arrival at Lexington, Virginia to shoulder the robes of educational leadership, General Lee wrote the former governor of Virginia expressing his views regarding the reunification efforts that were at hand. The following excerpts sample his resolve to accomplish that ultimate goal.

"The questions which for years were in dispute between the States and the General Government…having been decided against us, it is the part of wisdom to acquiesce in the result, and of candor to recognize the fact…The interests of the State are the same as those of the United States…The duty of its citizens, then, appears to me too plain to admit without doubt."

"We Must Look to the Rising Generation"

Speaking to Governor Letcher in August of 1865:

"We must look to the rising generation for the restoration of the country."

"Regardless of Self"

General Lee realized what must be done in order to restore peace and harmony after the long engagement. He knew it would be a long and difficult path requiring all to make sacrifices in order to preserve the dignity of the southern people.

"Our country requires now everyone to put forth all his ability, regardless of self."

"I Would Have Preferred to Die at Appomattox with My Brave Men"

Though General Robert E. Lee attempted to maintain a status quo and not comment upon the war and what might have been, on one occasion he let his passions override his marble stature. When speaking to Governor Stockdale of Texas regarding the outcome of the war and reconstruction, he forcefully uttered the following statement:

"Governor, if I had foreseen the use those people designed to make of their victory, there would have been no surrender at Appomattox Courthouse; no sir, not by me. Had I foreseen the results of subjugation, I would have preferred to die at Appomattox with my brave men, my sword in this right hand."

"Abandon Your Animosities"

Robert E. Lee speaking after the war on unification of the nation:

"Abandon your animosities and make your sons Americans."

"Save Us from Destruction"

"I look forward to better days, and trust that time and experience, the great teachers of men, under the guidance of an ever-merciful God, may save us from destruction and restore to us the bright hopes and prospects of the past."

"We Have But One Rule Here"

Speaking to his students while President of Washington College

"Young gentleman, we have no printed rules. We have but one rule here, and it is that every student must be a gentleman."

"Make No Needless Rules"

President Lee speaking to his faculty at Washington College. (R.E. Lee: A Biography; Freeman, Douglas Southall; New York; Charles Scribner's Sons, 1934)

"As a general principle, you should not force young men to do their duty, but let them do it voluntarily and thereby develop their characters…Make no needless rules."

"He Strives for That Nobleness of Self and Mildness of Character"

General Lee's philosophy on being always a gentleman is well stated in the following comments. Note the strength of his convictions and the example of brotherly love reiterated throughout his statement.

"The forbearing use of power does not only form a touchstone; but the manner in which an individual enjoys certain advantages over others, is a test of a true gentleman. The power which the strong have over the weak, the magistrate over the citizen, the employer over the employed, the educated over the unlettered, the experienced over the confiding, even the clever over the silly; the forbearing and inoffensive use of all this power or authority, or a total abstinence from it when the case admits it, will show the gentleman in a plain light. The gentleman does not needlessly and unnecessarily remind an offender of a wrong he may have committed against him. He cannot only forgive, he can forget; and he strives for that nobleness of self and mildness of character, which imparts sufficient strength to let the past be but the past. A true man of honor feels humbled himself when he cannot help humbling others."

"Be Sure We Attend Ourselves"

After the war, President Lee began the laborious task of rebuilding Washington College but more importantly, interweaving the highest of standards within that institution of higher learning. To his faculty, he stated the following regarding the attendance of chapel services: (Reminiscences of General Lee, J. J. William; 244)

"One of the best ways that I know of to induce the students to attend chapel is to be sure we attend ourselves."

The preceding is a picture taken of the beautiful chapel that was built during Lee's tenure as President of Washington College. Citizen Lee sat in the front isle to the viewer's right. It is known as Lee's Chapel.

"One That Will Harmonize the Surrounding Colors"

During the beautification of the college campus, President Lee was asked if he wanted the trees arranged in any order. Lee stated to have them planted, "Not in rows; Nature never plants trees in rows." When asked about a fence project to keep wandering cattle off the campus, Lee stated, "A fence is a blot on any lawn. We must have a fence; but select a color which will render the fence as inconspicuous as possible: one that will harmonize with the surrounding colors."

"I Would Love Him for That Yet"

During the semester, a boy from Kentucky attending Washington College received word that his mother had passed away. By the time he received the sad message it was too late for him to make arrangements to go home. He asked his roommates to go to the president and explain that he would not be attending classes for a few days. Fifty-six years late he expressed his feelings regarding that time in his life: "At the end of the month when my report came out there was not a single absent mark against me. This can only be accounted for by General Lee's going to each professor to whom I recited and telling him. To me this is a remarkable illustration of his kindness to and care for the boys entrusted to him. If I had no other reason, I would love him for that yet." (Lee, The Last Years; Flood, Charles Bracelen; Houghton Mifflin Company; N. Y; 1981; p 143)

"Tell them from me that it is Unworthy"

Christiana Bond remembered a valued lesson that the old general taught while at a social event. Several Pennsylvanians were in the ballroom but the Southerners were shunning their company. General Lee asked if some of the ladies would accompany him to be introduced to the Northerners. Finally, Christiana consented. Stopping underneath a chandelier, Lee told her "…of the grief with which he found a spirit of unreasoning resentment and bitterness in the young people of the South, of the sinfulness of hatred and social revenge, of the duty of kindness, helpfulness and consideration for others." The old sage then gave her a charge. "When you go home, I want you to take a message to your young friends. Tell them from me that it is unworthy of them as women, and especially as Christian women, to cherish feelings of resentment against the North. Tell them that it grieves me inexpressibly to know that such a state of things exists, and that I implore them to do their part to heal our country's wounds." (Lee, The Last Years; Flood, Charles Bracelen; Houghton Mifflin Company; New York; 1981; pages 165-166)

"That Heartbroken Look on His Face"

A reflection by a woman living in the Lexington area whose son had broken his leg recalled General Lee visiting her son on different occasions. One spring evening he came and she described his manner on that particular day:

"He would sit and talk in the twilight...Once, I remember he sat still for sometime by the window and his face looked so sad. He spoke of the Southern people, of their losses, privations, and sufferings, and also of our vain struggle. 'I cannot sleep,' he said, 'for thinking of it, and often I feel so weighted down with sorrow that I have to get up in the night and go out and walk till I thoroughly weary myself before I can sleep.' That was the only melancholy sentence I ever heard him utter, and the only time I ever saw that heartbroken look on his face." (Lee, The Last Years; Flood, Charles Bracelen; Houghton Mifflin Company; New York; 1981; page 153)

"If You Talk Disrespectfully of Grant"

In the year 1868 one of Lee's professors was discussing the political situation of the day and in particular downgrading General Grant who was a Republican candidate for the Presidency. He made it quite clear that this type of talk would not be tolerated in his presence.

"Sir, if you ever again presume to speak disrespectfully of General Grant in my presence, either you or I will sever his connection with this university."

"Education is the Most Efficacious Means"

Speaking to General Gordon in 1869 Lee defined his educational vision for a reunited America. (R. E. Lee, a Biography; Freeman Douglas Southall; four-volume; New York; Scribner; 1934-35; page 563)

"The thorough education of all classes of the people is the most efficacious means, in my opinion, of promoting the prosperity of the South. The material interests of its citizens, as well as their moral and intellectual culture, depend upon its accomplishment. The textbooks of our schools, therefore, should not only be clear, systematic, and scientific, but they should be acceptable to parents and pupils in order to enlist the minds of all in the subjects."

"I Received Your Tribute to the Merits of My Countrymen"

During this period of growth Lee received a special gift from Philip Stanhope Worsley, a noted poet and scholar from Oxford, England. According to his son Bertus (an affectionate name given Robert E. Lee Jr. by his father), Lee was deeply touched by the gift. It was a translation of the Iliad by Worsley. Also on the inside was an inscription that read, "To General Lee, the most stainless of living commanders and, except in fortune, the greatest. This volume is presented with the writer's earnest sympathy and respectful admiration...cios yap epveto Idiov Ektwp." Also attached was a hand-written poem in tribute to Lee and the South. General Lee's letter of gratitude expressed his delight in the gift. "My Dear Sir: I have received the copy of your translation of the Iliad which you so kindly presented to me. Its perusal has been my

220

evening's recreation, and I have never more enjoyed the beauty and grandeur of the poem than as recited by you. The translation is as truthful as powerful, and faithfully represents the imagery and rhythm of the bold original. The undeserved compliment in prose and verse, on the first leaves of the volume. I received your tribute to the merits of my countrymen, who struggled for constitutional government." (<u>Recollections and Letter of Robert E. Lee</u>; Lee, Robert E. Jr. Captain; Doubleday, Doran, and Company; 1904,1924; pages 118-119)

With great respect,
Your Obedient Servant
R. E. Lee
Lexington, Virginia, March 14, 1866

"What a Gentle Noble Soul"

During Lee's sixty-second year of life, an internationally known Swedish painter by the name of Franz Buchner came to Lexington to paint his picture. His idea was that if Lee posed, then Grant would follow suit. He even had the notion that he would recreate the surrender scene at Appomattox. But Lee quickly ended that suggestion when he simply stated, "I am a soldier no longer." Lee did consent to allow a portrait of him but he was to be dressed in the black suit that Rooney bought. The only hints of his days as a soldier were on a table. Beside him were his sword, belt, sash, binoculars, hat, and the uniform that he had worn at Appomattox. During the painting sessions and while living on the hospitality of the Lees, Frank became besotted with this legend called Lee. In his journal, he wrote, "What a gentle noble soul, how kind and charming the old white-haired warrior is! One cannot see and know this great soldier without loving him." His portrait of Lee is on permanent

221

display in the Swiss National Museum. (<u>Lee, The Last Years</u>; Flood, Charles Bracelen; Houghton Mifflin Company; New York; 1981; page 220)

"I Will More Willingly Follow"

In 1869, Lee made a profound statement on death, of faith and the hereafter. It attests to the spirit of man and the sweet reassurance that we will meet on the other shore. "Death, in its silent, sure march is fast gathering those whom I have longest loved, so that when he shall knock at my door, I will more willingly follow." (<u>May I Quote You General Lee?</u>; Bedwell, Randall; Cumberland House Publishing; Nashville; 1997; page 76)

"It is History That Teaches Us to Hope"

"The truth is this: The march of Providence is so slow and our desires so impatient; the work of progress is so immense and our means of aiding it so feeble; the life of humanity so long, that of the individual so brief, that we often see only the ebb of the advancing wave and are thus discouraged. It is history that teaches us to hope." (<u>May I Quote You General Lee?</u>; Bedwell, Randall; Cumberland House Publishing; Nashville; 1997)

"You Can Teach Your Children to Love and Cherish Her"

In May of 1870, Lee embarked upon what was destined to be his last trip to visit the South and the people in which he offered his all. While touring, he made an unscheduled stop to visit White Marsh, the home of Dr. Professor Tabb. Dr. Tabb had married a cousin of the general and she was determined that her children meet their famous cousin. His son Rob accompanied him and that

222

night slept in the same bed as he had done years before while growing up under the watchful eye of the Lee family. While staying at White Marsh, Dr. Tabb provided a traditional family dinner in which the topic fell upon the Reconstruction Movement that was weighing heavily upon the oppressed people of the South. One of Lee's cousins asked what was to become of, "us poor Virginians." His reply became the battle cry of the state and helped in the rebuilding of pride of being a Virginian. The old general turned and looked into his cousin's eyes and stated, "You can work for Virginia, to build her up again, to make her great again. You can teach your children to love and cherish her." (In the Footsteps of Robert E. Lee; Johnson, Clint; John H. Blair Publisher; Winston-Salem, North Carolina; 2001; pages 60-62)

"I Fear I Should Not Like to Say Any Evil"

General Lee was approached by a lady who wished to talk to him regarding the possibility of writing a biography of his life. He replied in a letter that he was honored but in his classic manner of expression he declined stating that;

"I know of nothing good I could tell you of myself, and I fear I should not like to say any evil."

"My Spirit Passeth By"

After reading so many of the quotes and letters that Lee had written to his loved ones, I started to sense the quintessence of the man. While pondering the many illustrations of Lee and the love he possessed for his family, I felt compelled to again sit down and write my interpretations of what must have ran through the mind of the old patriot as he deliberated over the question that each of us must face. This laborious task of love and tribute was one of deep thought and reflection, as should be the question of one's own mortality. This question has crossed the minds of millions as they waited on the roar of battle or the quiet whisper of the inevitable call of conviction to enter the secret garden.

My Spirit Passeth By

Oh Darling will you miss me
When I exist no more?
And will you long to kiss me
The way you did before?

Oh, will your heart be broken
And will you start to cry?
When ere my name is spoken;
My spirit passeth by.

If I should fall while fighting
Know my love shall remain.
My love for you I'm writing
On every drop of rain.

If I should fall in battle,
I'll feel your fingertips
Soothing my heart's death rattle;
Your name upon my lips.

My love for you is boundless
And every time you cry;
My love for you surrounds us
As my spirit passeth by.

THE LETTERS OF LEE
(An Assorted Assortment)

As the author of such an important man in our history, I feel that it is essential to offer the reader every opportunity to review the material that has been penned by the very person being written about. The family members of Lee were also prolific writers and their correspondence covers thousands of letters and documents. The Wartime Papers of Robert E. Lee alone contains over a thousand communications ironically dating from April 20, 1861 through April 20, 1865. (The Wartime Papers of Robert E. Lee; Dowdey, Clifford, Editor; Manarin, Louis H., Associate Editor; Da Capo Press; an unabridged reproduction of the edition published in Boston in 1961; Commonwealth of Virginia)

Through my research, I have found a vast quantity of letters that paint a much clearer portrait of the man called Lee than this novice fielder could ever express. The sources are vastly varied and are too exhaustive for this endeavor to be an all-exclusive enterprise. I therefore chose a sampling of letters from different periods of his life to get an inkling of the character of the man. I have made every effort to be as concise and accurate as possible. The first letter known to exist that was written by Lee was when he accepted his appointment to West Point. It consisted only of two lines and was written on April 1, 1824. For over forty-six years Lee would spend countless hours laboring at writing and answering correspondences. The end result is a tapestry of his life. The sources (Captain Lee, Agnes and Mildred Lee, Taylor, Jones, Alexander, Marshal, Flood etc.) are listed throughout this literary effort to acknowledge those that were privileged to have written about and/or to have personally known the legend called Lee. A full bibliography is included in the back in order to assist the reader further his/her knowledge regarding the moral fiber of Robert Edward Lee.

"I Am Engaged"

A nervous Robert Edward Lee wrote his brother Carter informing him of his forthcoming nuptials. Note that the adopted son of George Washington, George Washington Custis had not placed his seal of approval upon the wedding plans at that juncture but yielded to the ladies of the house desires. The date was set for June 30. They were married inside Arlington since a rain shower made it necessary to do so. The Reverand Reuel Keith, though soaked, performed the ceremony. The letter shows excitement and apprehension on the part of Lee. Lee would later humorously write of the ceremony that, "The minister had few words to say, though he dwelt upon them as if he had been reading my death warrant, and there was a tremulousness in the hand I felt that made me anxious for him to end." (Lee; Freeman, Douglas Southall; Touchstone Book; Simon & Schuster; New York; 1961, 1991)

226

"I am engaged to Miss Mary C.. Think of that…That is, she & her mother have given their consent. But the father has not yet made up his mind, though it is supposed will not object."

"History and Tradition Seemed to Breathe Their Legends"

The bulk of Robert E. Lee's correspondence comes after his wedding held on June 30, 1831. Being a lifetime soldier, he was away from home more than he was present. And the mold of maintaining that relationship came via the letters of love and devotion that was sent to one another. Regarding the wedding of two famous families, surprisingly not much was noted in the paper as previously reviewed. But his nephew Fitzhugh Lee noted that, "Arlington was in her glory that night. Its broad portico and widespread wings held out open arms, as if were, to welcome the coming guest. Its simple Doric columns graced domestic comfort with a classic air. Its halls and chambers were adorned with the patriots and heroes and with illustrations and relics of the great Revolution and of the 'Father of his Country', and without and within, history and tradition seemed to breathe their legends upon a canvas as soft as a dream of peace." (General Lee; Lee, Fitzhugh; Premier Civil War Classics; Fawcett Publications, Inc.; Greenwich, Conn., 1961; page 35)

"I Was Firm in My Demands and Constant in Their Enforcement"

General Lee spoke of the need for discipline in every aspect of his life. No greater love could he show for his children than to discipline them and to teach them in the laws of the Lord. On one

227

occasion while he was stationed in the wilds of the west, Lee learned that his son was falling from the path in which Lee expected him to follow. On October 16, 1837, he wrote the following letter to his wife seeking her assistance in realigning the child's directions before he fell into serious mischief that would result in intervention by the fatherly side of Lee.

"Our dear little boy seems to have among his friends the reputation of being hard to manage. A distinction not at all desirable, as it indicates self-will and obstinacy. Perhaps these are qualities which he really possesses, and he may have a better right to them than I am willing to acknowledge; but it is our duty, if possible, to counteract them and assist him to bring them under control. I have endeavored in my intercourse with him, to require nothing but what was in my opinion necessary or proper…I have also tried to show him that I was firm in my demands, and constant in their enforcement, and that he must comply with them; and I let him see that I look to their execution, in order to relieve him as much as possible from the temptation to break them…You must assist me in my attempts, and we must endeavor to combine the mildness and forbearance of the mother with the sternness and perhaps unreasonableness of the father…I pray God to watch over and direct our efforts in guarding our little son, that we may bring him up in the way that he should go."

"From a Coon Story to a Sea Serpent"

While stationed in St. Louis, Lee wrote his cousin Cassius asking for him to send him a copy of the Lee family coat of arms. In 1866 he again addresses his ancestry in a letter to a man interested in the Lee lineage. He also addressed a rumor that somehow was started regarding his son and that of his cousin Philippa's son. He asked his cousin Cassius to intercede and not to take stock in such rumors. (<u>Life & Letters of Gen. Robert Edward Lee</u>; Jones, W.J.; Sprinkle Publications; Harrisonburg, Virginia; 1986; @ by Neale Publishing Company in 1906; pages 32-33)

"I believe I once spoke to you on the subject of getting for me the crest, coat of arms, etc., of the Lee family, and which, sure enough you never did. My object in making the request is for the purpose of having a seal cut with the impression of said coat, which I think is due from a man of my large family to his posterity, and which I have thought, perhaps foolishly enough, might as well be right as wrong. If therefore, you can assist me in this laudable enterprise, I shall be much obliged, and by enveloping it securely, directed to me at this place, and sending it either by mail or some safe hand to the Engineer Office, Washington City, without any work or further direction, it would come safely to hand. I once saw in the hands of Cousin Edmund, for the only time in my life, our family tree, and as I begin in my old age to feel a little curiosity relative to my forefathers, their origin, whereabouts, etc., any information you can give me will increase the obligation.

"So sit down one of these hot evenings and write it off for me, or at any rate the substance, and tell my cousin Philippa not to let you forget it. I wish you would at the same time undeceive her on a certain point, for, as I understand, she is laboring under a grievous error.

"Tell her that it is farthest from my wish to detract from any of the little Lees, but as to her little boy being equal to Mr. Rooney (Lee's nickname for his son William Henry Fitzhugh), it is a thing not even to be supposed, much less believed, although we live in a credulous country, where people stick at nothing from a coon story to a sea serpent. You must remember us particularly to her, to Uncle Edmund, Cousins Sally, Hannah and the Lloyds.

"I believe I can tell you nothing here that would interest you, except that we are all well, although my dame has been a little complaining for a day or two. The elections are all over, the 'Vanities' have carried the day in the State, although the Whigs in this district carried their entire ticket, and you will have the pleasure of hearing the great expunger again thunder from his place in the Senate against banks, bribery, and corruption. While on the river I cannot help being on the lookout for the stream of gold that was ascend the Mississippi, tied in silent purses! It would be a pretty sight, but the tide has not yet made up here. Let me know whether you can enlighten me on the point in question. And believe me, Yours very truly, R. E. Lee"

"Alone in a Crowd is Very Solitary"

On June 5, 1839, Lee wrote a very personal letter to his beloved wife Mary. The letter was written while Robert E. Lee was on duty in Louisville, Kentucky. This excerpt captures the essence of a man away from his family, longing to be with them and his efforts to offer fatherly counsel while away from his home.

"I hope you are all well and will continue so; and therefore must again urge you to be very prudent and careful of those dear children. If I could only get a squeeze at that little fellow turning up his sweet mouth to 'keeze Baba!' You must not let him run wild in my absence, and will have to exercise

230

firm authority over all of them. This will not require severity, or even strictness, but constant attention, and an unwavering course. Mildness and forbearance, tempered by firmness and judgment, will strengthen their affection for you, while it will maintain your control over them…You do not know how much I have missed you and the children, my dear Mary. To be alone in a crowd is very solitary."

"It Was the Prettiest Sight I Have Seen"

In a letter dated September 4, 1840, Lee tells his wife of an encounter with several small little girls playing in the yard. In the letter, one can ascertain the feeling of his love and devotion for children, especially little girls. The letter was written in St. Louis. (General Lee; Lee, Fitzhugh; Premier Civil War Classics; Fawcett Publications, Inc.; Greenwich, Conn., 1961; page 38)

"A few evenings since, feeling lonesome, as the saying is, and out of sorts, I got on a horse and took a ride. On returning through the lower part of town, I saw a number of little girls all dressed up in their white frocks and pantalets, their hair plaited and tied up with ribbons, running and chasing each other in all directions. I counted twenty-three nearly the same size. As I drew up my horse to admire the spectacle a man appeared at the door with the twenty-fourth in his arms. 'My friend,' said I, 'are all these your children?' 'Yes,' he said, 'and there are nine more in the house, and this is the youngest.' Upon further inquiry, however, I found that they were only temporarily his, and that they were invited to a party at his house. He said, however, he had been admiring them before I came up, and just wished that he had a million of dollars and that they were all his in reality. I do not think the eldest exceeded seven or eight years old. It was the prettiest sight I have seen in the West and perhaps in my life..."

"Always the Epaulets"

General Lee's namesake, Robert E. Lee wrote regarding his childhood and the fond memories he had with his father. Within his writings contains the essence of not a soldier but a father that dearly loves and is entirely devoted to his family.

"We would drive to the harbor in a bus, and there take one of the boats of the fort, sent up to meet us, with a crew from among the employees there, and were rowed to Sollers Point. There I was generally left in charge of the people of the place while my father visited the works and the workmen at the fort, a short distance out in the river. Those days were very happy ones. The shipping, the river, the boat and oarsmen, and the country dinner at Sollers Point-all made a strong impression on me. But, above all, I remember my father-his gentle, loving care of me; his bright talk; his stories; his maxims and teachings. I was so proud of him, and of the evident respect for and trust in him that everyone showed. The impressions received at that time have never changed nor left me. When he and my mother went out in the evening to some entertainment, we were allowed to sit up and see them start. My father, as I remember, was in uniform; and always ready, waiting for my mother, who was generally late. He would chide her gently in a playful way, and with his bright smile. After telling us goodbye, I would go to sleep with this beautiful picture in my mind-the golden epaulets and all; always the epaulets!" (Recollections and Letter of Robert E. Lee; Lee, Robert E. Captain; Doubleday, Doran, and Company; 1904,1924)

"Boo Yob's Coming to ee Him"

While stationed at Fort Hamilton, New York, on an engineering assignment, Captain Lee took time to write his son. In this letter emerged a concerned father over his son's academic progress and demonstrated his discipline through consultation with his children. He also discussed an accident that cost Rooney portions of his fore and middle finger on his left hand. Note the somber tone of the messages. In the letter he expresses inexplicable joy in his son's improvements, pride in his accomplishments and a reminder to stay the course in math. No matter where Lee is stationed, the father in him always shined through like a beacon for his children to follow. The letter is printed in its entirety due to it possessing such insight into the character of the man. It is dated 30th November 1845. (Life & Letters of Gen. Robert Edward Lee; Jones, W.J.; Sprinkle Publications; Harrisonburg, Virginia; 1986; @ by Neale Publishing Company in 1906; pages 37-39)

"I received last night, my dear son, your letter of the 25th inst. and was much gratified to perceive the evident improvement in your writing and spelling and to learn that you were getting on well in your studies.

"You must endeavor to learn, or order to compensate me for the pain I suffer in being separated from you, and let nothing discourage or deter you from endeavoring to acquire virtue and knowledge.

"I am pleased with your progress so far, and the last report sent me by Mr. Smith gave you a very good standing in all your studies. I was surprised to see that you were lower in algebra than in any other. How was that?-for I thought you had some talent for mathematics. Louis Marshall writes his father that he finds he (Louis) has no sense, for he has to study his eyes out to get along, and finds great difficulty in his mathematics.

"I hope you will not make the same discovery. You may probably not of heard of the accident that has happened to our dear Rooney. Last Monday afternoon (24th) while I was in N.Y. and your mother had gone out to tell the neighbors good-by, preparatory to leaving for Arlington, he feeling lonesome, went down to the public barn where they were putting in some hay for the horses, and got up in the loft, and before Jim was aware of it, commenced to cut some hay with the straw cutter and took off the ends of the fore and middle fingers of the left hand. The first just at the root of the nail and the second at the first joint. Jim took him immediately into the fort to the hospital, but unfortunately Dr. Eaton was also in N. Y. so that more than an hour and a quarter elapsed before they could be dressed. All that time he sat in the hospital with his fingers bleeding profusely, without complaining, and frequently scolded Jim for making a fuss about it.

"Jim got on one of the horses and went for Dr. Carpenter, but he was not at home. As soon, however, as Dr. Eaton arrived, which was about sunset, he sewed the ends on and bound them up. The officers who were present said they were astonished to see so young a boy behave so well, that they had seen many men under less trying circumstances behave worse. They had brought him home before I arrived, and I found him sitting before the fire waiting for me, to take his supper. I sent up early next morning to N.Y. for Dr. Monroe to see what further could be done.

"He came down again this afternoon, but has not yet taken off the ligatures put on by Dr. Eaton, for fear of displacing the ends of the fingers, which would destroy all hope of their uniting. We do not know yet, therefore, whether the ends will unite with the fingers or not.

"I pray God that they may, and that his hand may be entirely restored. I hope, my dear son, this may be a warning to you to meddle or interfere with nothing with which you have no concern, and particularly to refrain from going where you have been prohibited, or have not the permission of your parents or teachers.

"Fearing that some accident might happen to Rooney for his recklessness, I had prohibited his leaving the yard without permission, and never to go to the stable without my assent, and Jim had told him never to go near the cutting-box; notwithstanding all this he did both, and you see the fruits of his disobedience. He may probably lose his fingers and be maimed for life. You cannot conceive what I suffer at that thought.

"Do take warning from the calamity that has befallen your brother. I am now watching his bedside lest he should disturb his hand in his sleep. I still hope his hand may be restored. Since the accident he had done all in his power to repair his fault. He has been patient and submissive, giving us no trouble and never complaining.

"He has been more distressed at your mother's sufferings and mine than his own, and says he can do very well without his fingers, and that we must not mind their loss. Although he is at times obstinate and disobedient, which are grave faults, he has some very good qualities, which give us much pleasure.

"I hope this will be a lesson to him, and that in time he will correct his evil ways. I read him your letter. He says he wants to see you very much, that he will not forget his skates, and hopes to have a great deal of fun with you when he comes to Arlington. Rob says I must tell "Boo Yob's coming to ee him." Your mother and A. send much love. Write to me whenever you can. Stephen hears Aleck his lessons now every day, and I am told he improves very fast. Your affectionate father, R. E. Lee"

"To Do That You Must Learn to be Good"

It seems that his letters always addressed the spiritual growth as well as the intellectual growth of his children. After hearing of a story about a young man killed by a tree limb and how his son found him and took his body back home, Lee sat down and wrote of his concerns in the event of his demise. He asks his boys to take care of the ladies as he had done with his mother, his wife and family. He then instructs them in the manner of achieving this wish and as always beseeches them to follow God's word in all things. The reader will note the young age of the child that he is instructing and that the fatherly Lee believed that the seed of salvation was to be planted upon the fertile tender years of youth.

"I cannot go to bed, my dear son, without writing you a few lines to thank you for your letter, which gave me great pleasure. I am glad to hear you are well, and hope you are learning to read and write, and that the next letter you will be able to write yourself. I want to see you very much, and to tell you all that has happened since you went away…You and Custis must take great care of your kind mother and dear sisters when your father is dead. To do that you must learn to be good. Be true, kind, and generous, and pray earnestly to God to enable you to 'keep his commandments, and walk in the same all the days of your life."

"You Will Want For Nothing"

In a letter to his beloved children Captain Lee writes of Christmas. In the brief note one can obtain a glimpse of a father longing to be with his little ones. It was written on Christmas Eve of 1846, near Saltillo, Texas.

"I hope good Santa Claus will fill my Rob's stocking to-night; that Mildred's, Agnes's, and Anna's may break down with good things. I do not know what he may have for you and Mary (his daughter), but if he only leaves for you one half of what I wish, you will want for nothing. I have frequently thought if I had one of you on each side of me riding on ponies, such as I could get you, I would be comparatively happy."

"So Beautiful in Their Flight and so Destructive in Their Fall"

During the siege of Vera Cruz, Captain Lee met his brother Sydney Smith Lee. Smith was a Lieutenant in the United States Navy and was involved in the bombardment of the city. In essence the two brothers were fighting the enemy together. Captain Lee reflected upon that encounter in a letter dated 1847. It demonstrates his brotherly love and his compassion for the innocent women and children of the city. This was his first test in battle and it forged the bond between him and his superior, General Scott. (General Lee; Lee, Fitzhugh; Premier Civil

War Classics; Fawcett Publications, Inc,; Greenwich, Conn., 1961; pages 42-44)

"The first day this battery opened, Smith served one of the guns. I had constructed the battery and was there to direct its fire.   No matter where I turned, my eyes reverted to him, and I stood by his gun whenever I was not wanted elsewhere. Oh! I felt awfully, and am at a loss what I should have done had he been cut down before me. I thank God that he was saved. He preserved his usual cheerfulness, and I could see his white teeth through all the smoke and din of the fire. I had placed three 32 and three 68 pound guns in position…Their fire was terrific, and the shells thrown from our battery were constant and regular discharges, so beautiful in their flight and so destructive in the fall. It was awful! My heart bled for the inhabitants. The soldiers I did not care so much for, but it was terrible to think of the women and children…I heard from Smith to-day: he is quite well, and recovered from his fatigue."

"Pray Earnestly to God"

In another letter previously noted to his son Robert Lee Jr., Lee gives some fatherly advice on how to live honorably. (Recollections and Letter of Robert E. Lee; Lee, Robert E. Captain; Doubleday, Doran and Company; 1904, 1924; page 16)

"Be true, kind and generous, and pray earnestly to God to enable you to keep His commandments and walk in the same all the days of your life."

"I Scribbled Off This to Assure You of My Love"

On June 30, 1848, Captain Lee had just returned from the Mexican campaign and wrote his brother

Smith who was in the navy. In this letter one is able to obtain insight into Lee's love for his family, his concern for others (also his horse) and his joking nature. It was written at Arlington during an interlude of assignments. (General Lee; Lee, Fitzhugh; Premier Civil War Classics; Fawcett Publications, Inc,; Greenwich, Conn., 1961; pages 56-57)

"Here I am once again, my dear Smith, perfectly surrounded by Mary and her precious children, who seem to devote themselves to staring at the furrows in my face and the white hairs in my head. It is not surprising that I am hardly recognizable to some of the young eyes around me and perfectly unknown to the youngest, but some of the older ones gaze with astonishment and wonder at me, and seem at a loss to reconcile what they see and what was pictured in their imagination. I find them too much grown, and all well, and I have much cause for thankfulness and gratitude to a good God who has once more united us. I was greeted on my arrival by your kind letter, which was the next thing to seeing you in person. I wish I could say when I shall be able to visit you, but I as yet know nothing of the intention of the Department concerning me, and can not tell what my movements will be. Mary has recently returned from a visit to poor Anne, and gives a pitiable account of her distress. You may have heard of her having hurt her left hand; she is now consequently without the use of either, and can not even feed herself. She has suffered so much that it is not wonderful her spirits should be depressed. She sent many injunctions that I must come to her before even unpacking my trunk, and I think of running over there for a day after the fourth of July, if practicable. You say I must let you know when I am ready to receive visits. Now! Have you any desire to see the celebration, etc., of the Fourth

of July? Bring Sis Nannie and the little ones; I long
to see you all; I only arrived yesterday, after a long
journey up the Mississippi, which route I was
induced to take for the better accommodation of my
horse, as I wished to spare her as much annoyance
and fatigue as possible, she already having
undergone so much suffering in my service. I
landed her at Wheeling and left her to come over
with Jim. I have seen but few of our friends as yet,
but hear they are all well. Cousin Anna is at
Ravensworth. I met Mrs. John Mason yesterday as
I passed through W. All her people are well. I hear
that pretty Rhett, hearing of my arrival, ran off
yesterday evening to take refuge with you. Never
mind, there is another person coming from Mexico
from whom she cannot hide herself. Tell her with
my regrets that I brought *muchas cosas* from her
young rifleman, who is as bright and handsome as
ever. No, Sis Nannie, your sister was not here
when I arrived. Are you satisfied? She had gone
to Alexandria to learn the news and do a little
shopping, but I have laid violent hands on her now.
An opportunity has just offered to the Post-office
and I scribbled off this to assure you of my love and
remembrance. With much love to Sis Nannie and
the children, and kind regards to Mrs. R. and
Misses V. and C., I remain, Affectionately your
brother, R. E. Lee."

"More Moschitoes than People"

In the year 1849, Colonel Lee was reappointed to
serve on the Board of Engineers for the Atlantic
Coast Defenses. He was required to travel by ship
to inspect the coast defenses from Florida to
Georgia. For some reason, the voyage began from
Mobile, Alabama and followed the coast around
Florida to the burial place of his father. But he did
not visit the site at this juncture. But he did write to

Mary regarding some of the conditions while on the U. S. Phoenix. The following excerpts offer the reader insight into that voyage. (Robert E. Lee, A Biography; Thomas, Emory M.; W.W. Norton & Company; New York-London; 1995; page 146)

"I have never been to Sea in a small vessel before...They had been to Apalchicola and then visited St. Marks-found more moschitoes than people & grounded in the channel...We had to lay under a treble reefed foresail...{he remained below for} as long as I could stand it & then sat on deck, watching the big waves tumbling around us."

"Did You Not Feel Your Cheeks Pale"

Lee was faithful in his writing. He was also faithful to his wife, as no evidence has reared to prove otherwise. But Lee did enjoy the company of beautiful ladies and wrote to them faithfully. One of his favorites was a distant cousin and a first cousin to his wife. Her name was Martha Custis Williams but was known as simply Markie. She was eighteen years his junior and lived for a time with Lee's daughter Mary. The letter was written sometime during the spring of 1851. Mrs. Lee was well aware of their friendship and seemed to approve of his needs to be around other ladies as well. Such was the love that they possessed for one another. (Robert E. Lee, A Biography; Thomas, Emory M.; W.W. Norton & Company; New York-London; 1995; page 149)

"You have not written to me for nearly three months. And I believe it is equally as long since I have written to you. On paper Markie, I mean, on paper. But oh, what lengthy epistles have I indited to you in my mind! Had I any means to send them, you would see how constantly I think of you. I have followed you in your pleasures, & your duties, in the house & in the streets, & accompanied you in your walks to Arlington, & in your search after flowers. Did you not feel your cheeks pale when I was so near you? You may feel pale Markie, You may look pale; You may even talk pale; But I am happy to say you never write as if you were pale; & to my mind you always appear bright and rosy."

"You Must Act Right Whatever the Consequences"

In a letter addressed to Custis Lee dated June 22, 1851, Lee advises his son on the value of righteousness.

"I am opposed to the theory of doing wrong that good may come of it. I hold to the belief that you must act right whatever the consequences."

"Fix Your Mind and Pleasures upon What is Before You"

In a letter dated March 28, 1852, which is addressed to his son Custis, Lee gives sound fatherly advice on happiness. Custis was in a period of depression while enrolled at West Point and his father was concerned. Note that Custis was first in his class. The fatherly advice must have stuck.

"Shake off those gloomy feelings. Drive them away. Fix your mind and pleasures upon what is before you...All is bright if you will think it so. All is happy if you will make it so."

"You Will Always Appear to Me as You are Now Painted on My Heart"

242

While Superintendent of West Point, Lee wrote a beautiful letter to his daughter Annie. In nine years Annie, would be taken from the Lee circle due to the dreaded typhoid fever epidemic. She would be the only biological child lost to the Lees during the struggle. Though disfigured around her eye due to an accident, the father's love of his daughter shines through and reminds us all that what really is essential is invisible to the eye. In Lee's eyes his precious Annie was perfect in every way, as it should be. In it he expresses his devotion, his expectations on how they are to behave and his family values. It is dated February 25, 1853. Note that Mim (and also Molly) is his pet name for his wife Mary and that Custis was a cadet at West Point while he was the Commandant. He referred to Agnes his third daughter in the correspondence. (Recollections and Letter of Robert E. Lee; Lee, Robert E. Captain; Doubleday, Doran and Company; 1904, 1924)

"My Precious Annie: I take advantage of your gracious permission to write to you, and there is no telling how far my feelings might carry me were I not limited by the conveyance furnished by the Mim's letter, which lies before me, and which must, the Mim says so, go in this morning's mail. But my limited time does not diminish my affection for you, Annie, nor prevent my thinking of you and wishing for you. I long to see you through the dilatory nights. At dawn when I rise, and all day, my thoughts revert to you in expressions that you cannot hear or I repeat. I hope you will always appear to me as you are now painted on my heart, and that you will endeavor to improve and so conduct yourself as to make you happy and me joyful all our lives. Diligent and earnest attention to ALL your duties can only accomplish this. I am told you are growing very tall, and I hope very straight.

I do not know what the Cadets will say if the Superintendent's Children do not practice what he demands of them. They will naturally say he had better attend to his own before he corrects other people's children, and as he permits his to stoop, it is hard he will not allow them. You and Agnes must not, therefore, bring me into discredit with my young friends, or give them reason to think that I require more of them than of my own. I presume your mother has told all about us, our neighbors, and our affairs. And indeed she may have done that and not said much either, so far as I know. But we are all well and have much to be grateful for. Tomorrow we anticipate the pleasure of your brother's company, which is always a source of pleasure to us. It is the only time we see him, except when the Corps comes under my view at some of their exercises, when my eye is sure to distinguish him among his comrades and follow him over the plain. Give much love to your dear grandmother, grandfather, Agnes, Miss Sue, Luretia, and all friends, including the servants. Write sometimes, and think always of your
Affectionate father
R .E. Lee

"I am Ready to Jump"

In the delightful journal of Agnes Lee, she speaks of the excitement of having her father, sister and brother return home. The name Tom refers to her cat Tom Nipper. Noting that this entry is from a child of twelve makes her entries even more remarkable. Her writings review keen insight into the times and offer an intimate portrait of life during the 1850s. Oh, the excited eyes of a twelve-year-old, waiting anxiously on her beloved papa, sissy and brother to show up upon the doorstep! Also, her pen shows the influence that religion played during those days of yesteryear. This wonderful little book should be considered a must to a person desiring to obtain a complete picture of the Lee family.

"Papa, Rob, & Mil are coming this evening. I am so glad, I am ready to jump. I don't know where exactly, but I can't help thinking of them. They will be so glad to see us. I suppose they have grown very much. I know how the buns will delight them, & doubtless they will be charmed with Tom. We went to the school house Sunday & saw the sacrament administered, it was very impressive." (Growing Up in the 1850s: The Journal of Agnes Lee; Edited and with a Foreword by deButts, Mary Custis Lee; Robert E. Lee Association, Inc.; University of North Carolina Press; Chapel Hill and London; 1984; page 16)

"I Yield to None In Admiration for Her Character"

While Superintendent of West Point, Colonel Lee received word that his wife's mother, Mrs. Custis had passed away. In a letter dated April 27, 1853, Lee the husband attempts to comfort his grieving wife. In this brief excerpt is the personification of his convictions in a life beyond the sunset. (General Lee; Lee, Fitzhugh; Premier Civil War Classics; Fawcett Publications, Inc,; Greenwich, Conn., 1961; page 57)

"May God give you strength to enable you to bear and say, 'His will be done.' She has gone from all trouble, care, and sorrow, to a holy immortality, there to rejoice and praise forever the God and Saviour she so long and truly served. Let that be our comfort and that our consolation. May our death be like hers, and may we meet in happiness in heaven." A couple of weeks later (May 10th) Lee stated that, "She was to me all that a mother could be, and I yield to none in admiration for her character, love for her virtues, and veneration for her memory."

"My Thoughts Sank to Those Who Rested Beneath the Tombs"

The loss of their grandmother profoundly affected his children. Mary Lee Fitzhugh Custis (1788-1853) was an institution to the family and upon her death the children witnessed a void. Agnes wrote a darkened letter describing her emotions while at Ravens worth. The letter is dated August 6, 1853.

"...I confess I felt something like fear or rather awe steal over me as I sat on that mouldy wall surrounded by dark cedars and other trees. The poisonous vines waving over and around me and looking down upon that mass of rank and poisonous weeds while my thoughts sank to those who rested beneath the tombs." (Growing Up in the 1850s: The Journal of Agnes Lee; Edited by and with a forward by deButts, Mary Custis Lee; Robert E. Lee Memorial Association, Inc.; University of North Carolina Press; Chapel Hill and London; 1984)

"We must learn not to be contaminated by Evil"

On September 16, 1853, Colonel Lee wrote Martha Custis Williams a letter in expressing his philosophy on evil and virtue. It offers a lesson for us all and reminds this author that when we teach the child, he will not depart from the teachings of the parent.

"Young men must not expect to escape contact with evil, but must learn not to be contaminated by it. That virtue is worth but little that requires constant watching and removal from temptation."

"The Winter Gaieties Have Commenced"

On February 2, 1854, Agnes made an entry into her diary while her father was Superintendent of West Point. It offers insight into the life of the Lee family while stationed at the Academy six years prior to the war. The man she referenced in her journal was John Pegram who became a Confederate general and was killed in 1865. Fitzhugh Lee was Robert E. Lee's nephew. He had fallen into trouble because he left the campus without permission. He would later ride by his uncle's side as a major general and go on to become the Governor of Virginia.

"Papa gave a dinner last Tuesday to Gen. Robies of the Mexican Army. To make sure of being out of the way Annie and I with Neva Bartlett bent our steps towards Flirtation. It was beautiful in the snow. We met Mrs. G. W. & Mr. Pegram, a great friend of hers. Also Fitzhugh Lee, our first cousin. He got into a scrape poor fellow and his punishment is walking post of course & he is not allowed to visit so I scarcely ever see him & he is more a stranger than almost any cadet in the corps.

"The winter gaieties have commenced, officers' concerts, cadets' ditto & dialectics-parties 7 hops which are frequent of course I don't attend."

"He Looked as Proud as Possible"

Lieutenant Colonel Lee had been transferred to the headquarters of the Second Cavalry in Louisville, Kentucky on April 20, 1855. He was then ordered to Jefferson Barracks, Missouri. While stationed at

247

that location, he wrote his wife Mary an insightful letter regarding the state of affairs at that garrison. (<u>General Lee</u>; Lee, Fitzhugh; Premier Civil War Classics; Fawcett Publications, Inc,; Greenwich, Conn., 1961; pages 62-63)

"The chaplain of the post, a Mr. Fish, is now absent; he is an Episcopal clergyman and well spoken of; we have therefore not had service since I have been here. The church stands out in the trees, grotesque in its form and ancient in its appearance. I have not been in it, but am content to read the Bible and prayers alone, and draw much comfort from their holy precepts and merciful promises. Though feeling unable to follow the one, and truly unworthy of the other, I must still pray to that glorious God without whom there is no help, and with whom there is no danger. That He may guard and protect you all, and more than supply to you my absence, is my daily and constant prayer. I have been busy all week superintending and drilling recruits. Not a stitch of clothing has as yet arrived for them, though I made the necessary requisition for it to be sent here more than two months ago in Louisville. Yesterday, at muster, I found one of the late arrivals in a dirty, tattered shirt and pants, with a white hat and shoes, with other garments to match. I asked him why he did not put on clean clothes. He said he had none. I asked him if he could not wash and mend those. He said he had nothing else to put on. I then told him immediately after muster to go down to the river, wash his clothes and sit on a bank and watch the passing steamboats till they dried, and then mend them. This morning at inspection he looked as proud as possible, stood in the position of a soldier with his little finger on the seams of his pants, his beaver cocked back, and his toes sticking though his shoes, but his skin and solitary two garments clean.

He grinned very happily at my compliments. I have got a fine puss, which was left me by Colonel Sumner. He was educated by his daughter, Mrs. Jenkins, but is too fond of getting up on my lap and on my bead; he follows me all about the house and stands at the door in an attitude of defiance at all passing dogs."

"I Must Not Indulge in Wishes that cannot be gratified"

The following excerpts are from a lengthy letter addressed to Agnes Lee. It is dated August 4, 1856, from Camp Cooper, Texas. Lee talks of the hardships of being away from his family, the agony of the heat in Texas during the summer, reminds her to continue her studies, and instructs her to do her duty in all things for her future. Imagine the horror that Ms. Agnes must have experienced to think that her father was living in such primitive conditions. Here was the man from Arlington, the man from Shirley, the man from the White House, the man of Stratford, and the man she lovingly called Papa living within the confines of a tent. But such was the manner of the humbled soldier.

"I cannot send off my letters to Arlington dearest Agnes without writing to you...Oh, that I could see you, kiss you, squeeze you! But that cannot be Agnes & I must not indulge in wishes that cannot be gratified...It is so hot in my tent now, that the spermaceti candles become so soft as to drop from the candlesticks. Sturine candles, have melted, & become liquid in the stand. On the right of the entrance of the tent, stands an iron camp bed. On the left a camp table and chair. The chair I sit in & table I write on is hot, disagreeably so, to the touch, & feel as if made of metal...At the far end a trunk. On the side near the entrance a water bucket, basin, and broom, clothes hang around within easy reach of all points, and a sword and pistol very convenient."...I unite with you in your wishes that we were all together & have no doubt we shall be, if it is best for us. You will still have around you, many, a great many. Your Grandfather, Mother, brothers & sisters. Custis I fear will not be able to join you. He and I must bide our time." (Growing Up in the 1850s: The Journal of Agnes Lee; Edited by and with a forward by deButts, Mary Custis Lee; Robert E. Lee Memorial Association, Inc.; University of North Carolina Press; Chapel Hill and London; 1984; pages 124-126)

"I Cannot Realize She Exists Only in My Imagination"

While stationed in that desolate area Lee received word of the death of one of his sisters. Catherine Mildred Childe was his younger sister and had died suddenly while in Paris. He wrote a mournful letter expressing his loss upon receiving the news of her demise. The following excerpt mourns her loss:

"It has cut short my early wishes and daily yearnings, and so vividly does she live in my imagination and affection that I cannot realize she exists only in my memory." (R. E. Lee: A Biography; Freeman, Douglas Southall; Charles Scibner's Sons; New York; 1934-1935; 4 volumes; 2,398 pages)

"We Are All in the Hands of a Kind God"

In a letter dated September 1, 1856, Lee expressed his unshakable faith in the Almighty. Throughout his life, he turned to his Creator and saw that He was looking out for his best interests. Sometimes we do not understand the great mystery of life, for we feebly see through the turbid vale of life's sunset searching in vain for the reasons but rest assured that the Creator of all things knows what is best and will supply all our needs. Such was the faith and character of the general. (Robert E. Lee: Man and Soldier; Page, Thomas Nelson; Charles Scribner's sons; New York; 1926; page 624)

"We are all in the hands of a kind God who will do for us what is best, and more than we deserve, and we have only to endeavor to deserve more and to do our duty to Him and to ourselves. May we all deserve His mercy, His care, and His protection."

"Slavery as an Institution, is a Moral and Political Evil"

In a letter to his wife dated December 27, 1856, Lee writes regarding his distaste for the institution of slavery. Lee was not a slave owner. One can readily see his distain for the institution as he lays the solution into the kind hands of Providence. His statement clearly shows that his sympathy lay with the man in bondage and that he did not want to see this matter explode into a war to resolve the issue.

"I was much pleased with the President's message. His views of the systematic and progressive efforts of certain people at the North to interfere with and change the domestic institutions of the South are truthfully and faithfully expressed. The consequences of their plans and purposes are also clearly set forth. These people must be aware that their object is both unlawful and foreign to them and to their duty, and that this institution, for which they are irresponsible and non-accountable, can only be changed by them through the agency of a civil and servile war. There are few, I believe, in this enlightened age, who will not acknowledge that slavery as an institution is a moral and political evil. It is idle to expatiate on its disadvantages. I think it is a greater evil to the white than to the colored race. While my feelings are strongly enlisted in behalf of the latter, my sympathies are more deeply engaged for the former. The blacks are immeasurably better off here than in Africa, morally, physically, and socially. The painful discipline they are undergoing is necessary for their further instruction as a race, and will prepare them, I hope, for better things. How long their servitude may be necessary is known and ordered by a merciful Providence. Their emancipation will sooner result from the mild and melting influences of Christianity than from the storm and tempest of fiery controversy. This influence, though slow, is sure. The doctrines and miracles of our Saviour have required nearly two thousand years to convert but a small portion of the human race, and even among Christian nations what gross errors still exist! While we see the course of the final abolition of human slavery is still onward, and give it the aid of our prayers, let us leave the progress as well as the results in the hands of Him who, chooses to work by slow influences, and with whom a thousand years are but as a single day. Although the abolitionist must know this, must know that he has neither the right not the power of operating, except by moral means; that to benefit the slave he must not excite angry feelings in the master; that, although he may not approve the mode by which Providence accomplishes its purpose, the results will be the same; and that the reason he gives for interference in matters he has no concern with, holds good for every kind of interference with our neighbor, still, I fear he will persevere in his evil course. . . . Is it not strange that the descendants of those Pilgrim Fathers who crossed the Atlantic to preserve their own freedom have always proved the most intolerant of the spiritual liberty of others?"

"The True Means of Establishing a Virtuous Character"

In a letter dated January 31, 1857, Colonel Lee expresses his belief that only through denying oneself and self control, can one obtain a truly virtuous character. The letter was written to his wife Mary on New Year's Eve.

"{The exercise of self-denial and self-control} is the true means of establishing a virtuous character, so far as it can be accomplished by human means."

"It Should Remain as He Bestowed It"

Upon the death of his grandfather George Washington Parke Custis (grandson of Martha Washington and adopted son of General Washington), Custis was named heir to the Arlington Estate upon the death of his mother. Custis Lee immediately wrote his father, wishing to transfer the estate to him. Family values and love of family are quite evident in this letter written at Arlington, dated March 17, 1858. This is Lee, the father's reply. (<u>Life & Letters of Gen. Robert Edward Lee</u>; Jones, W.J.; Sprinkle Publications; Harrisonburg, Virginia; 1986; @ by Neale Publishing Company in 1906; pages 90-91)

"My Dear Son, I received tonight your letter of the 18th Feb'y, and also the deed relinquishing to me all your right and title to Arlington, the mill, adjacent lands, personal property, etc., bequeathed you by your grandfather. I am deeply impressed by your filial feeling of love and consideration, as well as your tender solicitude for me, of which, however, I required no proof, and am equally touched by your generosity and disinterestedness. But from what I said in a previous letter, you will not be surprised at my repeating that I cannot accept your offer. It is not from any unwillingness to receive from you a gift you may think proper to bestow, or to be indebted to you for any benefit great or small, But simply because it would not be right for me to do so. Your dear grandfather distributed his property as he thought best and it is proper that it should remain as he bestowed it. It will not prevent me from improving it to the best of my ability, or of making it as comfortable a home for your mother, sisters, and yourself as I can. I only wish I could do more than I shall have in my power to do. I wish you had received my precious letter on this subject in time to have saved you the trouble of executing the deed you transmitted me. And indeed I also regret the expense you incurred, which I fear in that country is considerable, as I wish you to save all your money, and invest it in some safe and lucrative way, that you may have the means to build up old Arlington, and make it all we would wish to see it. The necessity I daily have for money has, I fear, made me parsimonious. In order that you may know the full intent of your grandfather's will, I enclose you a copy.

"I shall leave Mary the relation of all family matters. Rooney leaves us tomorrow on his return to New York, whence he will accompany the last batch of recruits for the "Relieving Army of Utah" to Leavenworth, and then join his regiment destined for that service. It is needless to say how pained I am at his departure. If I could only have my children around me, I could be happy. The court has acquitted Colonel Sumner, and, as far as I can judge, properly. Farewell my dear, dear son, Aff'y your father, R. E. Lee"

"My Heart Quails within Me"

On May 30, 1858, Lee the father wrote his son William H. Fitzhugh Lee a letter from Arlington gently reminding him of his mission in life in the first paragraph. But in the second section he offered sound advice for not only his son but to every father's son that must go out into the world to find his own course. Below is sound fatherly advice for an earthly world. (Life & Letters of Gen. Robert Edward Lee; Jones, W.J.; Sprinkle Publications; Harrisonburg, Virginia; 1986; @ by Neale Publishing Company in 1906; pages 93-94)

"I hope you will always be distinguished for your avoidance of the "universal balm," whiskey, and every immorality. Nor need you fear to be ruled out of the society that indulges in it, for you will rather acquire their esteem and respect, as all venerate if they do not practice virtue. I am sorry to say that there is great proclivity for spirit in the army in the field. It seems to be considered a substitute for every luxury. The great body may not carry it to extreme, but many pursue it to their ruin. With some it is used as a means of hospitality, and your—commanding used to value it highly in this way, and perhaps, partook of it in this spirit. I think it better to avoid it altogether, as you do, as its temperance use is so difficult. I hope you will make many friends, as you will be thrown with many who deserve this feeling, but indiscriminate intimacies you will find annoying and entangling, and they can be avoided by politeness and civility. You see I am following my old habit of giving advice, which I dare say you neither need or require. But you must pardon a fault which proceeds from my great love and burning anxiety for your welfare and happiness. When I think of your youth, impulsiveness, and many temptations, your distance from me, and the ease (and even innocence) with which you might commence an erroneous course, my heart quails within me, and my whole frame and being trembles at the possible result. May Almighty God have you in His holy keeping. To His Merciful Providence I commit you, and will rely upon Him, and the Efficacy of the prayers that will be daily and hourly offered up by those who love you."

"If They Peacefully Surrender Themselves"

In the month of October 1859, Colonel Lee received a message summoning him to see the Secretary immediately. The officer carrying the message to Lee was none other than Lieutenant Stuart, destined to become the greatest cavalier of all time. Accompanied by the Secretary and Lt. Stuart, Colonel Lee went to the White House. Upon arriving at the White House, the rumors of an insurrection were confirmed and Lee was ordered to take command of the forces from Fort Monroe and join with the Maryland militia. He was to take to the field immediately and deal with those responsible for stopping the trains and taking the arsenal by force. Lt. Stuart asked and was granted permission to accompany Colonel Lee. Their destination was Harper's Ferry and their adversary a noted antislavery activist by the name of John "Ossawatomie" Brown.

Upon arrival at Harper's Ferry they found that the insurgents were few in number but had taken refuge in a firehouse within the perimeters of the arsenal. They had also taken several hostages with them to barter for their demands. Lee took command of the situation and after careful study, made the decision to send the following message to the men holding the thirteen hostages. He gave the message to his trusted lieutenant, JEB Stuart and under the flag of truce he delivered it to John Brown. After Lt. Stuart gave a predetermined signal, Lee's soldiers in blue began sending a deadly volley into the building as they charged with fixed bayonets. Miraculously none of the hostages were injured by the violence. Four of John's men lay upon the ground, two dead from previous wounds. Brown himself was wounded. The dead and wounded was laid upon the ground and the others were taken into custody. A small performance with enormous consequences was set that day. The nation gasped in horror and terror as the clouds of war loomed in the sky. (Lee; Freeman Douglas Southall, An Abridgment by Richard Harwell of the Pulitzer Prize Winning four-volume Biography; New York; Touchstone; 1991; pages 99-103)

"He Could Have Wiped Me Out Like a Mosquito"

The 'soon-to-be-famous' cavalier volunteered to accompany Lee. JEB Stuart offers the following account of the events that transpired at Harper's Ferry. The message carried by JEB to John Brown, demanding his surrender follows: "Colonel Lee was sent to command the forces at Harpers Ferry. I volunteered as his aid...I was deputed by Colonel Lee to read to the leader, then called Smith, a demand to surrender immediately...he opened the door about four inches, and placed his body against the crack, with a cocked carbine in his hand: hence his remark after his capture that he could have wiped me out like a mosquito...I left the door and waved my cap and Colonel Lee's plan was carried out."

Headquarters Harper's Ferry,
October 18, 1859

"Colonel Lee, United States Army, commanding the troops sent by the President of the United States to suppress the insurrection at this place, demands the surrender of the persons in the armory buildings.

"If they will peaceably surrender themselves and restore the pillaged property, they shall be kept in safety to await the orders of the President. Colonel Lee represents to them, in all frankness, that it is impossible for them to escape; that the armory is surrounded on all sides by troops; and that if he is compelled to take them by force he cannot answer for their safety."

R.E. Lee
Colonel Commanding United States Troops

"I Have Been Received With Great Kindness"

The following excerpts from a letter addressed to Mary spoke of meeting Mrs. Brown. It was written on December 1st.

"I arrived here...yesterday about noon, with four companies from Fort Monroe...the feelings of the community seemed to be calmed down, and I have been received with every kindness...This morning I was introduced to Mrs. Brown, who...had come to have a last interview with her husband."

"Save in Defence, Will Draw my Sword on None"

Colonel Lee was very concerned with the war rhetoric that was being spoken throughout the country. The talk was nothing new except this time there loomed over the land the inevitability of the dissolving of the states. Torn between the Union that he had served for over thirty-six years and his beloved State of Virginia, Lee wrote of his quandary to his son. In the letter written in the month of January 1861, Lee states to his son Custis, "I can anticipate no greater calamity for the country than a dissolution of the Union. It would be an accumulation of all the evils we complain of, and I am willing to sacrifice everything but honor for its preservation. Still, a Union that can be maintained only by swords and bayonets, and in which strife and civil war are to take the place of brotherly love and kindness, has no charm to me. If the union is dissolved and the government disrupted, I shall return to my native state and share the miseries of my people; and, save in defence, will draw my sword on none."

"Virginia is my Country, Her I Will Obey"

Why did Lee feel so strongly about the individual loyalty to his state and the right of Virginia to voluntarily surrender her admission to the union? When glancing back upon Lee's past, he had two heroes that he admired more than any other. One was George Washington, the revolutionist and the other his father, Harry Lee. Both men stood upon the altar of freedom and stated that independence and freedom of choice was the cornerstone to America. Both made the commitment to give all if that was the will of providence for their beliefs. One of the main reasons was probably rooted in his childhood. His father was an ardent State's rights supporter and feverishly stated, "Virginia is my country; her I will obey, however lamentable the fate to which it may subject me." In a letter written to Mr. Madison that was dated January 1792, General Harry Lee stated that, "No consideration on earth could induce me to act a part, however gratifying to me, which could be construed into disregard of, or faithlessness to, this commonwealth." This doctrine was surely passed down to the son for it was the cornerstone belief of the Lee family. And then there was his mother. She had taught him the Christian values that require a person to stand against the wrong doing of others and to come to the aid of others in plight or suffering. And the people of the south suffered greatly with unfair taxation and being subjected to the rule of a central government. Lee was a product of his environment and values. The path he chose could be no other. (<u>Life & Letters of Gen. Robert Edward Lee</u>; Jones, W.J.; Sprinkle Publications; Harrisonburg, Virginia; 1986; @ by Neale Publishing Company in 1906; pages 18-19)

To Simon Cameron, Secretary of War

On April 20, 1861, while still residing at his home in Arlington, Colonel Lee made the agonizing decision to cast his lot with his native state. Lee sat down and wrote his final note as Colonel in the 1st Cavalry of the United States Army.

"Sir: I have the honor to tender the resignation of my commission as colonel of the 1st Regiment of Cavalry...Very resply your obt servt, R.E. Lee"

"I Shall Carry to the Grave the Most Grateful Recollections"

Lee composed another letter on April 20, 1861. The Navy Yard at Norfolk Virginia was under attack by the newly formed army. Upon hearing the news, Lee immediately penned the following letter. This letter was addressed to none other than his old commander and mentor, General Scott. General

260

Scott was a man that he truly admired and found this letter most difficult to compose. Both men held each other with such high regard and fondness that one can only imagine the saddened dispositions on the faces and hearts of the men; one as he wrote the correspondence and the other as he read it. Robert E. Lee wrote Lt. General Winfield Scott, Commander of the United States Army the following words resigning his commission to follow his heart and conscience:

"General: Since my interview with you on the 18th instant, I have felt that I ought no longer to retain my commission in the Army. I therefore tender my resignation, which I request you will recommend for acceptance. It would have been presented at once, but for the struggle it has cost me to separate myself from a service to which I have devoted all the best years of my life and all the ability I possessed.

"During the whole of that time-more than a quarter of a century-I have experienced nothing but kindness from my superiors, and the most cordial friendship from my comrades. To no one, General, have I been as much indebted as to yourself, for uniform kindness and consideration, and it has always been my ardent desire to merit your approbation. I shall carry to the grave the most grateful recollections of your kind consideration, and your name and fame will always be dear to me.

"Save in defence of my native State, I never desire again to draw my sword. Be pleased to accept my most earnest wishes for the continuance of your happiness and prosperity, and believe me, most truly yours, R.E. Lee"

"The Search"

I found "The Search" very challenging to write. I knew what I wanted to say but could not find the words to express it. I incubated the idea in the back of my mind for the longest time. I even thought that I would give this poem a rest within the perimeters of my mind but it just would not let me be. Something about it just had to be written. Was it the essence of the man's virtue demonstrated not only during the war but also throughout his life that kept calling me back to the desk? Was it the brute honesty of his meeting with General Scott that he admired so (it was reciprocated) and the agony of his decision? In one of Mary's letters she recalls hearing her husband pacing the floor most of the night and then falling to his knees in prayer. No doubt he was asking that the cup be taken away from him and given to another to bear the yoke. But once resolved, he followed God's will and always stated prior to battle that, "Its in God's hands." His sacrifices for what he believed should inspire all of us to live virtuously and in all things give thanks. It is the trials of life that make us who we are and ultimately make us stronger, if we prevail against the winds of change. The tribulations allow us, by our example, to encourage those around us to seek an honorable existence. Are we not required to do this for our future generations and can we afford to do less?

The Search

He went to Fuss and Feathers
To ask what should he do.
His course would change forever
The world that he now knew.

He listened with keen senses
But he could not be swayed.
No chance of mending fences.
The dealt hand must be played.

With head hung in submission
He offered his fond farewell
He gave up his commission:
The final curtain fell.

He rode for Old Dominion.
Defend her with his sword
And it was his opinion
He was led by the Lord.

He rode on into history;
Reluctant to his fate.
Hardships full of mystery
For him to contemplate.

He was but just a soldier;
A life of toil and grief.
But as he grew much older
He found his sweet relief.

His search on earth has ended.
His mission's now complete.
Old wounds have been mended;
There was honor in defeat.

"God May Yet Allay the Fury for War"

During the soul-searching period in the first of five
Aprils, Lee received an appeal from a friend's
daughter that lived in the North. She wanted an
autograph of Lee. He not only offered his signature
but also wrote an insightful letter in response to her
request. The following excerpt gives the reader a
feel of the dark times that loomed in the immediate

future for this great nation. (<u>Jackson & Lee;</u> <u>Legends in Gray</u>; Kunstler, Mort, paintings of; Text by Robertson, James I., Jr.; Rutledge Hill Press; Nashville, Tennessee; 1995; page 21)

"I can say in sincerity that I bear animosity against no one. Wherever the blame may be, the fact is that we are in the midst of a fratricidal war. I must side with my section of the country. I cannot raise my hand against my birthplace, my home, my children. I should like, above all things, that our difficulties might be peaceably arranged, and still trust that a merciful God, whom I know will not unnecessarily afflict us, may yet allay the fury for war."

"Believe That I Have Endeavored to do What I Thought Right"

At the onset of the war, Lee penned a letter to his sister Anne Lee Marshall (living in Baltimore, Maryland), stating his decision to go with the choice of his native state. The letter is dated April 20, 1861, and was written in the last days of Camelot while he was still residing at Arlington. It expressed the deep sorrow in which he was forced to cast his lot and the division of a nation from presidents to privates, as each person searched their souls for guidance in the direction to take. Ann lived in Baltimore and was married to William Marshall, a man who would remain on the side of the Union, as well as their son. Such was the tremendous price that was paid in what could be called the War Between The Brothers. (<u>The Wartime Papers of</u> <u>Robert E. Lee</u>; Dowdey, Clifford and Manarin, Louis H.; De Capo Press; Commonwealth of Virginia; 1961; pages 9-10)

I am grieved at my inability to see you. I have been waiting for a more convenient season, which has brought to many before me deep and lasting regret. Now we are in a state of war which will yield to nothing. The whole South is in a state of revolution, into which Virginia, after a long struggle, has been drawn; and though I recognize no necessity for this state of things, and would have forborne and pleaded to the end for redress of grievances, real or supposed, yet in my own person I had to meet the question whether I should take part against my native State.

"With all my devotion to the Union, and the feeling of loyalty and duty of an American citizen, I have not been able to make up my mind to raise up my hand against my relatives, my children, my home. I have therefore, resigned my commission in the Army, and save in defense of my native State (with the sincere hope that my poor services may never be needed) I hope I may never be called upon to draw my sword.

"I know you will blame me; but you must think as kindly of me as you can, and believe that I have endeavored to do what I thought right. To show you the feeling and struggle it has cost me I send you a copy of my letter resignation. I have no time for more. May God guard you and protect you and yours and shower upon you everlasting blessings, is the prayer of Your devoted brother, R. E. Lee"

"I Am Now a Private Citizen"

On the same day he wrote his brother, Sydney Smith Lee who was in Washington at this time. He expressed his regrets but that he must follow his heart and conscience. He stated that his desire was to never draw his sword again and to remain a private citizen. This would not be afforded him for a period of four years.

"My Dear Brother Smith: The question which was the subject of my earnest consultation with you on the 18th instant has in my own mind been decided. After the most anxious inquiry as to the correct course for me to pursue, I concluded to resign, and sent in my resignation this morning. I wished to wait till the Ordinance of Secession should be acted on by the people of Virginia; but war seems to have commenced, and I am liable at any time to be ordered on duty which I could not conscientiously perform. To save me from such a position, and to prevent the necessity of resigning under orders, I had to act at once, and before I could see you again on the subject, as I had wished. I am now a private citizen, and have no other ambition than to remain at home. Save in defense of my native State, I have no desire ever again to draw my sword. I send you my warmest love. Your affectionate brother, R. E. Lee"

"Trusting in Almighty God"

Private citizen Lee remained that way for a total of one day. On April 21, 1861, he met with the governor of Virginia and was unofficially appointed as major general, pending his approval by the Virginia Convention on the next day. With the fanfare of politicians, Lee's candidacy was announced and unanimously accepted. The Convention President, Mister John Janney offered the following oratory in recognition of the Federal soldier of thirty-six years that was now abandoning it all for what he felt was a higher calling. He was fifty-four years of age at the time of his appointment. Already he was being compared to the great liberator that he so admired, George

Washington. (<u>The Wartime Papers of Robert E. Lee</u>; Dowdey, Clifford and Manarin, Louis H.; De Capo Press; Commonwealth of Virginia; 1961; pages 4-11)

"In the name of the people of your native State, here represented, I bid you a cordial and heartfelt welcome to this hall, in which we may almost yet hear the echo of the voices of the statesmen, the soldiers and sages of by-gone days, who have borne your name, and whose blood flows in your veins...Sir, we have, by the unanimous vote, expressed our convictions that you are, at this day, among the living citizens of Virginia, 'first in war.' We pray to God most fervently that you may so conduct the operations committed to your charge, that it will soon be said of you, that you are, 'first in peace,' and when that time comes you will have earned the still prouder distinction of becoming 'first in the hearts of your countrymen.'"

The newly appointed general must have been awed by the honors and responsibility being placed upon his shoulders. In his short speech, he expressed his humility, his total trust in God and that for his state only would he ever have drawn his sword. His response is typical of this shy man of character. The legacy would continue and the legends of Lee would grow in proportion.

"Mr. President and Gentlemen of the Convention: Deeply impressed with the solemnity of the occasion on which I appear before you, & profoundly grateful for the honor conferred upon me, I accept the position your partiality has assigned me, though {I} would greatly have preferred your choice should have fallen on one more capable.

"Trusting to Almighty God, an approving conscience & the aid of my fellow citizen, I will devote myself to the defence & service of my native State, in whose behalf alone would I have ever drawn my sword."

"Permit Reason to Resume Her Sway"

As late as April 25, 1861, the newly commissioned Confederate General was praying for another solution short of going to war against the flag that he had served for thirty-six years. He wrote of his fear, his desire for divine intervention, his concept of defensive maneuvers and his feverish hope of reason to prevail upon the land.

"No earthly act would give me so much pleasure as to restore peace to my country, but I fear it is now out of the power of man, and in God alone must be our trust. I think our policy should be purely on the defensive, to resist aggression and allow time to allay the passions and permit reason to resume her sway."

"I am Very Anxious About You"

On April 26, 1861, while in Richmond, three days after accepting the command of the military and naval forces of Virginia, Major General Lee wrote an urgent letter to his wife. The words demonstrate his concern for the safety of his family, the inevitability of the war, and the character of the newly elected man who would become the greatest general and one of the utmost gentlemen amongst mortals. (The Wartime Papers of Robert E. Lee; Dowdey, Clifford and Manarin, Louis H.; De Capo Press; Commonwealth of Virginia; 1961; letter 9; page 12)

"My Dear Mary, I return with my signature the pay accounts forwarded by Custis. I doubt the propriety of presenting them, & if presented I doubt whether they will be paid. I would therefore suppress them but for the probability, in the settlement of my accounts with the United States, some stoppage or disallowance, of which I am ignorant, may have been made against me for which they may be an off set to pay all charges against me. I wish if Custis or Lawrence Williams think proper they may be presented, otherwise destroy them & say nothing about it. I am very anxious about you. You have to move, & make arrangements to go to some point of safety which you must select. The Mt. Vernon plate & pictures ought to be secured. Keep quiet while you remain & in your preparations. War is inevitable & there is no telling when it will burst around you. Virginia yesterday I understand joined the Confederate States. What policy they may adopt I cannot conjecture. I send a check for $500., which you had better apply, tell Custis, in settling up matters. May God keep & reserve you & have mercy on all our people is the constant prayer of your affectionate husband R.E. Lee"

"My Heart Would Have But the One Place to Leap"

In a letter to Mary dated May 2, 1861, Lee again talks about his concern for his family and that he sees no manner of avoiding the imminent conflict. His love for his wife and children is clearly earmarked by his remarks. His love of his state and the role that honor plays in his life will ultimately shape his fate and the destiny of our nation permeates his written passages. The excerpt also provides a look into the man's integrity of not accepting anything that he feels he has not earned. (The Wartime Papers of Robert E. Lee; Dowdey, Clifford and Manarin, Louis H.; De Capo

269

Press; Commonwealth of Virginia; 1961; letter 16; page 18)

"My Dear Mary, I received last night your letter of the 1st with the coat. It gave me great pleasure to learn that you were all well & in peace. You know how pleased I should be to have you & my dear daughters with me. That I fear cannot be. There is no place that I can expect to be but in the field & there is no rest for me to look to. But I want you to be in a place of safety. To spare me that anxiety. Nor can any one say where safety can be found. I am grateful to dear Cousin Anna for her invitation to you. She is always our friend in need. Ravensworth I suppose is as safe as any place, & if you could all be there comfortable together, my heart would have but the one place to leap to. I fear however it would add too much to Cousin Anna's anxiety & trouble. Of this you must judge, or where else you had better go. Do not go to Berkley, or the Shenandoah Valley. Those points are much exposed, but you must not talk of what I write. Nor is Richmond perhaps more out of harms way. I take it for granted that our opponents will do us all the harm they can. They feel their power & they seem to have the desire to oppress & distress us. I assume therefore they will do it. We have only to be resigned to God's will & pleasure & do all we can for our protection.

"Make your arrangements quickly, to be ready for any emergency... Do keep yourselves quiet & out of harms way. I hope Mr. McGuire is able to prosecute work on the farm. Give love to all. I hope Helena is not alarmed & that she will when she wishes be able to return to her friends in safety.

"I have just received Custis' letter of the 30th enclosing the acceptance of my resignation. It is stated it will take effect on the 25th April. I resigned on the 20th & wished it to take effect on that day. I cannot consent to its running on farther & he must receive no pay if they tender it beyond that day, but return the whole if need be. In answer to his question he had better I think, when he fully makes up his mind, tender his services formerly to the Governor." Truly & Affly R.E. Lee

"My Own Sorrows Sink into Insignificance"

On May 8, 1861, General Lee again wrote his wife concerning Arlington, the sacrifices that they must be willing to offer at the altar of freedom, and the cross that they must bear. But he summates his full devotion to the cause and to his principles when he states, "When I reflect upon the calamity impending over the country, my own sorrows sink into insignificance."

"The Times are Indeed Calamitous"

Five days later, May 13, 1861, the newly commissioned Confederate General wrote his wife from Richmond, Virginia. General Lee candidly expressed his belief that the war was inevitable, it would be long, and it would be costly not only in money, material, and merchandise but also in manpower. In this letter, he demonstrates his principles and will not intrude upon his son's decision regarding which side to join nor offer him advice other than say it is for every man to settle himself. The man of character lived his principles and wished for his children to do likewise. They decided to follow him and all united behind the 'grey banner'. (Robert E. Lee: Man and Soldier; Page, Thomas Nelson; Charles Scribner's sons; New York; 1926; pages 84-85)

"Do not put faith in rumors of adjustment. I see no prospect for it. It cannot be while passions on both sides are so infuriated. Make your plans for several years of war. If Virginia is invaded, which appears to be designed, the main routes through the country will, in all probability, be infested and passage interrupted. I agree with you in thinking that the inflammatory articles in the papers do us much harm. I object particularly to those in the Southern papers, as I wish them to take a firm, dignified course, free from bravado and boasting. The times are indeed calamitous. The brightness of God's countenance seems turned from us, and its mercy stopped in its blissful current. It may not always be so dark, and He may in time pardon our sins and take us under His protection. Tell Custis he must consult his own judgment, reason, and conscience as to the course he may take. I do not wish him to be guided by my wishes or example. If I have done wrong, let him do better. The present is a momentous question which every man must settle for himself and upon principle. Our good Bishop Meade has just come in to see me. He opens the convention to-morrow, and, I understood him to say, would preach his fiftieth anniversary sermon. God bless and guard you."

"My Husband Has Wept Tears of Blood"

Months after Lee had resigned his commission; Mary wrote a letter to a friend. In it she expresses her husband's dismay and torment regarding the condition of the country. (Lee; Freeman Douglas Southall; An Abridgment by Richard Harwell of the Pulitzer Prize Winning four-volume Biography; New York; Touchstone; 1991; page 112)

"My husband has wept tears of blood over this terrible war, but as a man of honor and a Virginian, he must follow the destiny of his state."

"I Hope God Will Again Smile on Us"

General Lee writing to his wife regarding the Battle of Manassas on July 21, 1861. Note the prophecy of another battle occurring upon that battlefield.

"I wished to partake in the battle and was mortified at my absence. But the President thought it more important that I should be here. I could not have done as well as has been done, but I could have helped and taken part in a struggle for my home and neighbors...the battle will be repeated there in greater force. I hope God will again smile on us and strengthen our hearts and arms."

"We are all in the Hands of a Kind God"

In a letter dated September 1, 1861, General Lee again attests to his faith in God and how it is His will, not mans, that will prevail in the end. (The Christian Character of Robert E. Lee; Weaver, John; Chaplain in Chief; Confederate Veteran; Volume Three 2002; page 80)

"We are all in the hands of a kind God, who will do for us what is best, and more than we deserve, we have only to deserve more and do our duty to Him and to ourselves. May we all deserve His mercy, His care, and His protection."

"I am Much Grieved"

Lee's compassion and grief over the loss of one of his favorite young officers is evident in this excerpt from a letter to his wife. It was dated September

17, 1861, and was written on Valley Mountain of Western Virginia (what would later become the child of the Civil War-the state of West Virginia). In the letter this man of constant sorrows described his strategy in attacking Cheat Mountain and how it had not been implemented according to his orders. Then he talks of the loss of a soldier that had accompanied his son Fitzhugh on a reconnaissance mission. One can read between the lines as he laments the loss and feels guilt in allowing the persistent young man to venture forth on such a precarious mission. (General Lee; Lee, Fitzhugh; Premier Civil War Classics; Fawcett Publications, Inc,; Greenwich, Conn., 1961; pages 122-123)

"...We met with one heavy loss which grieves me deeply: Colonel Washington, accompanied Fitzhugh on a reconnoitering expedition. I fear they were carried away by their zeal and approached within the enemy's pickets. The first they knew there was a volley from a concealed party within a few yards of them. Three balls passed through the colonel's body, three struck his horse, and the horse of one of the men was killed. Fitzhugh mounted the colonel's horse and brought him off. I am much grieved. He was always anxious to go on these expeditions. This was the first day I assented. Since I had been thrown in such immediate relations with him, I had learned to appreciate him very highly. Morning and evening have I seen him on his knees praying to his Maker. 'The righteous perisheth, and no man layeth it to heart; the merciful men are taken away, none considering that the righteous are taken away from the evil to come; May God have mercy on us all!"

"I Shall Not Sleep for Thinking of my Poor Men"

In a letter dated September 26, 1861, Lee again writes to his wife Mary about the loss of Colonel Washington while he was out on patrol with his own son. The letter talks of the conditions that not only he was experiencing but also those of his troops. It gives insight into the way Lee thinks of others before himself.

"It is raining heavily. The men are all exposed on the mountain, with the enemy opposite to us. We are without tents, and for two nights I have lain buttoned up in my overcoat. Today my tent came up and I am in it. Yet I fear I shall not sleep for thinking of my poor men. I wrote about socks for myself. I have no doubt the yarn ones you mention will be very acceptable to the men here or elsewhere. If you can send them here, I will distribute them to the most needy. Tell Rob I could not write to him for want of time. My heart is always with you and my children. May God guard and bless you all is the constant prayer of your devoted husband. R.E. Lee" (Recollections and Letters of General Robert E. Lee; Lee, Robert E. Jr.; Garden City Publishing Company; Garden City, New York; 1904)

I Wish I Could Purchase Stratford"

On December 25, 1861, with his beloved Arlington confiscated and turned into a cemetery by the Federalist, General Lee wrote his wife Mary the following letter about their beloved Arlington and his childhood home. He expressed his apprehension but also attempted to comfort her with soothing words of affectionate memories. But more importantly, he demonstrated his faith and the ability to accept the will of God in all things. Lee always prepared and then placed it in God's hands. The letter was written from Coosawhatchie, South Carolina. Mary was living in their "White House".

"I cannot let this day of grateful rejoicing pass without some communion with you. I am thankful for the many among the past that I have passed with you, and the remembrance of them fills me with pleasure. For those on which we have been separated we must not repine. If it will make us more resigned & better prepared for what is in store for us, we should rejoice. Now we must be content with the many blessing we receive. If we can only become sensible of our transgressions, so as to be fully penitent & forgiven, that this heavy punishment under which we labour may with justice be removed from us & the whole nation, what a gracious consummation of all that we have endured it will be...As to our old home, if not destroyed it will be difficult ever to be recognized. Even if the enemy had wished to preserve it, it would almost have been impossible. With the number of troops encamped around it, the change of officer, &c., the want of fuel, shelter, &c., & all the dire necessities of war, it is vain to think of its being in a habitable condition, I fear too books, furniture, & the relics of Mount Vernon will be gone. It is better to make up our minds to a general loss. They cannot take away the remembrances of the spot, and the memories of those that to us rendered it sacred. That will remain to us as long as life will last and that we can preserve. In the absence of a home I wish I could purchase Stratford. It is the only place I could go to, now acceptable to us, that would inspire me with feelings of pleasure and local love. You and the girls could remain there in quiet. It is a poor place, but we could make enough cornbread and bacon for our support and the girls could weave us clothes. I wonder if it is for sale and how

276

much. Ask Fitzhugh to try & find out when he gets to Fredericksburg." He never returned to Stratford. (The Wartime Papers of Robert E. Lee; Dowdey, Clifford and Manarin, Louis H.; De Capo Press; Commonwealth of Virginia; 1961; pages 95-97)

"Arlington House was surrounded by Groves of Stately Trees"

Arlington! Oh, that beautiful mansion perched on the hill overlooking the city of Washington! Arlington was the home of the adopted son of the first president of the United States. But it represented far more. It was the "museum" that contained the priceless pieces of American history that were possessions of George and Martha Washington, passed down to their child. It was the symbol of the high-water mark of the revolution and freedom itself. Miss Emily Mason wrote of the fair halls in the following manner:

"This fine mansion stands on the heights opposite Washington City, overlooking the Potomac, and was for many years an object of attraction to all visitors to Washington on account of its historical associations, and the Washington relics collected and preserved by the patriotic father of Mrs. Lee. Here were to be seen the original portraits of General and Mrs. Washington, painted at the time of their marriage, which have been so constantly reproduced; the portrait of Mrs. Washington's first husband, Col. Parke Custis, of many of his progenitors, and several pictures of the great Revolutionary battles, painted by Mr. Custis, whose delight perpetuate upon canvas the features of the great man who had been to him a father, and to commemorate the important scenes in which he had been an actor.

"Here, also, was the last original portrait of General Washington by Sharpless, a distinguished English artist who painted in crayons. Many of the pictures and much of the old furniture of Mount Vernon were here; the china presented to Mrs. Washington by certain English merchants, upon which was her monogram; that given to George Washington by the Society of the Cincinnati; the tea table at which Mrs. Washington always presided; a book case made by General Washington's own direction; and the bed upon which he died.

"Arlington House was surrounded by groves of stately trees, except in front, where the hill descended to a lovely valley spreading away to the river. The view from the height showed Washington, Georgetown, and a long stretch of the Potomac in the foreground, with wooded hills and valleys making a background of dark foliage. (Life & Letters of Gen. Robert Edward Lee; Jones, W.J.; Sprinkle Publications; Harrisonburg, Virginia; 1986; @ by Neale Publishing Company in 1906; pages 30-31)

"The Sacred Hallowed Ground of Arlington"

The Lees suffered along with the masses of Southern people. One of the more stringent punishments imposed upon them was the confiscation of Mrs. Mary Custis Lee's childhood home. The plantation was confiscated at the onset of the war. It was officially taken over by the government in January of 1864, as retribution for Robert E. Lee casting his lot with his native state. The Union government sold the property to itself for delinquent taxes owed. The Lees were unaware of any delinquent taxes when it was sold. And it was sold in such a manner that it was impossible for family members to attend.

Several of the family heirlooms were taken, including several items that belonged to George and Martha Washington. Adding insult to injury, the government declared that the garden area would be a cemetery for the fallen soldiers in blue. Mrs. Mary Custis Lee who had formally been a devout supporter of the preservation of the Union, became very antagonistic towards it after the war. She would never recover from the loss of her childhood home and became very bitter toward those that had dealt so cruelly with her children's inheritance. After the death of Robert and Mary Lee, the United States Supreme Court made a decision regarding the property. In 1883 the Supreme Court ruled that the wartime confiscation of Arlington was indeed illegal. The government paid Custis Lee the sum of $150,000 for the future national shrine.

Ironically, this act of retribution only added to the mystical image of the Lee legend. In a conspiracy to destroy Lee's memory, the Federal government assisted in immortalizing him and justice was finally served. The Lee family history was forever entwined and associated with that sacred and hallowed ground now known as our national treasure; the Arlington National Cemetery.

Arlington

Eleven Hundred acres
Overlooking the Dome.
She felt nothing could shake her;
She would always be their home.

Eight columns made of marble;
A mansion on a hill.
For years the world would marvel
At Fate's ironic will.

Her walls saw seven children
And heard their sweet refrains.
She'd give her all to shield them
From life's sorrow and pain.

They took away her garden,
Hid treasures 'neath her feet.
Refused her land a pardon;
But victory with defeat.

She stands as a reminder
The price they had to pay.
The wounds are now behind her;
We go to her and pray.

Now treasured by both nations,
She's earned a just reward.
Her death was her salvation.
She's more hallowed than before.

"I Send You Some Sweet Violets"

On that same Christmas day in 1861, Lee wrote his daughter a loving letter, revealing his fatherly affection and commitment to his family. Also he demonstrated that life was the precious gift not money. All that is really important in life is life itself.

"My Dear Daughter: Having distributed such poor Christmas gifts as I had to those around me, I have been looking for something for you. Trifles even are hard to get these wartimes, and you must not therefore expect more. I have sent you what I thought most useful in your separation from me, and hope it will be of some service...To compensate for such 'trash' {money} I send you some sweet violets, that I gathered for you this morning while covered with dense white frost, whose crystals glittered in the bright sun like diamonds, and formed a brooch of rare beauty and sweetness, which could not be fabricated by the expenditure of a world of money...Among the calamities of war, the hardest to bear perhaps, is the separation of families and friends."

"They Shoot at it Whenever Visible to Them"

In June of 1862, General Lee wrote a playful letter to his son Rooney's wife (his daughter-in-law) describing his dress and physical characteristics. In one short year, Lee had gone from being clean-shaven with a black moustache and his hair slightly sprinkled with the salt and pepper characteristics of age to solid white beard and hair. Such is the burden of war.

"My habiliments are not suited to this hot weather, but they are the best I have. My coat is of gray, of the regulation style and pattern, and my pants of dark blue, as is prescribed, partly hid by my long boots. I have the same handsome hat, which surmounts my gray head (the latter is not prescribed in the regulations), and shields my ugly face, which is marked by a white beard as stiff and wiry as the teeth of a card. In fact, an uglier person I have never seen, and so unattractive is it to our enemies that they shoot at it whenever visible to them."

"I Passed by You Friday Morning"

While encamped for the winter near Orange Court House, General Lee took time from his horrendous schedule to write his wife Mary an extended letter. In it he talks of personal matters but also relates the conditions of his boys, the strength of "those people" and his longing to be with his loved ones.

The excerpts from his writing are dated August 17, 1862. (<u>The Wartime Papers of Robert E. Lee</u>; Dowdey, Clifford and Manarin, Louis H.; De Capo Press; Commonwealth of Virginia; 1961; letter 268; page 257)

"My Dear Mary: I passed by you Friday morning when you were asleep. I looked very hard but could see no body. I should have liked so much to stop to have waked you all up. I was afraid at such an hour I should not have been welcome. But welcome or not I was obliged to go on & here I am in a tent instead of my comfortable quarters at Dabb's. The tent however is very comfortable & of that I have nothing to complain...I have not seen my precious Rob yet. I hear he is well. I presume he does not know I am here, & I have not had time to go to him. Give much love to everybody & plenty of kisses to Chass, Cousin Anne &c."
Truly & devotedly yours
R.E.Lee

"Our Sole Object is the Establishment of Our Independence"

General Lee was in constant contact with his superior and friend, President Jefferson Davis. He kept him appraised of the situations and was considered the President's number one advisor. While encamped near Fredericksburg, Lee wrote the President a fervent letter encouraging his endorsement for the perusing of peace on honorable terms. Note that the following letter was dated September 8, 1862, the same date that Lee issued the proclamation to the citizens of Maryland asking them to support the cause of the South. (<u>Robert E. Lee Man and Soldier</u>; Page, Thomas Nelson; Charles Scribner's sons; New York; 1926; page 218)

"His Excellency, Jefferson Davis,
President of the Confederate States, Richmond, Va.

Mr. President: The present position of affairs, in my opinion, places it in the power of the government of the Confederate States to propose with propriety to that of the United States the recognition of our independence. For more than a year both sections of the country have been devastated by hostilities which have brought sorrow and suffering upon thousands of homes without advancing the objects which our enemies proposed to themselves in beginning the contest. Such a proposition, coming from us at this time, could in no way be regarded as suing for peace, but, being made when it is in our power to inflict injury upon our adversary, would show conclusively to the world that our sole object is the establishment of our independence and the attainment of an honorable peace. The rejection of this offer would prove to the country that the responsibility of the continuance of the war does not rest upon us, but that the party in power in the United States elect to prosecute it for purposes of their own. The proposal of peace would enable the people of the United States to determine at their coming elections whether they will support those who favor a prolongation of the war or those who wish to bring it to a termination which can but be productive of good to both parties without affecting the honor of either. I have the honor to be, with high respect, your obedient servant, R.E. Lee, General"

"Has a Single Eye to the Good of the Service"

General Lee recognized the qualities of leadership that General Jackson possessed. He admired

Stonewall for his tenacity and aggressive actions and Christian spirit. General Jackson shadowed Lee in his Christian manner. After the battle of Antietam Lee became even more impressed and respectful of the contributions this one man made to the cause of Southern freedom. They seemed to think and move as one. Though their partnership lasted a little over a year, they became synonymous, forever riding together as friends and comrades in the minds of those that guard the true history of our nation. The eyes of historians see them as the greatest team to traverse the fields of warfare as well. In a letter dated October 2, 1862, Lee recommends promotion for both Longstreet and Jackson. He wrote specifically of Jackson in very gracious terms. (<u>Robert E. Lee Man and Soldier</u>; Page, Thomas Nelson; Charles Scribner's sons; New York; 1926; pages 287-288)

"My opinion of General Jackson has been greatly enhanced during this expedition. He is true, honest, and brave; has a single eye to the good of the service, and spares no exertion to accomplish his object."

"I was Startled and Shocked to See Him Overcome with Grief"

During October of 1862, while encamped at Winchester, General Lee learned of the death of his darling daughter, Anna. She died of typhoid fever in a place called Warren White Sulphur Springs, North Carolina. Colonel Taylor, one of his trusted staff members relates, "One morning the mail was received and the private letters were distributed as was the custom, but no one knew whether any home news had been received by the General. At the usual hour, he summoned me to his presence to know if there were any matters of army routine

284

upon which his judgment and action were desired. The papers containing a few such cases were presented to him; he reviewed them and gave his orders in regard to them. I then left him, but for some cause returned in a few moments and, with my accustomed freedom, entered his tent without announcement or ceremony, when I was startled and shocked to see him, overcome with grief, an open letter in his hands. That letter contained the sad intelligence of his daughter's death. His army demanded his first thought and care; to his men, to their needs, he must first attend, and then he would surrender himself to his private, personal affairs." (Four Years with General Lee; Taylor, Walter H.; D. Appleton-Century Company; New York; 1878)

"God has Mingled Mercy with the Blow"

In a letter to her son dated October 26, 1862, Mary Custis Lee expressed the loss of her child as only one experiencing that dreaded event could possibly do.

"I cannot express the anguish I feel at the death of our sweet Annie. To know that I shall never see her again on earth, that her place in our circle, which I always hoped one day to enjoy, is forever vacant, is agonising in the extreme. But God in this, as in all things, has mingled mercy with the blow, in selecting that one best prepared to leave us. May you be able to join me in saying, 'His will be done!'...I know how much you will grieve and how much she will be mourned. I wish I could give you any comfort, but beyond our hope in the great mercy of God, and the belief that He takes her at the time and place when it is best for her to go, there is none. May that same mercy be extended to us all, and may we be prepared for His summons." (Recollections and Letters of General

Robert E. Lee; Lee, Robert E. Jr.; Garden City Publishing Company; Garden City, New York; 1904; page 50)

My Darling Little Annie Lee

Her smile was like the sunshine
That breaks the morning dew.
Our love was the special kind
That father daughter knew.

While stationed at Winchester
I first received the news.
I wanted to caress her
And see her sickness through.

One day a tear-stained letter
Shocked me beyond belief.
Annie is gone forever!
I was overwhelmed with grief.

My darling little Anne
Went to her just reward.
She walks the fields of plenty
With her Savior and Lord.

Death crowds the lonely soldier
Yet somehow he survives.
But I'll never get over
The day my Annie died.

When I first read of the General's loss (Annie was in the spring of her life, being only twenty-three years of age) while both were away from home, it made me so sad for all the family members of every war that lost loved ones while away fighting for what they believed. How helpless and forlorn they must have felt. Oh, the devastated spirit and heartbroken agony of knowing that one will never look upon the face of that loved one ever again! But Lee was a man of faith and knew that he would see his beloved daughter again. On her marker, he had engraved the following words demonstrating his unshakable faith in the Almighty: "Perfect and true are all His ways, whom Heaven adores and earth obeys."

I grieved for his loss and those who have lost loved ones but it made me want to appreciate those around me more and to let them know while they are living just how important they are. It also made me realize that death is the great equalizer and comes to all mortals. For all the times, I failed to say the right words, and due to pride did not do the right thing, for all those loved that now are gone, allow me a personal moment to ask for forgiveness, and allow me to express my love and gratitude. We must treasure each other in the recognition that we will not always have one another. God in His mercy will allow us the final hope and assurance of being reunited forever, just as our General and dear Annie are now together walking hand in hand through the fields of plenty.

"I feel as if I Should be overwhelmed"

One month after the death of his darling daughter, Lee wrote to his sister Mary expressing his sorrow. He was encamped somewhere around Fredericksburg.

"The death of my dear Annie was, indeed, to me a bitter pang, but the Lord gave and the Lord has taken away; blessed be the name of the Lord. In the quiet hours of night, when there is nothing to lighten the full weight of my grief, I feel as if I should be overwhelmed. I have always counted, if God should spare me a few days after this Civil War has ended, that I should have her with me, but year after year my hopes go out, and I must be resigned." (Recollections and Letters of General Robert E. Lee; Lee, Robert E. Jr.; Garden City Publishing Company; Garden City, New York; 1904; page 50)

"You Have Now Two Sweet Angels in Heaven"

While still staggered by the loss of his daughter, General Lee received word of another personal loss, his granddaughter.   In his letter dated December 10, 1862, he laments her untimely death but offers words of comfort. His unshakable faith in life in the hereafter is quite evident throughout the text of the letter.   It was written at Camp Fredericksburg. (Christ in the Camp: Religion in the Confederate Army; Jones, J. William; Martin and Hoyt Company; Atlanta; 1904; page 72)

"I heard yesterday, my dear daughter, with the deepest sorrow of the death of your infant. I was so grateful at her birth. I felt that she would be such a comfort to you, such a pleasure to my dear Fitzhugh, and would fill so full the void still aching in your hearts. But you have now two sweet angels in heaven. What joy there is in the thought. What relief to your grief. What suffering and sorrow they have escaped. I can say nothing to soften the anguish you must feel, and I know you are assured of my deep and affectionate sympathy. May God give you strength to bear the affliction. He has imposed and produce future joy out of present misery, is my earnest prayer.

"I saw F (Fitzhugh) yesterday. He is well and wants much to see you. When you are strong enough, cannot you come up to Hickory Hill, or your grandpa's, on a little visit, where he could ride down and see you? My horse is waiting at my tent door, but I could not refrain from sending these few lines to recall to you the thought and love of your devoted father, R. E. Lee."

"My Heart Bleeds at the Death of Every One of Our Gallant Men."

During Christmas day of 1862, while in the vicinity of Fredericksburg, a brief reunion was held with two of his sons. Afterwards the graying general sat down and wrote a letter to his beloved wife (she was in Richmond, Virginia) expressing his thoughts that personify a man of war yearning for the sweet taste of peace. It also reveals his values and the character of his Christian heart. It also shows his desire for the cruel war to come to an end. (The Wartime Papers of Robert E. Lee; Dowdey, Clifford and Manarin, Louis H.; De Capo Press; Commonwealth of Virginia; 1961; pages 379-380; # 352)

"I will commence this holy day by writing to you. My heart is filled with gratitude to Almighty God for His unspeakable mercies with which He has blessed us in this day, for those He has granted us from the beginning of life, and particularly for those He has vouchsafed us during the past year. What should have become of us without His crowning help and protection? I have seen His hand in all the events of the war. Oh, if our people would only recognize it and cease from vain self-boasting and adulation, how strong would be my belief in final success and happiness to our country! For in Him alone I know is our trust & safety. Cut off from all communication with you & my children, my greatest pleasure is to write to you & them. Yet I have no time to indulge in it. You must tell them so, & say that I constantly think of them & love them fervently with all my heart. They must write to me without waiting for replies. I shall endeavour to write Mildred from whom I have not heard for a long time. Tell dear Charlotte I have received her letter & feel greatly for her. I saw her Fitzhugh this morning with his young aid, riding at the head of his brigade on his way up the Rappahannock. I regret so he could not get to see her. He only got her letter I enclosed him last evening. She ought not to have married a young soldier, but an old "exempt" like her papa, who would have loved her as much as he does. F{itzhugh} & R{obert} are very well. But what a cruel war this is; to separate and destroy families and friends, and mar the purest joys and happiness God has granted us in this world; to fill our hearts with the hatred instead of love of our neighbours, and to devastate the fair face of this beautiful world! I pray that, on this day when only peace and good-will are preached to mankind, better thoughts may fill the hearts of our enemies and turn them to peace. The confusion that now exists in their counsels will thus result in good. Our army was never in such good health and condition since I have been attached to it. I believe they share with me my disappointment that the enemy did not renew the combat on the 13th. I was holding back all day and husbanding our strength and ammunition for the great struggle for which I thought I was preparing. Had I divined that was to have been his only effort, he would have had more of it. But I am content. We might have gained more but we would have lost more, & perhaps our relative condition would not have been improved. My heart bleeds at the death of every one of our gallant men. Give much love to every one. Kiss Chass & Agnes for me & believe me with true affection. Yours, R.E. Lee" (<u>Recollections and Letters of General Robert E. Lee</u>; Lee, Robert E.

Jr.; Garden City Publishing Company; Garden City, New York; 1904)

"A More Noble Spirit was Never Displayed Anywhere"

On December 26, 1862, while camped at Fredericksburg, Lee wrote the following words to his daughter expressing his longing to be with his family, yet that he must share the sorrows of solitary with others suffering from the ravages of the war:

"My precious Little Agnes: I have not heard of you for a long time. I wish you were with me, for always solitary, I am sometimes weary, and long for the reunion of my family once again. But I will not speak of myself, but of you...I have seen the ladies in this vicinity only when flying from the enemy, and it caused me acute grief to witness their exposure and suffering. But a more noble spirit was never displayed anywhere. The faces of old and young were wreathed with smiles, and glowed with happiness at their sacrifices for the good of their country. Many have lost everything. What the fire and shells of the enemy spared, their pillagers destroyed. But God will shelter them, I know. So much heroism will not be unregarded. I can only hold oral communication with your sister (his daughter Mary, in King George county, within the lines of the enemy), and have forbidden the scouts to bring any writing, and have taken some back that I had given them for her. If caught, it would compromise them. They only convey messages. I learn in that way she is well. Your devoted father, R. E. Lee."

"May We Yet Meet in Peace and Happiness"

Upon hearing that his son had been wounded, General Lee wrote the following excerpt to Fitz:

"My Dear Son: I send you a dispatch, received from C. (Curtis) last night. I hope you are comfortable this morning. I wish I could see you, but I cannot. Take care of yourself, and make haste and get well and return. Though I scarcely ever saw you, it was a great comfort to know that you were near and with me. I could think of you and hope to see you. May we yet meet in peace and happiness…"

"Some good is Always Mixed with the Evil"

On the 11th he wrote the following letter to his daughter-in-law expressing his love, thankfulness, concern, and faith:

"I am so grieved, my dear daughter, to send Fitzhugh to you wounded. But I am so grateful that his wound is of a character to give us full hope of a speedy recovery. With his youth and strength to aid him, and your tender care to nurse him, I trust he will soon be well again. I know that you will unite with me in thanks to Almighty God, who has so often sheltered him in the hour of danger, for his recent deliverance, and lift your whole heart in praise to Him for sparing a life so dear to us, while enabling him to do his duty in the station in which he had placed him. Ask him to join in supplication that He may always cover him with the shadow of His almighty arm, and teach him that his only refuge is in Him, the greatness of whose mercy reacheth unto the heavens, and His truth unto the clouds. As some good is always mixed with the evil in this world, you will now have him with you for a time, and I shall look to you to cure him soon and send him back to me..." (<u>Recollections and Letters of General Robert E. Lee</u>; Lee, Robert E. Lee Jr.; Garden City Publishing Company; Garden City, New York; 1904)

"Every Exertion Be Made to Supply the Army with Bread"

On January 19, 1863, General Lee's fifty-sixth birthday, he sat down and wrote a letter to President Davis. The letter was composed at his headquarters near the banks of the Rappahannock. The correspondence offers you, dear reader, a glimpse into the typical daily duties of the general. He addresses his concern for feeding his men, for he knows that in order for the cause to be furthered, his men must eat. He informs the President that the wheat be delivered to the fifty wagons and that a barter of sugar for bacon be offered to the citizens in which he is trading with for the wheat. His tactfulness in addressing issues is noted and his ability to keep the President informed went a long way in providing his men the supplies that they so desperately needed. (<u>The Wartime Papers of Robert E. Lee</u>; Dowdey, Clifford and Manarin, Louis H.; De Capo Press; Commonwealth of Virginia; 1961; pages 391-392; #363)

"Mr. President, I go down this morning to examine the preparations which the enemy seem to be making of the banks of the Rappahannock. I understand that a redoubt (a small field fortification, often hastily constructed, that was enclosed on all sides-<u>The Encyclopedia of Civil War Usage</u>; Garrison, Webb; Cumberland House Publishing; Nashville, Tennessee; 2001; page 209) has been built on the hill overlooking the river where their causeway has been constructed. Since my arrival,

I have learned nothing more of the designs of the enemy than what had been previously received, except the enclosed notes from two of our scouts on their right & left flank. Everything combined seems to indicate a movement, and I believe that their army, instead of being diminished by detachments to North Carolina, has been reinforced since the ballet of the 13th December. I therefore have suspended the march of the brigades ordered to North Carolina until I can ascertain something more definitely. If in your opinion the necessity there is more urgent than here, I will dispatch them immediately, they are ready for the march.

"I have directed the Chief Quartermaster of this army to take fifty wagons belonging to its transportation, and apply them exclusively to convey the wheat that may be purchased by the agents of the Commissionary Department, at Richmond, in the counties lying between the Rappannock & Pamunky, to the Central Railroad at Hanover Court House. I think this a more convenient point than any on the Fredericksburg Railroad, and one from which transportation to Richmond can be more readily obtained. I would suggest that the Quartermaster General in Richmond collect all the wagons that can be spared from the posts at Gordonsville, Charlottesville, Staunton, Lynchburg, Richmond, &c., which may probably amount to fifty, & apply them to the transportations of the wheat in Greene, Madison & Culpeper Counties, &c., to the railroad for conveyance to Richmond. Our necessities make it imperative that every exertion be made to supply the army with bread.

"As the Commissionary Department proposes to issue sugar to the army in lieu of part of its meat ration, it has occurred to me that if its supply will warrant it, that by offering to exchange sugar for salt meat in the counties where grain is being collected, many persons might be tempted to part with bacon now retained for their own use. A few thousand pounds collected in this way would be of assistance to the army.

"I have the honor to be with great respect, your obt. Servt., R.E. Lee, General"

Also, note that at no juncture did he reference his birthday and it brings to mind the thought of what were the common soldiers doing on their birthday as well. On January 19, 1862, Lee was in Coosawhatchie, South Carolina, writing one of his sons, George Washington Custis Lee. In the correspondence he acknowledges receipt of two letters written by Custis and offers to send him money for repair on his home. He talks of his own impending financial ruin in a matter of fact fashion and asks his son to inquire of the character of one Lt. Col. Henry H. Walker who "is paying court" to Ms. Mary. (The Wartime Papers of Robert E. Lee; Dowdey, Clifford and Manarin, Louis H.; De Capo Press; Commonwealth of Virginia; 1961; pages 104-106; #104) Two years later (January 19, 1864) General Lee wrote to President Davis and to General Alexander R. Lawton (Quartermaster General). To General Lawton he writes of the desperate need of shoes for his men and implores him to do whatever needed to assure his men of the leather, even if it meant impression (a synonym for seizure and commandeering private property- The Encyclopedia of Civil War Usage; Garrison, Webb; Cumberland House Publishing; Nashville, Tennessee; 2001; page 117-118). In his writings to the President his manner is directed at "the abuse of the right of volunteering by conscripts and its effect upon the armies in the field." He asks the President to intervene and address the imbalance or he fears that the army will diminish. (The Wartime Papers of Robert E. Lee; Dowdey, Clifford and Manarin, Louis H.; De Capo Press; Commonwealth of Virginia; 1961; pages 653-654; #608-609)

On his fifty-eighth birthday (January 19, 1865), Lee wrote to President Davis and later to William P. Miles. In his letter to Mr. Davis he thanks him for the confidence in his leadership but questions his ability to lead the total army that Davis is planning to place under his dominion. In his last statement, Lee does relent and he states that, "I am willing to undertake any service to which you think proper to assign me, but I do not wish you to be misled as to the extent of my capacity." Again his humble nature shines through, as the inner man questions his ability. In answering William Miles' request (as stated by South Carolina Governor Magrath in a telegram) Lee sadly relates his dilemma and inability to send troops to aide against the march of Sherman. He recounts to Mr. Miles that only the War Department has the authority to send troops but if he had them to offer, he would be willing to do so with the blessing of the government. (The Wartime Papers of Robert E. Lee; Dowdey, Clifford and Manarin, Louis H.; De Capo Press; Commonwealth of Virginia; 1961; pages 884-886; # 938-939)

"That is all That Makes Life Valuable"

In an excerpt from a letter to his wife Mary, Lee shows his worry for his wife's health and again stresses the importance of doing good deeds. The letter was composed on January 29, 1863, while at Camp Fredericksburg. (The Wartime Papers of

Robert E. Lee; Dowdey, Clifford and Manarin, Louis H.; De Capo Press; Commonwealth of Virginia; 1961; pages 8395-396; # 368)

"I am grieved to hear of your sufferings. I trust now that the storm has passed, you are relieved. It has terminated here in a deep snow which does not improve our comfort. But as long as we can retain our health we can stand anything…You must endeavour to enjoy the pleasure of doing good. That is all that makes life valuable."

"The Cause Would be Very Much Jeopardized"

General Lee seemed to always tempt fate by placing himself as a readily recognizable target in which a sharp shooter could take advantage. He firmly believed that he could not lead from the rear, that his men needed to see him facing the enemy, and that once committed, it was all in God's hands. But that did not relieve the fears of those around him. His staff and his own foot soldiers were constantly reminding him to get back. On one juncture in which his safety was being questioned, he annoyingly stated, "I wish some one would tell me my proper place in battle. I am always told I should not be where I am." His son W. H. F. Lee was so alarmed upon hearing of his exposure to unnecessary dangers that he wrote his father begging him to not place himself in harm's way. (General Lee; Lee, Fitzhugh; Premier Civil War Classics; Fawcett Publications, Inc,; Greenwich, Conn., 1961; page 250)

"I hear from every one of your exposing yourself. You must recollect, if anything should happen to you, the cause would be very much jeopardized. I want very much to see you. May God preserve you, my dear father, is the earnest prayer of your devoted son."

"Our Resources in Men are Constantly Diminishing"

During the month of May 1863, as Lee completed the plans for the invasion of the North, he wrote a very insightful letter to President Davis. In the letter, he expresses his concerns for his armies' limited resources in manpower and supplies and the importance of pressing for peace in the event of a victory on Northern soil. The letter was written twenty-two months prior to his surrender at Appomattox.

"We should not conceal from ourselves that our resources in men are constantly diminishing, and the disproportion in this respect between us and our enemies, if they continue united in their efforts to subjugate us, is steadily augmenting...Should the belief that peace will bring back the Union become general, the war would no longer be supported, and that, after all, is what we are interested in bringing about. When peace is proposed to us, it will be time enough to discuss its terms, and it is not the part of prudence to spurn the proposition in advance." (<u>Lee</u>; Freeman Douglas Southall; An Abridgment by Richard Harwell of the Pulitzer Prize Winning four-volume Biography; New York; Touchstone; 1991; pages 311-312)

"Some Doctor Had Seen Our Son"

On August 2, 1863, after enduring the simultaneous devastating twin blows of Gettysburg and Vicksburg, General Lee wrote to his wife. His primary concern was his wounded and captured son Rooney. He then talked of the never-ending possibility of doing battle. (General Lee; Lee, Fitzhugh; Premier Civil War Classics; Fawcett Publications, Inc.; Greenwich, Conn., 1961; pages 296-297)

"I have heard of some doctor having reached Richmond who had seen our son at Fort Monroe. He said that his wound was improving, and that he himself was well and walking about on crutches. The exchange of prisoners that had been going on has for some cause been suspended, owing to some crotchet or other, but I hope will soon be resumed, and that we shall have him back soon. The armies are in such closed proximity that frequent collisions are common along the outposts. Yesterday the enemy laid down two or three pontoon bridges across the Rappahannock and crossed his cavalry and a large force of his infantry. It looked at first as if it were the advance of his army, and, as I had not intended to deliver battle, I directed our cavalry to retire slowly before them and to check their too rapid pursuit. Finding later in the day that their army was not following, I ordered out the infantry and drove them back to the river. I suppose they intended to push on toward Richmond by this or some other route. I trust, however, they will never reach there."

"I am so Dull That in Making Use of the Eyes of Others"

After the results of the three-day battle at Gettysburg, General Lee decides that it would be best for the country if he resigns. His prayer was that a more able individual would rise and succeed him. The letter is printed in its entirety so that the reader can feel Lee's unconditional regard for his men and his earnest desire to have the best man lead the gallant army. It also shows that Lee was quite aware of his failing health. On August 8, 1863, he wrote President Davis the following letter while at the Camp Orange. (The Wartime Papers of Robert E. Lee; Dowdey, Clifford and Manarin, Louis H.; De Capo Press; Commonwealth of Virginia; 1961; pages 589-590; #543)

"Mr. President, Your letters of July 28 and August 2 have been received, and I have waited for a leisure hour to reply, but I fear that will never come. I am extremely obliged to you for the attention given to the wants of this army, and the efforts made to supply them. Our absentees are returning, and I hope the earnest and beautiful appeal made to the country in your proclamation may stir up the virtue of the whole people, and that they may see their duty and perform it. Nothing is wanted but that their fortitude should equal their bravery to insure the success of our cause. We must expect reverses, even defeats. They are sent to teach us wisdom and prudence, to call forth greater energies, and to prevent our falling into greater disasters. Our people have only to be true and united, to bear manfully the misfortunes incident to war, and all will come right in the end.

"I know how prone we are to censure and how ready to blame others for the non-fulfillment of our expectations. This is unbecoming in a generous people, and I grieve to see its expression. The general remedy for the want of success in a military commander is his removal. This is natural, and in many instances proper. For no matter what may be the ability of the officer, if he loses the confidence of his troops disaster must sooner or later ensue.

"I have been prompted by these reflections more than once since my return from Pennsylvania to propose to Your Excellency the propriety of selecting another commander for this army. I have seen and heard of expression of discontent in the public journals at the result of the expedition. I do not know how far this feeling extends in the army. My brother officers have been to kind to report it, and so far the troops have been too generous to exhibit it. It is fair, however, to suppose that it does exist, and success is so necessary to us that nothing should be risked to secure it. I therefore, in all sincerity, request Your Excellency to take measures to supply my place. I do this with the more earnestness because no one is more aware than myself of my inability for the duties of my position. I cannot even accomplish what I myself desire. How can I fulfill the expectations of others? In addition I sensibly feel their growing failure of my bodily strength. I have not yet recovered from the attack I experienced the past spring. I am becoming more and more incapable of exertion, and am thus prevented from making the personal examinations and giving the personal supervision to the operations in the field which I feel to be necessary. I am so dull that in making use of the eyes of others I am frequently misled. Everything, therefore, points to the advantages to be derived from a new commander, and I the more anxiously urge the matter upon Your Excellency from my belief that a younger and abler man than myself can readily be attained. I know that he will have as gallant and brave an army as ever existed to second his efforts, and it would be the happiest day of my life to see at its head a worthy leader, one that would accomplish more than I could perform and all that I wished. I hope Your Excellency will attribute my request to the true reason, the desire to serve my country, and to do all in my power to insure the success of her righteous cause.

"I have no complaints to make of any one but myself. I have received nothing but kindness from those above me, and the most considerate attention from my comrades and companions in arms. To Your Excellency I am specially indebted for uniform kindness and consideration. You have done everything in your power to aid me in the work committed to my charge, without omitting anything to promote the general welfare. I pray that your efforts may at length be crowned with success, and that you may long live to enjoy the thanks of a grateful people. With sentiments of great esteem, I am very respectfully and truly yours, R. E. Lee"

President Davis replied swiftly and firmly. He made it quite clear that the general leading the grand army was the only choice. "To ask me to substitute you by some one in my judgment more fit to command, or who would possess more of the confidence of the army, or of the reflecting men of the country, is to demand an impossibility." The issue was settled. Lee would continue in the position that had been ordained by destiny.

"The Defenders of a Just Cause Should be Pure in God's Eyes"

Just a little over a month after the defeat at Gettysburg, in an address dated August 21, 1863, General Lee talks of purity and the just cause of battle:

"We have not remembered that the defenders of a just cause should be pure in {God's} eyes; that our times are in His hands, and we have relied too much on our own arms for the achievement of our independence."

"I Could Not Bear to Expose Them to Certain Suffering"

On the 19th of October 1863, Lee wrote Mary about the condition of his army. His letter reveals his love for his men, as a father would try to shelter his children from all harm. It is a very moving passage and quite candid.

"I have returned to the Rappahannock. I did not pursue with the main army beyond Bristoe or Broad Run. Our advance went as far as Bull Run, where the enemy was entrenched, extending his right as far as Chantilly, in the yard of which he was building a redoubt. I could have thrown him farther back, but I saw no chance of bringing him to battle, and it would have only served to fatigue our troops by advancing farther. If they had been properly provided with clothes, I would certainly have endeavored to have thrown them north of the Potomac; but thousands were barefooted, thousands with fragments of shoes, and all without overcoats, blankets or warm clothing. I could not bear to expose them to certain suffering on an uncertain issue."

"We Have Thousands of Barefooted Men"

The date of October 28, 1863, was one in which Lee sat down and again wrote a letter expressing his concern for his son and soldiers' needs. Lee was well aware that his army was in dire need of supplies and throughout his correspondences, he expressed his dismay about the deplorable conditions that infused the army. His anguish over his son's condition and precarious predicament is evident. Lee was well aware that his army was in dire need of supplies and throughout his correspondences, he expressed his dismay about the deplorable conditions that infused the army. He addressed the shoeless conditions and need for supplies. But he also reveals his sense of humor and his undying fighting spirit. (<u>Robert E. Lee Man and Soldier</u>; Page, Thomas Nelson; Charles Scribner's sons; New York; 1926; pages 368-369)

"I moved yesterday into a nice pine thicket, and Perry is to-day engaged in constructing a chimney in front of my tent which will make it warm and comfortable. I have no idea when F. {his son, Brigadier-General W.H. F. Lee} will be exchanged. The Federal authorities still resist all exchanges, because they think it is to our interest to make them. Any desire expressed on our part for the exchange of any individual magnifies the difficulty, as they at once think some great benefit is to result to us from it. His detention is very grievous to me, and, besides, I want his services. I am glad you have some socks for the army. Send them to me. They will come safely. Tell the girls to send all they can. I wish they could make some shoes, too. We have thousands of barefooted men. There is no news. General Meade, I believe, is repairing the railroad, and I presume will come on again. If I could only get some shoes and clothes for the men, I would save him the trouble."

"If A Gracious God Will Give Us Our Independence"

Lee shared everything with his wife. On November 21, 1863, the general reflected on God's will and that he would submit to it no matter the cost. The following excerpt demonstrates quite pointedly his willingness to give his all for the cause.

"I am content to be poor, and to live on corn bread the rest of my life if a gracious God will give us our independence."

"I Believe a Kind God Has Ordered All Things for Our Good"

Lee's greatest confidant was his beloved wife Mary. He shared with her so many of his secret disappointments, desires and asked for her advice in some of his decisions. He sometimes discussed the battles and described them in detail. At times, he would simply talk of family matters and remind them all of his love. On the 4th day of December of 1863 he wrote his beloved Mims the following letter addressing his disappointment in the movements of General Meade when he withdrew across the Rappahannock. Yet Lee once again affirms his faith in a merciful providence.

"You will probably have seen that General Meade has retired to his old position on the Rappahannock without giving us battle. I had expected, from his movements and all that I have heard, that it was his intention to do so, and after the first day, when I thought it necessary to skirmish pretty sharply with him on both flanks to ascertain his vies, I waited patiently his attack. On Tuesday, however, I thought he had changed his mind, and that night made preparations to move around his left next morning and attack him. But when day dawned he was nowhere to be seen. He had commenced to withdraw at dark Tuesday evening. We pursued to the Rapidan, but he was over. Owing to the nature of the ground, it was to our advantage to receive rather than to make the attack, and as he about doubled us in numbers, I wished to have that advantage. I am greatly disappointed at his getting off with so little damage, but we do not know what is best for us. I believe a kind God has ordered all things for our good."

"Their Privation Was Beyond His Means of Present Relief"

A letter written by Colonel Charles Marshall (Lee's aide-de-camp) also reflects upon the hardships endured by the soldiers during winter encampment. Imagine being barefoot and hungry with limited rations available. There were few blankets to be passed among the men and the amazing fact is that General Lee chose to endure the same hardships as his men. He could have found the basic creature comforts and would have been a welcomed guest in all homes but he chose to stay among his beloved men. The following letter is a testament to fortitude and determination of those men in gray as they embraced their cause with unflinching devotion.

"While the army was on the Rapidan, in the winter of 1863-1864, it became necessary, as was often the case, to put the men on very short rations. Their duty was hard, not only on the outposts during the winter, but in the construction of roads, to facilitate communication between the different parts of the army. One day General Lee received a letter from a private soldier whose name I do not now remember, informing him of the work that he had to do, and stating that his rations were not sufficient to enable him to undergo the fatigue. He said, however, that if it was absolutely necessary to put him upon such short allowance, he would make the best of it, but that he and his comrades wanted to know if General Lee was aware that his men were getting so little to eat, because if he was aware of it he was sure there must be some necessity for it. General Lee did not reply directly to the letter, but issued a general order in which he informed the soldiers of his efforts in their behalf, and that their privation was beyond his means of present relief, but assured them that he was making every effort to procure sufficient supplies. After that there was not a murmur in the army, and the hungry men went cheerfully to their hard work."

"That You May Know My Sorrow in all its Breath"

Lee was ever faithful in writing to his beloved family. On Christmas, he always took time to write and share his love with them. But on this occasion he could only express his sorrow for his daughter-in- law that was ebbing to the other shore. His love for her and his family is readily evident in the compassionate letter written of Christmas night. Sweet Charlotte's passing would deeply sadden the general and would remain a burden that he carried to his grave. (The Wartime Papers of Robert E. Lee; Dowdey, Clifford and Manarin, Louis H.; De Capo Press; Commonwealth of Virginia; 1961; pages 644-645; # 599)

"I am filled with sadness dear Mary at the intelligence conveyed in your letter of last evening. I have been oppressed with sorrowful forebodings since parting with Charlotte. She seemed to me stricken with a prostration I could not understand. Dear child she promised to be better the next morning & I wrote to her in a cheerful & hopeful mood which I could not feel. That you may know my sorrow in all its breath & depth, As far as I know my own heart, I feel for her all the love I feel for Fitzhugh. That is very great. I pray she may be spared to us. Yet God's will be done. The blow so grievous to us is intended I believe in mercy to her. She was so devoted to Fitzhugh. Seemed so bound up in him that apparently she thought of & cared for nothing else. They seemed so united, that I loved them as one person. I would go down tomorrow, but from your letter have no hope of finding her alive, or of being able to do anything for her. I feel that all will be done for her that human power can, & oh I pray that our Merciful Father will yet spare her, or gently take her to Himself. Telegraph me if I can yet reach there in time…Truly & Affly, R.E.Lee"

"Link by Link the Strong Chain Broken"

In a letter dated December 27, 1863, General Lee expresses his anguish over the loss of Charlotte, his daughter-in-law that was as deeply loved as if his own offspring. Her husband, W. H. F. Lee was imprisoned at Fortress Monroe. His brother General Custis Lee had offered to exchange himself for his brother so that his brother could be by his wife's side during those last moments. General Butler declined this act of humanity.

"Custis's dispatch which I received last night demolished all the hopes, in which I had been indulging during the day, of dear Charlotte's recovery. It has pleased God to take from us one exceedingly dear to us, and we must be resigned to His holy will. She, I trust, will enjoy peace and happiness forever, while we must patiently struggle on under all the ills that may be in store for us. What a glorious thought it is that she has joined her little cherubs and our angel Annie (his second daughter) in Heaven. Thus is link by link the strong chain broken that binds us to the earth, and our passage soothed to another world. Oh, that we may be at last united in that heaven of rest, where trouble and sorrow never enter, to join in an everlasting chorus of praise and glory to our Lord and Saviour! I grieve for our lost darling as a father only can grieve for a daughter, and my sorrow is heightened by the thought of the anguish her death will cause our dear son and the poignancy it will give to the bars of his prison. May God in His mercy enable him to bear the blow He has so suddenly dealt, and sanctify it to his everlasting happiness!" (<u>Recollections and Letters of General Robert E. Lee</u>; Lee, Robert E. Lee Jr.; Garden City Publishing Company; Garden City, New York; 1904)

"There Are Too Many Lees on the Committee"

While at winter camp Lee wrote a letter revealing his dismay over his officers and own son's frailty during perilous times. In the letter one quickly notes his concern for his army, their health and well being far out weighing the "trivial amusements" of a ball. The letter was written on January 17, 1864, at Orange Court House. Note the unorthodox tone of sarcasm of his correspondence. (<u>Robert E. Lee Man and Soldier</u>; Page, Thomas Nelson; Charles Scribner's sons; New York; 1926; page 374)

"I enclose a letter for you which has been sent to my care. I hope you are well and all around you. Tell Fitz I grieve over the hardships and sufferings of his men in their late expedition. I would have preferred his waiting for more favorable weather. He accomplished much under the circumstances, but would have done more in better weather. I am afraid he was anxious to get back to the ball. This is a bad time for such things. We have too grave subjects on hand to engage in such trivial amusements. I would rather his officers should entertain themselves in fattening their horses, healing their men, and recruiting their regiments. There are too many Lees on the committee. I like them all to be present at battles, but can excuse them at balls. But the saying is: "Children will be children!" I think he had better move his camp farther from Charlottesville, and perhaps he will get more work and less play. He and I are too old for such assemblies. I want him to write me how his men are, his horses, and what I can do to fill up his ranks."

"I Fear They Suffer"

General Lee continually worried and showed concern with the status and condition of his men under his command. They had needs that had to be addressed before his personal affairs could be handled. That was the nature and greatness of the man.

In the dead of winter Lee was camped on the Rapidan. The boys of valor were away from their loved ones and for some, experiencing their first northern Virginia winter. Many were barefoot and lacked socks. They seemed always hungry and the provisions were lacking in their content. But yet they clung to their dreams of independence and willingly made the self-sacrifices that set them apart from others. Within the confines of a state of destitution: within the perimeters of suffering; yet within that determination of spirit a sense of pride emerged and continued to defy the odds that still lives today in the true American heart. It pays homage to the men of gray. Lee addressed the wants of his men and in a letter to Mary dated January 24, 1864. In it he describes the condition of the army.

"I have had to disperse the cavalry as much as possible to obtain forage for their horses, and it is that which causes trouble. Provisions for the men, too, are very scarce, and with very light diet and light clothing, I fear they suffer, but still they are cheerful and uncomplaining. I received a report from one division the other day, in which it was stated that over 400 men were barefooted and over 1,000 were without blankets. (Robert E. Lee Man

310

and Soldier; Page, Thomas Nelson; Charles Scribner's sons; New York; 1926; page 373)

"I Loved Them as One Person"

In a letter to his wife Mary Custis Lee, he again shares his sorrow over the loss of Charlotte. In his correspondence Lee gives an unending tribute to the love he held in his heart for his children and the bond that Rooney and Charlotte possessed for each other. (Lee, The Last Years; Flood, Charles Bracelen; Houghton Mifflin Company; New York; 1981; page 42)

"That you may know my sorrow in all its breadth and depth, as far as I know my own heart, I feel for her all the love I bear Fitzhugh. That is very great...she was so devoted to Fitzhugh, seemed so bound up in him, that apparently she thought of and cared for nothing else. They seemed so united that I loved them as one person."

"How I Mourn Her Loss"

Lee the father also wrote his grief stricken son who had been captured and was currently a prisoner of war. In his letter, he tries to console his child and shield him from the ravages of death. But through the darkness of the night, a ray of hope riding on the wings of faith permeates the correspondence. The letter was written in April on the 24th of 1864. (Christ in the Camp: Religion in the Confederate Army; Jones, J. William; Martin and Hoyt Company; Atlanta; 1904; pages 74-75)

"I received last night, my dear son, your letter of the 22nd. It has given me great comfort. God knows how I loved your dear, dear wife, how sweet her memory is to me, and how I mourn her loss. My grief could not be greater if you had been taken from me. You were both equally dear to me. My heart is too full to speak on this subject, nor can I write. But my grief is for ourselves, not for her. She is brighter and happier than ever--safe from all evil, and awaiting us in her heavenly abode. May God in His mercy enable us to join her in eternal praise to our Lord and Savior. Let us humbly bow ourselves before Him, and offer perpetual prayer for pardon and forgiveness. But we cannot indulge in grief, however mournfully pleasing. Our country demands all our strength, all our energies. To resist the powerful combination now forming against us will require every man at his place. If victorious, we have everything to hope for. I have not heard what action has been taken by the department in reference to my recommendations concerning the organization of the cavalry. But we have no time to wait, and you had better join your brigade. This week will, in all probability, bring us active work, and we must strike fast and strong. My whole trust is in God, and I am ready for whatever He may ordain. May He guide, guard and strengthen us, is my constant prayer. Your devoted father, R. E. Lee."

"Texans Always Lead Them!"

During the battle of the Wilderness, the Federal forces broke the centerline, as a worried Lee watched. Just then a Texas Regiment made their way from the march and charged. Taking his hat off his graying hair, waving it above his head vigorously, as he raised out of his saddle, Lee proclaimed, "Texans always lead them!" Immediately, the roar of the rebel yell resounded over all the lines and the battle tide was turned. A courier watching the exhalation of the men and the love and admiration this man of men held in the

312

hearts of his troop, broke down and with tears streaming down his face exclaimed, "I would charge hell itself for that old man!"

"Citizens Defending Their Country"

In May of 1864, A. P. Hill became dissatisfied with performance of an officer under his command. General Lee expressed his belief that his men fight not as an army of conquest but for their citizenship. In every situation, the general was always teaching. (The Wit and Wisdom of Robert E. Lee; edited by Cannon, Devereaux D.; Pelican Publishing Company; Gretna, Louisiana; Third Edition; 2000; page 88)

"These men are not an army, they are citizens defending their country. General Wright is not a soldier; he's a lawyer. I cannot do many things that I could do with a trained army. The soldiers know their duties better than the general officers do, and they have fought magnificently…you'll have to do what I do: when a man makes a mistake, I call him to my tent, and use the authority of my position to make him do the right thing the next time." (Lee, The Last Years; Flood, Charles Bracelen; Houghton Mifflin Company; New York; 1981; page 20)

"I Do Not Know What Will Become of Us"

On June 16, 1864, the Army of Northern Virginia was in dire straits. It was held together only by the man that had become the symbol of the Southern Cause. The second Cold Harbor had yielded a dreadful toll of over 7,000 Union dead in less than one hour but still they came. Not only did Lee must worry about the approaching army but also, he had to worry about the welfare of his men and how to meet their basic needs. He also had to provide provisions for his animals. This was not a menial task. The following extract from a communiqué' to President Davis voices the desperation of the times and his disappointment with the proficiency of the railroads in meeting the needs of all.

"For some few days back we have been only able to get sufficient corn for our animals from day to day. Any accident to the railroads would cut short our supplies. Genl Lawton is doing everything he can, but cannot provide more than about 2000 bushels per day. We require 3200 bushels daily for our animals-I think it is clear that the railroads are not working energetically & unless some improvement is made, I do not know what will become of us." (Lee's Dispatches: Unpublished Letters of General Robert E. Lee, C. S. A., to Jefferson Davis and the War Department of the Confederate Sates of America 1862-1865; Lee, Robert E.; From the private Collection of Wymberley Jones de Renne, of Wormsloe, Georgia (edited by Freeman, Douglas S. Freeman); G.P. Putnam's Sons; New York; 1915; Page 400)

"That Reverent Worshiper Who Kneels in the Dust"

In June of 1864, Lee's army was crossing the James River in an attempt to head off General Grant at Petersburg. Richmond had to be saved at all costs! Lee was bombarded with messages, intelligence reports and concerns of for his men. Though barraged with the burden of leadership and saving Richmond, the man who followed Christ stopped in the road, got off his mount, and knelt in the dust with his pastor. Chaplain J. William Jones offered the following regarding Lee's pious and humble nature:

314

"Let us go some bright Sabbath morning to that cluster of tents in the grove across the Massaponas, not far from Hamiltons Crossing. Seated on the rude logs, or on the ground, may be seen fifteen hundred or two thousand men, with upturned faces, eagerly drinking in the truths of the gospel. That reverent worshiper who knees in the dust during prayer, or listens with sharpened attention and moist eyes as the preacher delivers his message, is our loved Commander-in-Chief, General R.E. Lee." (Robert E. Lee The Christian; Johnson, William J.; Christian Liberty Press; Arlington Heights, Illinois; pages 40-41)

"I Fear a Great Calamity Will Befall Us"

In November, General Lee wrote President Davis at Richmond expressing the desperateness of the situation. He would pen several more but to no avail.

"Unless we can obtain a reasonable approximation to his (speaking of Grant) force I fear a great calamity will befall us."

"He Added the Brighter Graces of Pure Life"

After the Battle of Yellow Tavern, it became evident that General Stuart was mortally wounded and would soon die. Note that it was almost a year to the day (May 12, 1863 vs. May 10, 1864) that Jackson had fallen in battle. Lee was visibly shaken and stated he could not think of him without weeping. In the form of General Orders No. 44 Lee announced the death of General Stuart to his men. Lee paid his highest regards to Stuart and demonstrated the character of the man that he mourned with heartfelt sorrow.

"Among the gallant soldiers who have fallen in this war, General Stuart was second to none in valour, in zeal, and in unflinching devotion to his country. His achievements form a conspicuous part of the history of this army, with which his name and services will be forever associated. To military capacity of high order and to the noble virtues of the soldier he added the brighter graces of pure life, guided and sustained by the Christian's faith and hope. The mysterious hand of an all-wise God has removed him from the scene of his usefulness and fame. His grateful countrymen will mourn his loss and cherish his memory. To his comrades in arms he has left the proud recollections of his deeds and the inspiring influence of his example." (Recollections and Letters of General Robert E. Lee; Lee, Robert E. Lee Jr.; Garden City Publishing Company; Garden City, New York; 1904)

"We are a Dull People in the Army"

A letter addressed to Mary by General Lee was written on December 17, 1864. Mary was still living around Richmond and General Lee was under siege at Petersburg. Note that mood of the letter is somber and he does not mention Christmas. Although he is grateful for the gifts and polite he seems to be preoccupied. This is one of the few letters penned by him that he does not mention his Creator. Times were bleak and he was hurried by the horrors of the siege. The letter expresses an undercurrent of soberness that hints of the sad conditions of the grand army of Northern Virginia during this Christmas season. (The Wartime Papers of Robert E. Lee; Dowdey, Clifford and Manarin, Louis H.; De Capo Press; Commonwealth of Virginia; 1961; pages 877-878; # 928)

316

"My Dear Mary-I received day before yesterday the box with the hat, gloves & socks & also the bushel of apples. You had better have kept the latter, as it would have been more useful to you than to me, & I should have enjoyed its consumption by yourself & the girls, more than by me. The gloves brought by Mrs. Grinnell are very nice. You must thank her for them & express my sympathy for her loss & present distress. I hope however her husband is in a fair way to recover. I can do very well without the boots. You must also thank Mrs. Lyons for the fur, & beg the kind people to send me nothing more. I fear the furs will be more needed by Mr. Lyons than by me & that he may consequently suffer. Send them down when convenient. The reason you were troubled by visits of the courier about the box, in your first note, the 12th, apprising me of having sent it, you did not state it was through Major Wood. I was out when the courier brought the note & asking for the box, no one could give any explanation. We are a dull people in the army, & it is requisite you should be very explicit. You had better sent the socks to Major Ferguson, to be forwarded as the bundle appears to be large. I am some distance from the railroad depot now, & our little couriers have as much as they can carry.

"Robert can select any of my hats he prefers. I have offered them repeatedly, but he declines. Custis has the same privilege, also Fitzhugh. When last here Robt had a nice black hat with cord, &c., new. He said he wanted no other. Give much love to everybody, Very truly & affly R.E.Lee"

"The Country is Swept Clear"

In the winter month of January of 1865, General Lee, recognizing the desperation of the situation, sent a message to the Confederate Secretary of

317

War. In it he pleads for supplies to sustain his army. Lee knew that his army could not endure much longer without them. One can sense his desperation. The dispatch is dated the 11th of that month.

"Hon. J. A. Seddon,

"There is nothing within reach of this army to be impressed. The country is swept clear. Our only reliance is upon the railroads. We have but two days' supplies.
R. E. Lee"

"I Begged Them to Bring Nothing but Kisses"

No matter where he traveled General Lee was always receiving gifts from grateful admirers. He deeply appreciated the items but staying true to his nature would rather others have them. He especially had a tender spot in his heart for children. He loved them dearly. His whole countenance would light up when he talked with them. One incident reported by his son Rob talks of three young ladies that brought him gifts during the winter month of January 1865. This narrative offers a personal glimpse into the heart of the man.

"…Yesterday afternoon three little girls walked into my room, each with a small basket. The eldest carried some fresh eggs, laid by her own hens; the second, some pickles made by her mother; the third, some popcorn grown in her garden. They were accompanied by a young maid with a block of soap made by her mother. They were the daughters of a Mrs. Nottingham, a refugee from Northampton county, who lived near Eastville, not far from 'old Arlington.' The eldest of the girls, whose age did not exceed eight years, had a small wheel on which she spun for her mother, who wove all the cloth for her two brothers-boys of twelve and fourteen years. I have not had so pleasant a visit for a long time. I fortunately was able to fill their baskets with apples, which distressed poor Bryan {his mess-steward}, and I begged them to bring me nothing but kisses and to keep the eggs, corn, etc., for themselves. I pray daily and almost hourly to our Heavenly Father to come to the relief of you and our afflicted country. I know He will order all things for our good, and we must be content."

"You Must Not be Surprised if Calamity Befalls Us"

General Lee was always concerned with the state of affairs of his men. He worried about their clothing, food, shelter, and safety. He wrote several letters addressing the plight of his army. One of the most revealing correspondences was written to the Secretary of War while Lee's army was entrenched at Petersburg, two months before the inevitable occurred. In the manner of Lee as only he could express, he described the sad condition of the army and a prophecy of calamity if intersession wasn't offered on behalf of his boys. He pleaded for his boys but it went unheeded because of exhausted resources and the bureaucratic quagmire that had drained the South. The tragic result would be the calamity that was foreseen by the general. The letter was dated February 8, 1865. (Robert E. Lee Man and Soldier; Page, Thomas Nelson; Charles Scribner's sons; New York; 1926; page 511) (The Boys' Life of Robert E. Lee; Horn, Stanley F.; Harper Brothers Publishers; New York and London; 1935; page 279)

"Sir: All the disposable force of the right wing of the army has been operating against the enemy beyond Hatcher's Run since Sunday. Yesterday, the most inclement day of the winter, they had to be retained in line of battle, having been in the same condition the two previous days and nights. I regret to be obliged to state that under these circumstances, heightened by assaults and fire of the enemy, some of the men had been without meat for three days, and all were suffering from reduced rations and scant clothing, exposed to battle, cold, hail, and sleet. I have directed Colonel Coler, chief commissary, who reports that he has not a pound of meat at his disposal, to visit Richmond and see if nothing can be done. If some change is not made and the Commissary Department reorganized, I apprehend dire results. The physical strength of the men, if their courage survives, must fail under such treatment. Our cavalry has to be dispersed for want of forage. Fitz Lee's and Lomax's Divisions are scattered because supplies cannot be transported where their services are required. I had to bring William H. F. Lee's Division forty miles Sunday night to get him in position. Taking these facts in connection with the paucity of our numbers you must not be surprised if calamity befalls us..." R. E. Lee, General

APPOMATTOX
April 7-9, 1865

"The Offer of Surrender"

The end was now at hand. After a brilliant strategic withdrawal and a gallant but desperate attempt to reach his supply lines, the Great General halted his army of approximately twenty-five thousand (only eight thousand of the Army of Northern Virginia were able to do combat) at Appomattox. Upon realizing that his once invincible army was all but surrounded, General Lee held a council of war with his Lieutenants regarding the futile situation at hand.

"A little after nightfall a flag of truce appeared under torchlight in front of Mahone's line bearing a note to General Lee:

"Headquarters Armies of the United States,
5 P.M., April 7, 1865

General R. E. Lee,

Commanding Confederate States Army:

"General-The results of the last week must convince you of the hopelessness of further resistance on the part of the Army of Virginia in this struggle. I feel that it is so, and regard it as my duty to shift from myself the responsibility of any further effusion of blood by asking of you the surrender of that portion of the Confederate army known as the Army of Northern Virginia.

Very respectfully, your obedient servant,
U. S. Grant
Lieutenant General, Commanding Armies of the United States."
"I was sitting at his side when the note was delivered. He read it and handed it to me without referring to its contents. After reading it I gave it back, saying, 'Not yet.' General Lee wrote in reply:

"I Reciprocate Your Desire to Avoid Useless
Effusion of Blood"

April 7, 1865

Lieutenant General Grant,
Commanding Armies of the United States."

"General,-I have received your note of this day. Though not entertaining the opinion you express on the hopelessness of further resistance on the part of the Army of Northern Virginia, I reciprocate your desire to avoid useless effusion of blood, and therefore, before considering your proposition, ask the terms you will off on condition of its surrender.

R.E. Lee
General

"I was not informed of the contents of the return note, but thought, from the orders of the night, it did not mean surrender." (From Manassas to Appomattox; Longstreet, Major General James; Chapter XLIII, Appomattox)

On April 8, 1865, General Grant sent the following proposal of surrender after receiving General Lee's reply dated April 7, 1865:

General R. E. Lee, Commanding C.S.A.

"Your note of last evening in reply to mine of the same date, asking the conditions on which I will accept the surrender of the Army of Northern Virginia, is just received. In reply I would say that, peace being my great desire, there is but one condition I would insist upon,-namely, that men and officers surrendered shall be disqualified for taking up arms against the government of the United States until properly exchanged. I will meet you, or will designate officers to meet any officers you may name for the same purpose, at any point agreeable to you, for the purpose of arranging definitely the terms upon which the surrender of the Army of northern Virginia will be received."

U.S. Grant,
Lieutenant General

To which General Lee answered a very deliberately worded reply:

"The Restoration of Peace Should be the Sole Object of All"

April 8th

323

"General, I received at a late hour your note of today. I did not intend to propose the surrender of the Army of Northern Virginia, but to ask the terms of your proposition. To be frank, I do not think the emergency has arisen to call for the surrender of this army; but, as the restoration of peace should be the sole object of all, I desire to know whether your proposals would lead to that end. I cannot therefore meet you with a view to surrender the Army of Northern Va., but, as far as your proposal may affect the Confederate States forces under my command, & tend to the restoration of peace, I should be pleased to meet you at 10 A.M. tomorrow on the old stage road to Richmond between the picket lines of the two armies." R.E. Lee, Genl.

"The Confederacy has failed"

In General Edward Porter Alexander's memoirs, he reflects upon the conversation that he had with General Lee after receiving the above correspondences. General Potter suggests that the Commanding General order his boys to disperse and return to their native area and/or join General Johnston in North Carolina. In essence he was proposing guerilla warfare tactics to allow a regrouping of the troops. After listening to General Alexander's tactical suggestions, General Lee made the following statement to end forever the idea that continued fighting could achieve a victory over such overwhelming odds.

"There are here only about 15,000 men with muskets. Suppose two thirds, say 10,000, get away. Divided among the states their numbers would be too insignificant to accomplish the least good. Yes! The surrender of this army is the end of the Confederacy. As for foreign help I've never believed we could gain our independence except

324

by our own arms. If I ordered the men to go to Gen. Johnston few would go. Their homes have been overrun by the enemy and their families need them badly. We have now simply to look the fact in the face that the Confederacy has failed.

"And as Christian men, Gen. Alexander, you & I have no right to think for one moment of our personal feelings or affairs. We must consider only the effect which our action will have upon the country at large.

"Suppose I should take your suggestion & order the army to disperse & make their way to their homes. The men would have no rations & they would be under no discipline. They are already demoralized by four years of war. They would have to plunder & rob to procure subsistence. The country would be full of lawless bands in every part, & a state of society would ensue from which it would take the country years to recover. Then the enemy's cavalry would pursue in the hopes of catching the principal officers, & wherever they went there would be fresh rapine & destruction.

"And as for myself, while you young men might afford to go to bushwhacking, the only proper & dignified course for me would be to surrender myself & take the consequences of my actions.

"But it is still early in the spring, & if the men can be quietly and quickly returned to their homes there is time to plant crops & begin to repair the ravages of the war. That is what I must now try to bring about. I expect to meet Gen. Grant at ten this morning in rear of the army & to surrender this army to him." (Fighting for the Confederacy: The Personal Recollections of General Edward Porter Alexander;

Alexander, Edward Porter; The University of North Carolina Press; Chapel Hill; 1989; pages 528-535)

The decision to relent and fight no more must have been one filled with the deepest despair. After four long years, his boys were still ready to offer up their lives for what they believed. His decision to withdraw from the field of honor was his and his alone to make. He sought guidance from the Almighty and then slowly bowed his head in submission. The dream was over. The Confederacy had failed and he alone must bear the burden of climbing that mountain of surrender after riding through the valley of decisions. He bore the burden with such pride and dignity that his enemies saluted him with awe recognizing that a giant walked among mortal men.

Valley of Decisions

His valley of decisions
Lay menacing his sky.
What would be the conditions?
How many more would die?

Oh, should his army exit
Or fight until the death?
Would the enemy wreak it:
Dreams of a nation's breath?

Should he face the enemy
In one more gallant stand?
In the hands of Divinity
He left his tiny band.

Tortured by a thousand souls
That lay on freedom's altar.
From his knees, he slowly rose
While thinking of his daughters.

Realizing what he must do
He slowly rode away.
Surrenders to the boys in blue
The fading of the grey.

"I Now Ask for an Interview for That Purpose"

On April 9th, 1865, General Grant penned the following correspondence to General Lee:

"General: Your note of yesterday is received. I have no authority to treat on the subject of peace. The meeting proposed for 10 A.M. today could lead to no good. I will state, however, that I am equally desirous for peace with yourself, and the whole North entertains the same feeling. The terms upon which peace can be had are well understood. By the South laying down their arms, they would hasten that most desirable event, save thousands of human lives, and hundreds of millions of property not yet destroyed. Seriously hoping that all our difficulties may be settled without the loss of another life, I subscribe myself, etc.," U.S. Grant, Lieutenant General.

To which Lee swiftly replied:

April 9, 1865

"General: I received your note of this morning on the picket line, whither I had come to meet with you and ascertain definitely what terms were embraced in your proposal of yesterday with reference to the surrender of this army. I now ask an interview, in accordance with the offer contained in your letter of yesterday, for that purpose."
R.E. Lee, General

Common Ground

They met there in the middle;
They called it Common Ground.
Each side gave a little;
Solutions must be found.

They signed a piece of paper.
He bowed and took his leave.
And as the morning tapered,
The end was now conceived.

They saluted in respect.
He stepped upon the ground.
His sad sigh of regrets
Made a deafening sound.

The gray clad old gentleman
Dressed in his Sunday best.
Moved slowly among his clan;
A burning in his chest.

They asked had he surrendered?
With tears came his reply,
"I've done my best remember"
He turned away and cried.

His men cried out, "We love you!"
As tears rowed down their vest.
"We'll always be proud of you.
We know you've done your best."

The old man slowly faded
Without another sound.
Our nation was created
Upon that common ground.

The preceding poem was inspired by the writings in which I was privileged to read. I felt it necessary to interject and offer my interpretation of this sacred event. Without this gallant closure and the manner in which both sides handled themselves during those closing days of the great American Conflict, this nation may never have been truly one nation under God, indivisible. It took that Common Ground, that holy soil; now a shrine honoring the very fiber that makes America great. Very rarely does an event in history defy the terms in which it can be described. Those other than the privileged few privy to the event must be the writers and recorders of this moment in the making of America.

"You Have Killed Your Beautiful Mare"

During the transpiring of the communications between the new armies, General Fitz Lee had been looking for a possible escape route. He found an area that he felt was unguarded in which the entire army could escape. He immediately notified General Longstreet. Upon reading the message, Longstreet sent Haskell straight away with a message to try and prevent Lee from surrendering. John Haskell always rode beautiful mounts and the mare that was under him was no exception. She was swift and beautifully proportioned. Longstreet expressed to him that he must ride with the wind and if need be, "To kill his horse if necessary but to overtake Gen. Lee & tell him of the chance to escape." Upon finding Lee, his poor horse was lathered badly. Lee said to Haskell, "What is it? What is it?" Upon gazing upon the little mare Lee gave him an unusual admonishment. "Oh, you have killed your beautiful mare! What did you do it for?" During this terrible period of decision-making, Lee's love and respect for animals shined through the darkened horizon. General Lee listened to the report but he determined it to be of no consequence and presented his letter to the courier requesting a summit to discuss the terms of surrender. (Fighting for the Confederacy: The Personal Recollections of General Edward Porter Alexander; Alexander, Edward Porter; The University of North Carolina Press; Chapel Hill; 1989; pages 528-535)

"This Will Live in History"

Lee determined to meet Grant. Colonel Marshall, Colonel Babcock and Sergeant Turner accompanied General Lee to the McLean home. Marshall had previously secured it for the historical meeting. Sgt. Turner remained holding Traveller as the party of three entered the home. General Lee was dressed in his last new suit and had it buttoned to his throat. The coat possessed three stars on each side of the collar, top boots with red silk and exquisite spurs. In his possession was a beautiful sword attached close to his beautiful red sash. The sword's handle was white with a lion's head at the top. It was wrapped with gilt wire, with gilt guard and the scabbard was of blue steel with gilt trimmings. Where the rings are attached, on one side of the blade, are the words, "General Robert E. Lee, from a Marylander, 1863"; on the other, "Aide-toi et Dieu t'aidera." According to writings of Fitzhugh Lee, his uncle General Robert E. Lee was at that moment possessed, "With a magnificent physique, not a pound of superfluous flesh, ruddy cheeks bronzed by exposure, grave and dignified, he was the focus of all eyes." From head to toe he looked the part of a conqueror. (General Lee; Lee, Fitzhugh; Premier Civil War Classics; Fawcett Publications, Inc,; Greenwich, Conn., 1961; pages 374-375)

He sat down and waited for approximately one half hour before General Grant and twelve or more of his staff arrived. The crowd around the little farmhouse grew as word spread of the meeting of the two warriors. After formalities were exchanged, Grant talked of their brief encounter over eighteen years ago, during the Mexican War. General Lee asked General Grant if he could speak to General Lawrence Williams. Earlier that morning General Williams sent word to Lee that his son was alive and in captivity. This was a major relief for the old general for earlier reports had indicated that his son had been killed at Sailor Creek. General Grant yielded to the request and sent for General Williams. Upon arriving, General Lee thanked the Union general for his act of kindness. (Lee's Aid-De-Camp; Marshall, Charles; University of Nebraska Press; Lincoln and London; @1927; First Bison Books printing: 2000; pages 269-270)

Cordial conversation continued until Lee diplomatically reminded Grant of the purpose of the meeting. Terms were discussed and Lee found Grant very lenient in the terms of surrender. Provisions for Lee's starving troops and Union soldiers held prisoners were provided. With the terms agreed upon, Lee shook the hand of Grant, bowing slightly to the others present and slowly began walking towards the exit. For just a moment time stood still, hesitating between the two worlds of war and peace: victory and surrender. It was the four o'clock prelude to destiny.

"It Will Do Much toward Conciliating Our People"

In his three volumes masterpiece (The Civil War: A Narrative: Red River to Appomattox; Foote, Shelby; First Vintage Books Edition; Random

House; New York; 1986; pages 946-948) Shelby Foote describes the manner in which General Lee reviewed the proposed terms of surrender as a form of a ritual on the part of Lee. In his eloquent manner of expression, Mr. Foote captured the moment for prosperity to relive. He stated that it was "no doubt in an effort to master his nerves" but a ritual in nature. The old general "took out his steel-rimmed spectacles, polished them very carefully with a handkerchief, crossed his legs, set the glasses deliberately astride his nose, and at last began to read. Nothing in his expression changed until he reached the closing sentences. Having read them he looked up at Grant and remarked in a warmer tone than he had used before: "This will have a happy effect on my army." When his adversary said that he would have a fair copy made for signing, "Unless you have some suggestions in regard to the form in which I have stated the term," Lee hesitated before replying. "There is one thing I would like to mention. The cavalrymen and artillerists own their own horses in our army. Its organization in this respect differs from that of the United States." Grant overlooked what he later called "this implication that we were two countries," but said flatly: "You will find that the terms as written do not allow this." Lee perused again the two sheets of yellow flimsy. He was asking a favor, and he did not enjoy the role of supplicant. "No," he admitted regretfully, "I see the terms do not allow it. That is clear." Then Grant relented. Perhaps recalling his own years of hardscrabble farming near St. Louis before the war-or Lincoln's remark at City Point, less than two weeks ago, that all he wanted, once the time came, was 'to get the men composing the Confederate armies back to their homes, at work on their farms or in their shops'-he relieved Lee of the humiliation of having to plead a modification of terms already generous.

"Well, the subject is quite new to me,' he mused, feeling his way as he spoke. 'Of course I did not know that any private soldiers owned their animals, but I think this will be the last battle of the war-I sincerely hope so-and that the surrender of this army will be followed soon by all the others, and I take it that most of the men in the ranks are small farmers, and as the country has been so raided by the two armies it is doubtful whether they will be able to put in a crop to carry themselves and their families through the next winter without the aid of the horses they are now riding, I will arrange it this way; I will not change the terms as now written, but I will instruct the officers I shall appoint to receive the paroles to let all the men who claim to own a horse or mule take the animals home with them to work their little farms." Lee's relief and appreciation were expressed in his response. "This will have the best possible effect upon the men," he said, "It will be very gratifying, and will do much toward conciliating our people." Grant had been generous with the terms of surrender and very respectful to the commanding officer that he so admired. The terms reached offered hope to the men of a fading army.

Prior to the actual 'signing' of the terms of surrender, General Forsyth could get a brief look at the Commander and Chief of the Confederate Army. General Forsyth was pressing against the door threshold to get a closer glimpse of his old adversary. He gave the following description of his impression of this ordeal. "As I did so (pressed against the opening of the doorway) General Lee stood before me. As he paused for a few seconds...I took my first and last look at the great Confederate chieftain...A clear, ruddy, complexion-just then suffused by a crimson flush, that rising from his neck overspread his face and even tinged his broad forehead, which, bronzed where it had been exposed to the weather, was clear and beautifully white where it had been shielded by his hat-deep brown eyes, a firm but well-shaped Roman nose."

"His Demeanor Was That of a Thoroughly Possessed Gentleman"

A Northern journalist was privileged to witness the scene and he reported his observations of the legend of the South. One can sense the admiration felt by this man as he described the general's demeanor. All that encountered him sensed that this man was cast from a greater mold.

"General Lee looked very much jaded and worn, but nevertheless presented the same magnificent physique for which he has always been noted. He was neatly dressed in gray cloth, without embroidery or any insignia of rank, except the three stars worn on the turned portion of his coat-collar. His cheeks were very much bronzed by exposure, but still shone ruddy underneath it all. He is growing quite bald, and wears one of the side locks of his hair thrown across the upper portion of his forehead, which is as white and fair as a woman's. He stands fully six feet one inch in height, and weighs something over two hundred pounds, without being burdened with a pound of superfluous flesh. During the whole interview he was retired and dignified to a degree bordering on taciturnity, but was free from all exhibition of temper or mortification. His demeanor was that of a thoroughly possessed gentleman who had a very disagreeable duty to perform, but was determined to get through it as well and as soon as he could." (Grey Fox: Robert E. Lee and the Civil War; Davis,

Burke; Wings Books, an imprint of Random House Value Publishing; New York; 1956; pages 411-422)

One of the most powerful descriptors of the character of Lee and the love possessed by his boys for the man comes at the lowest point in the general's life. He had just "signed" the terms of surrender at Appomattox and rose to shake hands with General Grant. He acknowledged the other officers in the room by bowing and carried his hat and gauntlets into the hallway. Colonel Marshall (the grandson of Chief Justice John Marshall) followed him silently. For a brief moment the weary general paused in the hallway as he gathered himself to step outside. A Union general by the name of Forsyth saw him in the hallway. He stated that Lee was turning red, "A deep crimson flush, that rising from his neck overspread his face and even tinged his broad forehead...Booted and spurred, still vigorous and erect, he stood bareheaded, looking out of the open doorway, sad-faced and weary."

As he placed his hat upon his gray head several Union officers recognized him and immediately jumped up and out of respect, saluted him. He reciprocated as he stopped at the top of the stairs and put on his gauntlets, gazing in the direction of his encamped boys that was so dear to his heart. He called for his orderly (Sergeant G. W. Tucker) and immediately he brought Traveller to the grief stricken general. At the bottom of the steps, Lee again paused with Colonel Marshall and Sgt. Tucker, being the only gray in a sea of blue. Remorsefully looking towards his boys that had followed him so faithfully he, "Thrice smote the palm of his left hand slowly with his right fist in an absent sort of way." He then gingerly fondled his beloved mount, "As the orderly was buckling the throat latch, the general reached up and drew the forelock out from under the brow band, parted and smoothed it, and then gently patted the gray charger's forehead in an absent-minded way, as one who loves horses, but whose thoughts are far away." The Civil War: A Narrative: Red River to Appomattox; Foote, Shelby; First Vintage Books Edition; Random House; New York; 1986; page 950)

Lee, "Swung himself slowly and wearily, but nevertheless firmly, into the saddle...as he did so there broke unguardedly from his lips a long, low, deep sigh, almost a groan in its intensity, while the flush on his neck seemed, if possible, to take on a still deeper hue." He waited for Colonel Marshall and Sergeant Tucker and the broken procession consisting of three gray clad men in an ocean of blue began meandering back to the hearts awaiting to be broken.

General Grant had just stepped from the McLean house and upon realizing that General Lee was departing, took off his hat. His soldiers followed suit. No one moved as the old general with his two faithful servants in gray made their way between the parted seas of blue. One of Grants officers turned to him and stated, "This will live in history." The Fading of the Grey was now a reality.

As Lee rode into the safety of his gray clad boys, they raised their hats but noted the look upon their general's face. "General, are we surrendered?" they inquired. With tears streaming down his face he said, "Men, we have fought the war together, and I have done the best I could for you. You will all be paroled and go to your homes." He could say no more as tears of sorrow filled his eyes and ran unabatedly down his battle weary face. Somehow he managed to move along and whispered one last goodbye.

George Mills, a Lieutenant of the 16th North Carolina remembered, "General Lee…took off his hat and made a short speech: 'Boys, I have done the best I could for you. Go home now, and if you make as good citizens as you have soldiers, you will do well, and I shall always be proud of you. Goodbye, and God bless you all.' He seemed so full that he could say no more.

General Longstreet offered his interpretation of the event that unfolded before his very eyes. "Those who could speak said goodbye, those who could not speak, and were near, passed their hands gently over the sides of Traveller. Lee had sufficient control to fix his eyes on a line between the ears of Traveller and look neither to right nor left until he reached a large white oak tree, where he dismounted to make his last headquarters, and finally talked a little." (Grey Fox: Robert E. Lee and the Civil War; Davis, Burke; Wings Books, an imprint of Random House Value Publishing; New York; 1956; page 426)

"And the Dreaded Deed was done"

The Confederacy had failed! Not because of the dream being unworthy but the reality of overwhelming resources on the part of 'those people' and their seemingly endless supply of manpower. With a stroke of a pen the dreams of a Southern Confederacy were dissolved and would rest in the havens of history forever. This poem began to take form as I was reading a description of General Grant versus General Lee. I witnessed the dignified appearance of royalty in Lee's persona versus the unrefined look of Grant as described by

Richard H. Dana: "A short, round-shouldered man, in a very tarnished major-general uniform.... There was nothing marked in his appearance. He had no gait, no station, no manner, rough, light brown whiskers, a bye eye, and rather a scrubby look withal.....I saw that the ordinary, scrubby-looking man, with a slightly seedy look, as if he was out of office and on half-pay, and nothing to do but hang round the entry of Willard's, cigar in mouth, had a clear blue eye, and a look of resolution, as if he could not be trifled with, and an entire indifference to the crowd about him. Straight nose too.... He gets over the ground queerly. He does not march, nor quite walk; but pitches along as if the next step would bring him on his nose. But his face looks firm and hard, and his eye is clear and resolute, and he is certainly natural, and clear of all appearance of self-consciousness. How war, how all great crises, bring us to the one-man power!" But there they were facing each other, both with the same resolve but of different opinions. The generosity of Grant at the surrender must be noted along with his order to his troops to desist with their celebration over the fall of the Army of Northern Virginia stating that, "The war is over, the rebels are our country men again." Grant was following in the footsteps of Lee's example and character by paying homage to the men that fought so gallantly for so long, as one American welcomed another American home.

The prose matured at the Wilderness, were both generals wearing the blue and gray faced off in a death struggle that would last from May of 64 until April of 65. Each determined to end it at once and each committed to the final volley. Til' the dreaded deed is done was my way of expressing my awe and admiration at those events that occurred within the perimeters of those eleven months and

338

recognition of those two leaders that demonstrated their greatness not only on the battlefield but also with their humanity and dignity; as the two former adversaries embrace each other as Americans once again.

Til The Dreaded Deed Is Done

The test of resolution
Would play upon the fields.
Both seeking a solution
But neither side would yield.

The Wilderness was calling
And Lee's boys were entrenched
Like snowflakes Yanks were falling
As the fighting commenced.

But Grant would be persistent
Where other men would stop.
And the more Lee resisted.
The more soldiers would drop.

But Grant just kept on coming;
Giving up two for one.
The sound of fife and drumming
Said the fighting wasn't done.

They fought around the Angle,
Courthouse and South Anna.
The blue and gray were mangled
In the name of Hosanna!

They formed a line at P'burg.
Lee feared it was too thin.
All whispered the rumored words
That the fighting would soon end.

But yet Grey Fox persisted

Til supply lines were snapped.
His army now consisted
Of men ready to collapse.

So in a borrowed dwelling
By April's daylight sun.
Signatures stopped the shelling.
The dreaded deed was done.

"In an Instant They Were About Him"

In Thomas N. Page's magnificent portrayal of that moment eternally captured in the prism of time, he states that there 'occurred one of the most notable scenes in the history of war.' The cheers for their beloved general entwined with sobs could be heard for miles, as a forlorn rebel yell echoed over the mountains and valleys of Old Virginia. (Robert E. Lee Man and Soldier; Page, Thomas Nelson; Charles Scribner's sons; New York; 1926; page 639)

"In an instant they were about him, bare-headed, with tear-wet faces; thronging him, kissing his hand, his boots, his saddle; weeping; cheering him amid their tears; shouting his name to the very skies." Never before or since has a commander captured the hearts of his men. Though some Northern papers reported that the sounds that were heard were those of "jubilation at the surrender"; it was not. It was the sound of unconditional love for a man that they all would have gladly surrendered their lives before they would surrender their leader. It was the sound of pride in who they were because of who he was. It was a sound celebrating the Christian character that Lee represented. It was not the sound of surrender but the echo of submission to the "Commander of their hearts."

"With Cheers and Sobs"

While resting at an apple orchard and gathering his composure, word of Lee's surrender spread like a wildfire. Upon returning to his pilgrimage, he was met by eleven thousand faithful soldiers lining the road on both sides: The Seas of Grey. Colonel Blackford, an eyewitness to the event, offered this portrayal of the moment. "As soon as he entered this avenue of these old soldiers, the flower of the army, the men who had struck to their duty through thick and thin in so many battles, wild heartfelt cheers arose which so touched General Lee that tears filled his eyes and trickled down his cheeks as he rode on his splendid charger, hat in hand, bowing his acknowledgments...Each group began in the same way, with cheers, and ended in the same way, with sobs, all along the route to his quarters. Grim, bearded men threw themselves on the ground, covered their faces with their hands and wept like children. Officers of all ranks made no attempt to conceal their feelings, but sat on the horses and cried aloud...A dirt-crusted soldier embodied the broken heart of the Confederacy when he reached out his arms and shouted, 'I love you, just as well as ever, General Lee!' while another later pleaded with the angel Gabriel to, 'Blow, Gabriel, blow! My God, let him blow, I am ready to die!" (Lee, The Last Years; Flood, Charles Bracelen; Houghton Mifflin Company; New York; 1981; page 12-18) (The Civil War: A Narrative: Red River to Appomattox; Foote, Shelby; First Vintage Books Edition; Random House; New York; 1986; page 951)

"They Raised Their Heads and Looked at Him with Swimming Eyes"

One of his engineers noted that, "He seemed to be in one of his savage moods and when these moods were on him it was safer to keep out of his way." Unfortunately, the union officers came to either bid him farewell or to steal a moment from history. In either case, it was a cool reception of respect and reflection. It was said that when visitors approached, "He would halt in his pacing, stand at attention, and glare at them with a look which few men but he could assume." The noted exception supposedly occurred when General Meade visited him. General Meade had served with General Lee during his service to the union army and both thought highly of one another. After a brief time of the customary gentlemen comments, General Lee noted that General Meade had not been so gray in his beard on their last encounter. Meade quickly reminded that great general that he had not but that it was Lee that had added to the turning of the gray prematurely. "What are you doing with all that gray in your beard?", Lee asked. "You have to answer for most of it," was General Meade's reply. Later both old friends rode off together and as they approached some Confederate soldiers who were cheering, Meade ordered his color to, "Unfurl the flag.' Immediately he was reprimanded from the crowd as a veteran dressed in butternut yelled, "Damn your old rag! We are cheering General Lee." Such was the love that endeared the hearts of Lee's boys to their general, as they were still willing to offer their lives if he simply speak the order.

Finally, the parade of curiosity seekers ended and he retreated to a position less demanding. It was by the white oak tree where he had slept the previous night. Approaching the ranks of the First Corps, General Longstreet later noted that, "The road was packed by standing troops as he

342

approached. The men with hats off, heads and hearts bowed down. As he passed they raised their heads and looked at him with swimming eyes. Those who could find voice said goodbye; those who could not speak, and were near, passed their hands gently over the sides of Traveller." The scene would be repeated on several occasions as every one offered their tribute to the man that personified the South and their cause. (The Civil War: A Narrative: Red River to Appomattox; Foote, Shelby; First Vintage Books Edition; Random House; New York; 1986; pages 951-953)

"I Fell Into Violent Weeping"

The once proud general who rode in awe of his men so gracefully in front of over eighty thousand soldiers was reduced to a rag tag following of an old wagon (with no canvas, only a blanket covering the contents), a captured ambulance (that had served as an office), approximately twenty horses that were in dire straits and a couple of other vehicles that were being slowly pulled by bone weary mounts. Accompanying him was his faithful officers Lt. Colonel Charles Marshall and Lt. Colonel Walter H. Taylor. Major Giles B. Cooke was riding in the ambulance due to the recent wounds he had sustained in defense of his country. Others included a few enlisted men and a few black servants. He had overtaken a few of Stonewall's boys and they marched behind him as well. He had been escorted by a Union patrol (ordered by General Grant to ensure his safety and was instructed to follow Lee's every desire) to within a few miles of Richmond at which time he turned to the Union officer and stated, "You see I am in my own country and among friends and do not need an escort. I am giving you unnecessary trouble, and now request you to withdraw your men and rejoin your command." He shook the young lieutenant's hand and with "tears in his eyes, wished me a safe return to my home."

As the old warrior's arcade slowly approached Richmond, he shuttered at the sight of destruction and devastation. The war had been at such a large price for his beloved state. Everywhere were strode wagons, houses shelled and shot, bridges that had been blown to bits, dead livestock, horses and mules. Smoke scarred remnants were a part of the landscape and destruction had wreaked havoc among the masses. The stench was appalling. Yet he rode on through the mud and depravation. He rode with dignity and grace, all the while carrying the burden of a defeated nation and a broken heart. A burden that he knew that he must endure to ease the suffering of his people. For by example he led. He must offer them hope through his example and teach his people how to survive the hand of the conquering horde that he simply called, "those people". For the south, would be changed forevermore by the conquest and he only knew too well what it took to survive from the old south to the new "reconstructed" one as envisioned by the conquerors. Hence the statement, "I'd rather die a thousand deaths."

It was pouring the rain as the knight of a thousand battles rode through Manchester. Weary to the bone but yet full of spirit he rode on towards his destiny. A local Baptist minister recognized Lee and wrote the following description of that moment. "His steed was bespattered with mud, and his head hung down as if worn by long traveling. The horseman himself sat his horse like a master; his face was ridged with self-respecting grief; his garments were worn in the service and stained with travel; his hat was slouched and spattered with mud…even in the fleeting moment of his passing by my gate, I was awed by his incomparable dignity. His majestic composure, his rectitude and his sorrow, were so wrought and blended into his visage and so beautiful and impressive to my eyes that I fell into violent weeping."

"And All the Masses Cried"

All along the gauntlet, Lee was overwhelmed with the sweet sentiments of the population. At one point, when people discovered who was approaching, "Little girls dashed into the road, half-hiding their faces with aprons, and presented him with bouquets of hyacinths and daffodils." Women appeared from their homes with offerings of food and lovingly smiled at their hero. It was too much for the old warrior to endure. He turned to Taylor and burst out, "Colonel, these people are kind-too kind. Their hearts are as full as when we began our campaigns in eighteen sixty-one. They do too much-more than they are able to do-for us."

Somewhere close to Richmond the General saw the familiar form of his six foot three inch son. The one that he lovingly called Rooney. Rooney who was wounded and while recuperating at his mother in laws home was captured. Rooney, the young man that had lost his two children due to illness and while he was imprisoned, his loving wife succumbed to death's call. Rooney that brave general, offering his support during his father's time of greatest need, rode slightly behind father. As word spread of the passing of the legend, all heeded the call. The streets were lined with those adoring well-wishers showing their love for the man that was in essence the Cause. Men cheered, men cried. Women stood on each side and waved their handkerchiefs as they wept. Recognizing this unparalleled fleeting moment in history, those occupational soldiers in blue raised their hats and held them in veneration "honoring the man they wished had ridden with them instead of against them." The kindly gentleman frequently recognized their devotion by raising his hat and nodding. The procession followed; some touching him, some silently marching behind him, some stroking the mud stained charger, running their fingers against his boots and gently allowing their fingers to brush his sword. Men grasped his hand, speaking their devotion and the unspoken groans of a broken nation could be heard as the Legend of Lee opened his wrought iron gate on Franklin (house number 707), climbed the eight stairs, took off his hat, bowed and submitted to his destiny. And all the masses cried. (Lee, The Last Years; Flood, Charles Bracelen; Houghton Mifflin Company; New York; 1981; pages 30-40)

And All the Masses Cried

Tho' all Virginia's behind him

346

He traveled on alone.
With victory denied him,
His heart let out a groan.

Two Colonels and a Major
Young Rooney at his side
No more war would they wager;
It was his last ebb tide.

With all Virginia weeping
He pressed on through the rain.
And even when he's sleeping,
He's tortured by the pain.

Tho' crowds gather around him,
He feels so all-alone.
War's destruction surrounds him
And chills him to the bone.

The crowd pressed ever nearer,
To touch this mortal man.
The message was made clearer
Upon shaking his hand.

He could not keep from thinking
Of all his men that died.
His dream of freedom's shrinking
And all the masses cried.

FAREWELL TO THE ARMY OF NORTHERN VIRGINIA

"Many Bosoms Heaved With Emotion"

The Reverend J. W. Jones offers insight into that historical moment. He tells of a Reverend Doctor A. C. Hopkins having lost his regiment at Spottsylvania Court House, who was attached to General Gordon's staff. The Reverend Doctor is known for his bravery and does not realize that the great general has yielded to the overwhelming forces that faced him. The following is an excerpt from Rev. Jones' dynamic book. (<u>Life & Letters of Gen. Robert Edward Lee</u>; Jones, W.J.; Sprinkle Publications; Harrisonburg, Virginia; 1986; @ by Neale Publishing Company in 1906; pages 375-376)

The Reverend Doctor Hopkins, "Eagerly asked if the enemy had sent in to surrender their force on that road, thinking that in flanking us Grant had pushed a part of his force too far. They had no dream that they were to be surrendered. But gradually the truth broke upon them, and great was their chagrin when these high-mettled victors in the last battle of the Army of Northern Virginia learned that they must 'Yield to overwhelming numbers and resources'-that after all their marches, battles, victories, hardships and sufferings that the cause that they loved better than life itself must succumb to superior force. Many bosoms heaved with emotion and 'something on the soldier's cheeks washed off the stains of powder.

"The next day General Lee published to the troops the following order, -the last which ever emanated from this peerless soldier, -which will go down the ages as a touching memento of that sad day at Appomattox court House."

"His Feelings towards His Men Were Strongly Expressed"

The following account is by Lieutenant Colonel Charles Marshall (General Lee's staff) to General Bradley T. Johnson regarding the writing of the surrender order. It was dated September 27, 1887. In his correspondence, he offers more insight into the actual writing of the famous document. Note that Marshall is credited with writing several of the orders given by Lee, which demonstrates the level of confidence that Lee possessed in Colonel Marshall (Battles and Leaders of the Civil War; Bradford, Ned; First Meridian Printing, Dec. 1989)

"General Lee's order to the Army of Northern Virginia at Appomattox Court House was written the day after the meeting at McLean's house, at which the terms of the surrender were agreed upon. That night the general sat with several of us at a fire in front of his tent, and after some conversation about the army, and the events of the day, in which his feelings toward his men were strongly expressed, he told me to prepare an order to the troops.

"The next day it was raining, and many persons were coming and going, so that I was unable to write without interruptions until about 10 o'clock, when General Lee, finding that the order had not been prepared, directed me to get into his ambulance, which stood near his tent, and placed an orderly to prevent any one from approaching me.

"I sat in the ambulance until I had written the order, the first draft of which (in pencil) contained an entire paragraph that was omitted by General Lee's direction. He made one or two verbal changes, and I then made a copy of the order as corrected, and gave it to one of the clerks in the adjutant-general's office to write in ink. I took the copy, when made by the clerk, to the general, who signed it, and other copies were then made for transmission to the corps commanders and the staff of the army. All these copies were signed by the general, and a good many persons sent other copies which they had made or procured, and obtained his signature. In this way many copies of the order had the general's signature, as if they were originals, some of which I have seen."

General Orders No. 9
"An Affectionate Farewell"

Appomattox Courthouse-April 10, 1865

"After four years of arduous service, marked by unsurpassed courage and fortitude, the Army of Northern Virginia has been compelled to yield to overwhelming numbers and resources. I need not tell the survivors of so many hard-fought battles who have remained steadfast to the last that I have consented to this result from no distrust of them; but feeling that valor and devotion could accomplish nothing that could compensate for the loss that would have attended the continuance of the contest, I determined to avoid the useless sacrifice of those whose past services have endeared them to their countryman.

"By the terms of the agreement, officers and men can return to their homes and remain until exchanged. You may take with you the satisfaction that proceeds from the consciousness of duty faithfully performed, and I earnestly pray that a merciful God will extend to you his blessing and protection.

"With an unceasing admiration of your constancy and devotion to your country, and a grateful remembrance of your kind and generous consideration of myself, I bid you all an affectionate farewell."

Report of General Robert E. Lee, C.S. Army, Commanding Army of Northern Virginia.

Surrender at Appomattox
Near Appomattox Courthouse, Va.,
April 12, 1865

His Excellency Jefferson Davis.

"Mr. President: It is with pain that I announce to Your Excellency the surrender of the Army of Northern Virginia. The operations which preceded this result will be reported in full. I will therefore only now state that, upon arriving at Amelia Court House on the morning of the 4th with the advance of the army, on the retreat from the lines in front of Richmond and Petersburg, and not finding the supplies ordered to be placed there, nearly twenty-four hours were lost in endeavoring to collect in the country subsistence for men and horses. This delay was fatal, and could not be retrieved. The troops, wearied by continual fighting and marching for several days and nights, obtained neither rest nor refreshment; and on moving, on the 5th, on the Richmond and Danville Railroad, I found at Jetersville the enemy's cavalry, and learned the approach of his infantry and the general advance of his army toward Burkeville. This deprived us of the use of the railroad, and rendered it impracticable to procure from Danville the supplies ordered to meet us at points of our march. Nothing could be obtained from the adjacent country. Our route to the Roanoke was therefore changed, and the march directed upon Farmville, where supplies were ordered from Lynchburg. The Change of route threw the troops over the roads pursed by the artillery and wagon trains west of the railroad, which impeded our advance and embarrassed our movements. On the morning of the 6th General Longstreet's corps reached Rice's Station, on the Lynchburg railroad. It was followed by the commands of Generals R.H. Anderson, Ewell, and Gordon, with orders to close upon it as fast as the progress of the trains would permit or as with orders to close upon it as fast as the progress of the trains would permit or as they could be directed on roads farther west. General Anderson, commanding Pickett and B.R. Johnson's divisions, became disconnected with Mahone's division, forming the rear of Longstreet. The Enemy's cavalry penetrated the line of march through the interval thus left and attacked the wagon train moving toward Farmville. This caused serious delay in the march of the center and rear of the column, and enabled the enemy to mass upon their flank. After successive attacks Anderson and Ewell's corps were captured or driven from their position. The latter general, with both of his division commanders, Kershaw and Custis Lee, and his brigadiers, were taken prisoners. Gordon, who all the morning, aided by General W.H.F. Lee's cavalry, had checked the advance of the enemy on the road from Amelia Springs and protected the trains, became exposed to his combined assaults, which he bravely resisted and twice repulsed; but the cavalry having been withdrawn to another part of the line of march, and the enemy massing heavily on his front and both flanks, renewed the attack about 6 p.m., and drove him from the field in much confusion.

"The army continued its march during the night, and every effort was made to reorganize the divisions which had been shattered by the day's operations; but the men being depressed by fatigue and hunger, many threw away their arms, while others followed the wagon trains and embarrassed their progress. On the morning of the 7th rations were issued to the troops as they passed Farmville, but the safety of the trains requiring their removal upon the approach of the enemy all could not be supplied. The army, reduced to two corps, under Longstreet and Gordon, moved steadily on the road to Appomattox Court-House; thence its march was ordered by Campbell Court-House, through Pittsylvania, toward Danville. The roads were wretched and the progress slow. By great efforts the head of the column reached Appomattox Court-House on the evening of the 8th, and the troops were halted for rest. The march was ordered to be resumed at 1 a.m. on the 9th. Fitz Lee, with the cavalry, supported by Gordon, was ordered to drive the enemy from his front, wheel to the left, and cover the passage of the trains; while Longstreet, who from Rice's Station had formed the rear guard, should close up and hold the position. Two battalions of artillery and the ammunition wagons were directed to accompany the army, the rest of the artillery and wagons to move toward Lynchburg. In the early part of the night the enemy attacked Walker's artillery train near Appomattox Station, on the Lynchburg railroad, and were repelled. Shortly afterward their cavalry dashed toward the Court-House, till halted by our line. During the night there were indications of a large force massing on our left and front. Fitz Lee was directed to ascertain its strength, and to suspend his advance till daylight if necessary. About 5 a.m. on the 9th, with Gordon on his left, he moved forward and opened the way. A heavy force of the enemy was discovered opposite Gordon's right, which, moving in the direction of the Appomattox Court-House, drove back the left of the cavalry and threatened to cut off Gordon from Longstreet, his cavalry at the same time threatening to envelop his left flank. Gordon withdrew across the Appomattox River, and the cavalry advanced on the Lynchburg road and became separated from the army.

"Learning the condition of affairs on the lines, where I had gone under the expectations of meeting General Grant to learn definitely the terms he proposed in a communication received from him on the 8th, in the event of the surrender of the army, I requested a suspension of hostilities until these terms could be arranged. In the interview which occurred with General Grant in compliance with my request, terms having been agreed on, I surrendered that portion of the Army of Northern Virginia which was on the field, with its arms, artillery, and wagon trains, the officers and men to be paroled, retaining their side arms and private effects. I deemed this course the best under all the circumstances by which we were surrounded. On the morning of the 9th, according to the reports of the ordnance officers, there were 7,892 organized infantry with arms, with an average of seventy-five rounds of ammunition per man. The artillery, though reduced to sixty-three pieces, with ninety-three rounds of ammunition, was sufficient. These comprised all the supplies of ordnance that could be relied on in the State of Virginia. I have no accurate report of the cavalry, but believe it did not exceed 2,100 effective men. The enemy were more than five times our numbers. If we could have forced our way one day longer it would have been at a great sacrifice of life, and at its end I did not see how a surrender could have been avoided. We had no subsistence for man or horse, and it could not be gathered in the country. The supplies ordered to Pamplin's Station from Lynchburg could not reach us, and the men, deprived of food and sleep for many days, were worn out and exhausted."

With great respect, your obedient servant,
R. E. LEE,
General.

"To Save Useless Effusion of Blood"

Upon returning from Appomattox to Richmond, Virginia, General Robert E. Lee penned his final letter to President Davis as the Supreme Commander of the Confederate Army. In his writing, he summated the hopelessness of continuing the struggle, the devastated countryside's inability to sustain an army and the need to begin rebuilding the south. The correspondence addressed his concerns over those (including the president) that wanted to continue the struggle on a guerilla war basis instead of being subjected to a formal surrender. The letter is dated April 20th, 1865. (The Wartime Papers of Robert E. Lee; Dowdey, Clifford and Manarin, Louis H.; De Capo Press; Commonwealth of Virginia; 1961; pages 938-939; #1006)

"Mr. President,

"The apprehensions I expressed during the winter, of the moral condition of the Army of Northern Virginia, have been realized. The operations which occurred while the troops were in the entrenchments in front of Richmond and

355

Petersburg were not marked by the boldness and decision which formerly characterized them. Except in particular instances, they were feeble, and a want of confidence seemed to possess officers and men. This condition, I think, was produced by the state of feeling in the country, and the communications received by the men from their homes, urging their return and the abandonment of the field. The movement of the enemy on the 30th March to Dinwiddie Court House was consequently not as strongly met as similar ones had been. Advantages were gained by him which discouraged the troops, so that on the morning of 2d April. When our lines between the Appomattox and Hatcher's Run were assaulted, the resistance was not effectual: several points were penetrated and large captures made. At the commencement of the withdrawal of the army from the lines on the night of the 2d, it began to disintegrate, and straggling from the ranks increased up to the surrender on the 9th. On that day, as previously reported, there were only seven thousand eight hundred and ninety-two (7,892) effective infantry. During the night, when the surrender became known, more than ten thousand men came in, as reported to me by the Chief Commissary of the Army. During the succeeding days stragglers continued to give themselves up, so that on the 12th April, according to the rolls of those paroled, twenty-six thousand and eighteen (26,018) officers and men had surrendered. Men who had left the ranks on the march, and crossed James River, returned and gave themselves up, and many have since come to Richmond and surrendered. I have given these details that Your Excellency might know the state of feeling which existed in the army, and judge of that in the country. From what I have seen and learned, I believe an army cannot be organized or supported in Virginia, and as far as I know the condition of affairs, the country east of the Mississippi is morally and physically unable to maintain the contest unaided with any hope of ultimate success. A partisan war may be continued, and hostilities protracted, causing individual suffering and the devastation of the country, but I see no prospect by that means of achieving a separate independence. It is for Your Excellency to decide, should you agree with me in opinion, what is proper to be done. To save useless effusion of blood, I would recommend measures be taken for suspension of hostilities and the restoration of peace. I am with great respect, yr obdt svt, R.E. Lee, Genl"

"Their Conduct Must Conform to the New Order of Things"

After the war, General Lee's correspondence with General Beauregard articulates his opinion on what needed to be done for the good of the country. An excerpt from the October 3, 1865 letter shows Lee as an advocate for change and a man seeking peace for all.

"After the surrender of the Southern armies in April the revolution in the opinions and feelings of the people seemed so complete, and the return of the Southern States into the union of all the States so inevitable, that it became in my opinion the duty of every citizen, the contest being virtually ended, to cease opposition, and place himself in a position to serve the country…True patriotism sometimes requires of men to act exactly contrary, at one period, to that which it does at another, and the motive which impels the desire to do right is precisely the same. The circumstances which govern their actions change; and their conduct must conform to the new order of things."

357

"I Am a Poor Genealogist"

On November 20, 1865, the newly appointed president of Washington College wrote a letter to a man that was persistent into the lineage of Lee. The old gray haired general relented when he was informed that the man had relatives that had fought in the Revolutionary War and that he had lost two of his nephews in the service to the southern cause.   The following letter was written in Lexington, Virginia and gives Robert E. Lee's own account of his ancestry. (<u>Life & Letters of Gen. Robert Edward Lee</u>;   Jones, W.J.;   Sprinkle Publications; Harrisonburg, Virginia; 1986; @ by Neale Publishing Company in 1906; pages 22-23)

"My Dear Sir: I received by the last mail your letter of the 13th inst., inquiring into my family history. I am a poor genealogist and my family records have been destroyed or are beyond my reach. But as you 'insist' on my furnishing the information asked for, and desire it for your 'own private use,' I will endeavor to give you a general account.

"I am the youngest son of Henry Lee of the Revolutionary War, who commanded Lee's Legion under General Greene in the Southern Department of the U. S., and was born at Stratford on the Potomac, Westmoreland County, Va., the 19th of January, 1807. My mother was Anne Hill Carter, daughter of Mr. Charles Carter, of Shirley on James River. My father was twice married, first to Miss Lee then to Miss Carter. 'Major Henry Lee' of the war of 1812, of whom you inquire, was the only son of the first marriage, and consequently my half brother. 'Charles Carter Lee,' of whom you also ask, and Sydney Smith Lee are my full brothers. I had two sisters, Mrs. Anne R. Marshall, and Mrs. C. Mildred Childe, neither of whom are living. The first

358

left one son, Colonel Louis H. Marshall of the U. S. Army, and the second a son and daughter who reside in Europe. 'Gen. Fitzhugh Lee' is the eldest son of my second brother, Sydney Smith Lee, who has five other sons. My eldest brother, Charles Carter Lee, has also six children, the oldest of whom, George, is about 18 years old. I have three sons, Custis, Wm. H. Fitzhugh, and Robert, and three daughters, Mary, Agnes, and Mildred. My father died in 1818; my mother in 1829. My grandfather was Henry Lee of Strafford County; my great-grandfather, Henry Lee, son of Richard Lee, who first came from England to Americas and from whom the Southern Lees are descended. Richard Henry, Arthur, and Francis Lightfoot Lee, of the Revolution, were cousins of my father. 'John Fitzgerald Lee,' whom you mention, is the grandson of Richard Henry Lee.

"I believe I have answered all your questions and must now express the pleasure I feel in learning that your ancestors were fellow-soldiers with mine in the great war of the Revolution. This hereditary bond of amity has caused me, at the risk of being tedious, to make to you the foregoing family narrative. I am also led by the same and other feeling to grieve with you at the death of your brave nephews who fell in the recent war. May their loss be sanctified to you and to your country.-+ Very respectfully, Yr. Obdt. Svt., R. E. Lee"

"The Desire to Do Right"

During his early tenure as president of Washington College President Lee was bombarded with letters. He was constantly writing. Some of the letters were heart wrenching. They asked of the last moments of their loved ones. They asked Lee for assurance to advice on what to do now that the war

359

was a part of history. One of his Lieutenants, General Beauregard wrote him asking for his advice. The letter became legendary.

"I am glad to see no indication in your letter of an intention to leave the country. I think the south requires the aid of her sons now more than at any period in her history. As you ask my purpose, I will state that I have no thought of abandoning her unless compelled to do so...I need not tell you that true patriotism sometimes requires of men to act exactly contrary, at one period, to that which it does at another, and the motive which impels them-the desire to do the right-is precisely the same. The circumstances that govern their actions, change, and their conduct must conform to the new order of things. History is full of illustrations of this: Washington himself is an example of this. At one time he fought in the service of the King of Great Britain; at another he fought with the French at Yorktown, under the orders of the continental congress of America, against him. He has not been branded by the world with reproach for this, but his course has been applauded." (Lee, The Last Years; Flood, Charles Bracelen; Houghton Mifflin Company; New York; 1981; page 102)

"My Prayers are Always Offered for Your Prosperity"

Lee's Post-war correspondence to Longstreet, dated January 19, 1866 demonstrates his devotion to his old warhorse and Christian demeanor.

"You must remember me very kindly to Mrs. Longstreet and all your children. I have not had an opportunity yet to return the compliment she paid me. I had, while in Richmond, a great many inquiries after you, and learned that you intended commencing business in New Orleans. If you become as good a merchant as you were a soldier, I shall be content. No one will then excel you, and no one can wish you more success and more happiness than I. My interest and affection for you will never cease, and my prayers are always offered for your prosperity."

"I Beg to Express the Gratitude I Have Felt All My Life"

While President of Washington College, Lee invited his old grammar teacher, Mr. W.B. Leary to come and be a guest of the family in Lexington, Virginia. Upon visiting Lee expressed his appreciation, giving him much credit and respect as the gentleman that had been instrumental in his formal and well as character education. The following letter dated December 15, 1866, from Lexington, Virginia, provides the reader with a glimpse of one of the great men of all times paying tribute to a man who was his mentor in life and helped mold him into his personality. It has been said that, "A teacher touches eternity, he never knows where his influence will end." With Lee his teacher held a place of honor within his heart and that gift was acknowledged with the deepest of heartfelt gratitude. (Life & Letters of Gen. Robert Edward Lee; Jones, W.J.; Sprinkle Publications; Harrisonburg, Virginia; 1986; @ by Neale Publishing Company in 1906; page 24)

"My Dear Sir: Your visit has recalled to me years long since passed when I was under your tuition, and received daily your instruction. In parting from you, I beg to express the gratitude I have felt all my life for the affectionate fidelity which characterized your teaching and conduct towards me.

"I pray that the evening of your days may be blessed with peace and tranquility, and that a merciful God may guide and protect you to the end.

"Should any of my friends, wherever your lot may be cast, desire to know your qualifications as a teacher, I hope you will refer them to me: for of them I can speak knowingly and from experience. Wishing you health, happiness, and prosperity, I am, Affectionately, your friend, R.E. Lee"

"Tell Her I Bear Toward Her the Love I Feel for You"

Lee also kept in contact via correspondence with his former adjutant, William Taylor. In one letter, he talks of Taylor's family members and inquiries of his wife. (Lee's Adjutant: The Wartime Letters of Colonel Walter Herron Taylor; Taylor, Walter H.; Edited by Tower, R. Lockwood; University of South Carolina Press; 1995; pages 30)

"Remember me most kindly to your mother, brothers and sisters. Though you would never show me your wife, tell her I bear toward her the love I feel for you." In another letter, Lee states, "You will have to bring Mrs. Taylor and the babies to Lexington to see us. I fear I shall never be able to get to Norfolk to see you." In 1870 he did visit Norfolk and was given a royal welcome and tour by his ever-faithful Colonel Taylor.

"A Continuous and Speedy Exchange of Prisoners of War"

General Lee penned the following letter while he was at Lexington, Virginia. It was sent to Doctor Charles Carter, his cousin. The letter addressed his concerns regarding rumors of the mistreatment of prisoners held by the Confederacy. He demonstrates his commitment to humane treatment and a speedy exchange of all soldiers held within the confines of the fences. It is dated April 17, 1867.

"DR. CHARLES CARTER,
"No. 1632 Walnut Street, Philadelphia, Pa.:

"My Dear Dr. Carter - I have received your letter of the 9th inst., inclosing one to you from Mr. J. Francis Fisher, in relation to certain information which he had received from Bishop Wilmer. My respect for Mr. Fisher's wishes would induce me to reply fully to all his questions, but I have not time to do so satisfactorily; and, for reasons which I am sure you both will appreciate, I have a great repugnance to being brought before the public in any manner. Sufficient information has been officially published, I think, to show that whatever sufferings the Federal prisoners at the South underwent, were incident to their position as prisoners, and produced by the destitute condition of the country, arising from the operations of war. The laws of the Confederate Congress and the orders of the War Department directed that the ration furnished prisoners of war should be the same in quantity and quality as those furnished enlisted men in the army of the Confederacy, and that the hospitals for prisoners should be placed on the same footing as other Confederate States hospitals in all respects. It was the desire of the Confederate authorities to effect a continuous and speedy exchange of prisoners of war; for it was their true policy to do so, as their retention was not only a calamity to them, but a heavy expenditure of their scanty means of subsistence, and a privation of the services of a veteran army. Mr. Fisher or Bishop Wilmer has confounded my offers for the exchange of prisoners with those made by Mr. Ould, the Commissioner of the Confederate States. It was he that offered, when all hopes of effecting the exchange had ceased, to deliver all the Federal sick and wounded, the amount of fifteen thousand, without an equivalent, provided transportation was furnished. Previously to this, I think, I offered to General Grant to send into his lines all the prisoners within my department, which then embraced Virginia and North Carolina, provided he would return me man for man; and when I informed the Confederate authorities of my proposition, I was told that, if it was accepted, they would place all the prisoners at the South at my disposal. I offered subsequently, I think to the committee of the United States Sanitary Commission, who visited Petersburg for the purpose of ameliorating the condition of their prisoners, to do the same. But my proposition was not accepted. Dr. Joseph Jones has recently published a pamphlet termed "Researches upon Spurious Vaccination," etc., issued from the University Medical Press, Nashville, Tenn., in which he treats of certain diseases of the Federal prisoners at Andersonville and their causes, which I think would be interesting to you as a medical man, and would furnish Mr. Fisher with some of the information he desires. And now I wish you to understand that what I have written is for your personal information and not for publication, and to send as an expression of thanks to Mr. Fisher for his kind efforts to relieve the sufferings of the Southern people.

"I am very much obliged to you for the prayers you offered for us in the days of trouble. Those days are still prolonged, and we earnestly look for aid to our merciful God. Should I have any use for the file of papers you kindly offer me I will let you know.

"All my family united with me in kind regards to your wife and children. And I am, very truly, your cousin, R. E. LEE

"I Fear You Will Fall in Love with Celibacy"

In a letter dated August 5, 1867, Lee speaks very frankly as a concerned father over the single status of Rob. He begins by the usual niceties of writing, talks about the harvest, about missing all his children around the house and then begins by talking of his son building a house, as stated in the following quotation.

"...I think you had better also begin to make arrangements to build yourself a house. If you can do nothing more than prepare a site, lay out a garden, orchard, etc., and get a small house partly finished, so as to inhabit it, it will add to your comfort and health. I can help you in that too. Think about it. Then, too, you must get a nice wife. I do not like you being so lonely. I fear you will fall in love with celibacy. I have heard some very pleasing reports of Fitzhugh. I hope that his desires, if beneficial to his happiness, may be crowned with success. I saw the lady when I was in Petersburg, and was much pleased with her." (Recollections and Letters of General Robert E. Lee; Lee, Robert E. Lee Jr.; Garden City Publishing Company; Garden City, New York; 1904)

"I Can Say Nothing to Mitigate Your Grief"

On March 19, 1868, President Lee wrote a letter to the father of a student that while attending Washington College had drowned. Apparently two boys had been long time friends and were enjoying the dangers and temptations of youth while throwing caution to the wind. Lee, the man who had witnessed the death of so many, found the time to write a very vivid letter to the family of one of the young men. The letter shows his genuine empathy for the bereaved family as he offers his condolences on behalf of himself and the entire college community. (<u>Recollections and Letters of General Robert E. Lee</u>; Lee, Robert E. Lee Jr.; Garden City Publishing Company; Garden City, New York; 1904)

"Mr. Dear Sir: Before this you have learned the affecting death of your son. I can say nothing to mitigate your grief or to relieve your sorrow; but if the sincere sympathy of his comrades and friends and of the entire community can bring you any consolation, I can assure you that you possess it in its fullest extent. When one, in the pureness and freshness of youth, before having been contaminated by sin or afflicted by misery, is called to the presence of his Merciful Creator, it must be solely for his good. As difficult as this may be for you not to recognize, I hope you will keep it constantly in your memory and take it to your comfort; and I pray that He who in His wise Providence has permitted this crushing sorrow may sanctify it to the happiness of all. Your son and his friend, Mr. Birely, often passed their leisure hours in rowing on the river, and, on last Saturday afternoon, the 4th inst., attempted what they had more than once been cautioned against-to approach the foot of the dam, at the public bridge. Unfortunately, their boat was caught by the return-current, was struck by falling water, and was immediately upset. Their perilous position was at once seen from the shore, and aid was hurried to their relief, but before it could reach them both had perished. Efforts to restore your son's life, though long continued, were unavailing. Mr. Birely's body was not found until the next morning. Their remains were, yesterday, Sunday, conveyed to the Episcopal church in this city, where the sacred ceremony for the dead were performed, by the Reverend Dr. Pendleton, who nineteen years ago, at the far-off home of their infancy, placed upon them their baptismal vows. After the service a long procession of the professors and students of the college, citizens of Lexington accompanied their bodies to the packet-boat for Lynchburg, where they were placed in charge of Messrs. Wheeler & Baker to convey them to Frederick City. With great regard and sincere sympathy, I am, Most respectfully, R. E. Lee"

"A Load of Sorrow was lifted"

Prior to the beginning of the 1867-1868 school year, Lee took a long overdue vacation. He visited several areas and was always received with open arms and grateful hearts. During his visit to Petersburg (a place that he had not visited since the siege) he discovered a sweet peace that he had not felt for the longest time. He wrote his son Rooney expressing,

"When I saw the cheerfulness with which the people were working to restore their condition, and witnessed the comforts with which they were surrounded, a load of sorrow which had been pressing upon me for years was lifted from my heart." (Lee; Freeman, Douglas Southall; Touchstone Book; Simon & Schuster; New York; 1961, 1991; page 544)

"She is Too Weak to Speak"

During 1868 Robert E. Lee was taking his family to the Warm Springs Resort (approximately forty miles from Lexington), when his youngest daughter became desperately ill. It was the dreaded Typhoid Fever that had taken his darling little Annie Carter Lee only a few summers ago. He was determined not to let this villain take the prize of his heart. He placed a cot next to her bed and tended to her every bidding. During those dark hours as his precious daughter lay in and out of delirium, Lee wiped the sweat from her brow and lovingly held her hand that had become a family tradition of affectionately touching one another (Mildred later held Lee's hand whenever he would take his afternoon nap and also held it tightly as he slipped into oblivion). During those tense moments in which Mildred was between two worlds hesitating, Lee wrote his son Rooney a letter. "I am writing in Mildred's room, who is very grateful for your interest in her behalf. She is too weak to speak." She later recovered much to the delight of a devoted father. The bond between them would last in legends throughout generations.

"Mingling My Sorrow for a Brief Season"

While Lee was with his wife at the Rockbridge Baths he received the news of the sudden death of his brother Smith. Robert and Smith were very close and the news shook him to the core. He immediately went to his brother's family. He arrived too late for the funeral but a letter to his wife dated July 25, 1869, attests to the love he possessed for Smith. In the correspondence, he talks of his own looming fate and the great promise of being reunited again in a land of milk and honey. (Recollections and Letters of General Robert E. Lee; Lee, Robert E. Lee Jr.; Garden City Publishing Company; Garden City, New York; 1904)

"My Dear Mary: I arrived here last evening too late to attend the burial of my dear brother, an account of which I have clipped from the Alexandria Gazette and inclose to you. I wish you would preserve it. Fitz and Mary went up to Ravensworth the evening of the funeral services, Friday, 23rd so that I have not seen them, but my nephew Smith is here, and from him I have learned all the particulars. The attack of his father was short, and his death apparently unexpected until a short time before it occurred. Mary was present, and I hope of some comfort to her uncle and assistance to her aunt. Fitz came here the afternoon of his father's death, Thursday, 22nd, made all arrangements for the funeral, went out to Ravensworth to announce the intelligence to our aunt. He carried down, Friday morning, on the steamer, Mrs. Cooper and Jennie, to stay with his mother, and returned that afternoon with his father's remains, which were committed to earth as you will see described.

"John returned the next morning, yesterday, in the mail-boat, to his mother, with whom Dan stayed. Robert arrived this morning and has gone to Ravensworth to announce my arrival. I shall remain here until I see or hear from Fitz, for, as you will see by the Gazette's account, the last resting place of the body has not been determined upon. Fitz, I understand, wishes it interred at Hollywood, Richmond; Nannie at the cemetery here where her father, mother, and daughter are buried; and Mrs. Fitzhugh at Ravensworth. I think Nannie's wishes should be consulted. I shall probably leave today or tomorrow, and, after seeing all that remains to us of our dear brother deposited in its last earthly home, and mingling my sorrow for a brief season with that of his dear wife and children, I shall return to you. Please send the letter after perusal to Agnes and Mildred, as I shall be unable to write to them. I am staying at the Mansion House. Our Aunt Maria did not come down to the funeral

369

services, prevented, I fear, by her rheumatic attack. May God bless us all and preserve us for the time when we, too, must part, the one from the other, which is not close at hand, and may we all meet again at the foot-stool of our merciful God, to be joined by His eternal love never more to separate.

Most truly and affectionately, R.E. Lee"

"I Have a Wretched Cold"

Some of the letters documents written by others indicated that Lee was a very sick man. In October of 69 he apparently had an attack accompanied by muscular pain on the back and the right side, which later extended to his arms. (Medical Histories of Confederate Generals; Welsh, Jack D.; Kent State University Press; Kent, Ohio, 1995; page 297). Lee was aware of his infirmaries and wrote to his beloved son Rooney of his weakened state. He talked of Traveller and his own personal lack of strength to ride him for any duration of time without being bone weary. But the letter reveals that he still had a keen sense of humor and was in good spirits despite his ailment. The letter is dated December 2, 1869.

"I have had a wretched cold. The effects of which have not left me, but I am better. The doctors still have me in hand, but I fear can do no good...Traveller's trot is harder to me than it used to be and fatigues me. We are all as usual-the women of the family very fierce and the men very mild."

"My Years of Labor are Nearly Over"

In the year of 1870, those close to Lee noted a steady decline in his health. He was also aware and in March after receiving an invitation to manage an association for the development of trade in Alexandria, Lee wrote a letter declining due to the following reasons:

"My health has been so feeble this winter that I am only waiting to see the effect of the opening spring before relinquishing my present position. I am admonished by my feelings that my years of labor are nearly over." Acting out of genuine concern and alarm for his declining physical state, the college staff met to discuss ways of addressing their concerns to their president. Three of his former soldiers (Johnston, Whit and Allan) were chosen to approach him to beseech him to take a long overdue vacation. Upon seeing the man, Johnston noted that, "The General was not looking well." After the usual curiosities that are afforded a man of his stature and his reciprocation of the respect, a letter was handed to him begging him to consider a vacation. With tears in his eyes, he spoke of his wish to have a permanent home for his invalid wife, his ailments, his age and his desire to farm. His final comment brought an air of sadness amongst the delegation. "He also said that he felt he might at any moment die." The three former soldiers, now professors still under guidance of their beloved commander, said their ado's and walked reflectively back to their homes believing that Lee would leave the college and indeed may live up to his prophecy. It was a dark night that foreshadowed the following days of those whom loved him.

"I Have Always Promised Myself to Go"

In March of 1870, Lee finally accepted the advice of his family, Doctors, and constituents. He was going to take a brief vacation in order to regain his health. He had the perfect destination in mind. It was near the White Sulphur Springs, in Warren County, North Carolina. This was the permanent resting place of his lovely little Annie that had died during the war of typhoid fever. Speaking to Rooney he stated, "I have always promised myself to go {there} and I think, if I am to accomplish it, I have no time to lose." His daughter Agnes accompanied him on the trip. The father and daughter had arrived that evening and were waiting at the depot while trying to figure out their next move when a former veteran who was waiting for his sister to arrive spotted them. After he offered his hospitality in an almost reverence fashion, they stayed at the home of Will White. The next morning, Willie White had a buggy harnessed and ready for Lee and Agnes to go to the cemetery to visit Annie's grave. Will's wife had picked some white hyacinths and handed them to Agnes. As they traveled down the road, thoughts of Annie must have filled their hearts. "The purest and the best" was Lee's favorite expression when speaking of his daughter. There are no photographs of Annie, maybe due to a youthful accident that left her eye badly scarred. But his child's loving nature and Christian spirit must have been felt as they drew ever nearer to their beloved Annie. Around a bend and there was the cemetery.

"Who Never Gave Me Aught but Pleasure"

Lee must have reflected upon the invitation that he received from the citizens of Warren County to attend the dedication of the gravesite after the end of the war. His reply was very moving. "I have always cherished the intention of visiting the tomb of her who never gave me aught but pleasure...Though absent in person, my heart will be with you, and my sorrow and devotions will be mingled with yours...I inclose, according to your request, the date of my daughter's birth and the inscription proposed for the monument over her tomb. The later are the last lines of the hymn which she asked for just before her death." The inscription cut in stone reads, 'Annie C. Lee, daughter of General R.E. Lee and Mary C. Lee'— on opposite Born at Arlington, June 18, 1839 and died at White Sulphur Springs, Warren County, North Carolina, Oct. 20, 1862.' The hymn verse simply read, 'Whom heaven adores and earth obeys.' (Recollections and Letters of General Robert E. Lee; Lee, Robert E. Lee Jr.; Garden City Publishing Company; Garden City, New York; 1904)

Getting out of the buggy the Lee's began searching for their love and the memorial that had been placed by the local citizens. And indeed, the fair citizens had remembered the Lee family and his child. The poor country folk of North Carolina, that brave state that offered so much for the cause in which they believe; those wondrous people had taken it upon themselves and had placed a twelve-foot memorial honoring the daughter of Robert E. Lee. The General was overcome with tears of grief and gratitude. He left that hallowed ground satisfied in the knowledge that they would soon be united. This would be the only visit Lee would make to his daughter's burial place. But it would suffice and the visit gratified his soul. Anna's remains would later be exhumed and taken to Washington and Lee College to be reunited with her family in the basement sepulchers of Lee's Chapel.

"Glad to do Him Honor"

While on what turned out to be his farewell tour of his beloved south, word spread like a wildfire of his pending arrivals and the multitudes dropped what they were doing to line the railroad stations just to get a glimpse of the legend. Charleston was no exception. They planned a grand parade in his honor. The Charleston Courier later stated that: (<u>Personal Reminiscences, Anecdotes, and Letters of General Robert E. Lee</u>; Jones, J. William; Appleton; New York; 1875; pages 223-224)

"Old and young, the gray beards and sages of the country, the noble, pure, honorable, poor and wealthy, with hardly an exception, were present, and glad to do him honor. Stately dames of the old school, grandmothers of seventy, and a long train of granddaughters, all flocked around the noble old chief, glad of a smile, of a shake of the hand, and happy was the girl of twelve, or fourteen, who carried away on her lips the parting kiss of the grand old soldier."

"He is Mighty like His Pictures"

After visiting for a while the gravesite of Annie, he traveled by rail toward Savannah. At Warren Plains, four words that electrified the masses were sent ahead to his next destination, "General Lee is aboard." The waiting crowds were shouting Lee's name, throwing their hats up into the air as they offered the old rebel yell in tribute, and ladies dressed in their Sunday best to see the idol of the south. At each stop the crowds grew, looking for the man that meant so much to them. Savannah

374

provided the largest crowd and the biggest reception for their hero. Jacksonville, Florida heard the roars of the people as Lee approached and a great reception was held. But within the confines of a place known as Palatka, the greatest tribute of all was given. There were no marching bands, no dignitaries, and no politicians wanting by association to make a mark. Here in awe and honor, the crowd that came to see their hero reverently uncovered their heads, as they looked upon each other in total silence. In a letter to her mother Agnes spoke about the reception that her father received. "Crowds came...wounded soldiers, servants, and workingmen even. The sweetest little children-namesakes-dressed to their eyes, with bouquets of japonica-or tiny cards in their little fat hands-with their names." In another correspondence, it was stated that, "Namesakes appeared on the way, of all sizes. Old ladies stretched their heads into the window at way-stations and then drew back and said, 'He is mighty like his pictures'." (Lee; Freeman, Douglas Southall; Touchstone Book; Simon & Schuster; New York; 1961, 1991; pages 567-571)

"The Pain is Ever Present"

While visiting the South for the last time, Lee's health problems continued. Although he complained of rheumatism and a heart cold, most scholars concur that he probably was stricken with angina pectoris. This shy man of bold deeds possessed a sick heart that slowly drained him of his essence. While in Savannah, Georgia, Lee took time to correspond. One of the individuals that he wrote was Colonel William Preston Johnston. The letter is dated April 21, 1870.

"My Dear Colonel, I am much obliged to you for your kind letter. I recd a telegram from the Proprietor of the Galt House Louisville, which I answered, stating that it would be out of my power to return to that city. I presume that will be sufficient, but should you think otherwise please give him my thanks etc - I wish the same information could reach the other places, as our kind of people seem to think that I am running loose or have a roving commission to traverse the country -I feel benefited by my visit to the South; am stronger & have less rheumatic pains, though the pain in my chest is ever present when I make any exertion & I still have a cough though it is not troublesome.

"I suppose that I have derived all the advantages I can receive from my visit to Savannah, & shall therefore on Monday next, 25t Inst: commence my journey homewards - Should nothing prevent, I will stop at Charleston & other points for rest, & shall have to be some days in Richmond, as the Physicians there wish to rexamine & consult over my case. I will not therefore reach Lexington before the 10t or 15t of May, when I hope the cold weather will have left the mountains -Please present my kindest regards to all the members of the Faculty & other friends - Agnes joins me in remembrances to Mrs. Johnston & your family & in best wishes for yourself.

"Tell Col: Allan I have recd his letter but may not answer it till I return - I am glad to hear that all are doing well at the College - I hope that it may continue -With great regard, very truly yours, R E Lee"

Robert E. Lee also wrote to his brother about his condition expressing his pain in his chest as being "ever present' and that he became fatigued whenever he attempted to walk. It was a 'coldness of heart' that left him drained and tired. Towards the last, his step was humbled as he walked with a slower gait. But he complained not to others but glorified his Maker for all that he had been given. He was a man destined to deny himself while in service to a higher calling.

"I feel better, am stronger and my rheumatism pains have diminished, but the pain in my chest, along the heart bone is ever present when I walk or make any exertion." (Lee Papers; Lee to Charles Carter Lee; Washington and Lee College; April 18, 1870)

"It is the Last Tribute of Respect That I Shall Ever be Able to Pay"

During his 1870 trip to reacquire his fleeting health, Lee visited Cumberland Island where his father was buried. Here he and Agnes had a moment to pay homage to Lee's father who is buried upon that island. The scene can only be imagined as the son stepped upon the sacred ground in which his father lay. Lee reported to his brother Carter that,

"Agnes strewed it with beautiful fresh flowers-I presume it is the last tribute of respect that I shall ever be able to pay it." Lee never returned to that location.

"There was a Great Fund of Amusement and Information in it, if it Could be Extracted"

In January of 1870, the ailing General Lee answered a letter that the family had received from Mildred, the one affectionately called Life. In it one readily sees that Lee's sense of humor was intact and that he delighted in playfully chastising her for her hurried penmanship. His wit is quite evident.

"My Precious Life,

"I received yesterday your letter of the 4th. We held a family counsel over it. It was passed from eager hand to hand, and attracted wondering eyes and mysterious looks. It produced few words, but a deal of thinking, and the conclusion arrived at, I believe unanimously was that there was a great fund of amusement and information in it, if it could be extracted. I have therefore, determined to put it carefully away till your return, then seize a leisure day and get you to interpret it. Your mother's commentary, in a suppressed soliloquy, was that you had succeeded in writing a wretched hand. Agnes thought it would keep this cold weather-her thought running on jellies and oysters in the storeroom. But I, indignant at such aspersions upon your accomplishments, retained your epistle and read in an elevated tone an interesting narrative of travels in sundry countries, describing gorgeous scenery, hair-breath events by flood and field, not a work of which, they declared, was in your letter. Your return I hope will prove the correctness of my version of your annals."

"The Ailing General"

According to D. Savage's book Lee had suffered heart problems: During the five months of his retreat from Pennsylvania, General Lee suffered a series of three heart "attacks". On September 20th, the chest and back pains were so severe that he was confined to an ambulance until October 10. A third coronary seizure on October 31, 1863, laid him in his ambulance until November 5, 1863. (The Court Martial of Robert E. Lee: a Novel; Savage,

Douglas; Warner Brothers). It is well documented that General Lee contracted a severe sore throat during the war and a result of that was rheumatic inflammation of the sac surrounding the heart. In October of 1869, the attack flared again resulting in rheumatism of the back, right side, both arms and probably a weakened heart due to the stress and strain of the war. The ultimate cost on his body was fatigue, weariness and depression leading to an earlier demise. (<u>Recollections and Letters of General Robert E. Lee</u>; Lee, Robert E. Lee Jr.; Garden City Publishing Company; Garden City, New York; 1904)

THE FINAL CURTAIN IS DRAWN

(General Lee Prior to His Death)

"Strike the Tent and He Spoke No More"

One of the most gripping descriptions of the death of General Lee comes from the written genius of Douglas Southall Freeman. In this fielder's mind Mr. Freeman captured the essence of the event better than any writer to date. The following excerpt is from his masterpiece.

"In Lexington apprehension battled with hope. The doctors remained confident, and Mrs. Lee talked of the time "when Robert gets well," but in her heart she was haunted by the look that had come into his eyes when he had tried vainly to answer her at the supper table and then had sat upright. "I saw he had taken leave of earth," she afterwards wrote. The superstitious whispered that his end was at hand because his picture had fallen down from the wall of his house; and when a flashing aurora lighted the sky for several nights some saw in it a beckoning hand. One Lexington woman took down a copy of *The Lays of the Scottish Cavaliers* and pointed significantly to this quatrain:

"All night long the northern streamers
Shot across the trembling sky:
Fearful lights, that never beckon
Save when kings or heroes die."

"A week passed, and General Lee's improvement, though slight, was apparent and seemed to be progressive. On October 8, 1870, a Richmond paper quoted his physicians as saying he would soon be out again. He still talked very little, and once, when Agnes started to give him his medicine, he said: "It is no use." But she prevailed on him to take it. Conscious of nearly all that went on around him, he was manifestly glad to have the members of the family come in to see him. He did not smile during his whole illness, but he always met greetings of his wife and children with the pressure of his hand. On the morning of October 10, Doctor Madison thought his patient was mending. "How do you feel today, General?" he inquired. "I . . . feel . . . better," said Lee, slowly but distinctly. "You must make haste and get well; Traveller has been standing so long in the stable that he needs exercise."

"The General shook his head deliberately and closed his eyes again. It had been much the same when Custis Lee had spoken of his recovery. Lee had then moved his head from side to side and had pointed upward. That afternoon, without warning, his pulse began to flutter. His breathing became hurried. Exhaustion was apparent. The evening brought no improvement. At midnight he had a chill, and his condition was so serious that Doctor Barton had to warn the family. One of his

381

professors, son of his old comrade, Sidney Johnston, sat by him that night, fully appreciative of the life that was ending. "Never," he recorded, "was more beautifully displayed how a long and severe education of mind and character enables the soul to pass with equal step through this supreme ordeal; never did the habits and qualities of a lifetime, solemnly gathered into a few last sad hours, more grandly maintain themselves amid the gloom and shadow of approaching death. The reticence, the self-contained composure, the obedience to proper authority, the magnanimity and Christian meekness that marked all his actions, preserved their sway, in spite of the inroads of disease, and the creeping lethargy that weighed down his faculties. As the old hero lay in the darkened room, or with the lamp and hearth fire casting shadows upon his calm, noble front, all the massive grandeur of his form, and face, and brow remained; and death seemed to lose its terrors, and to borrow a grace and dignity in sublime keeping with the life that was ebbing away. The great mind sank to its last repose, almost with the equal poise of health."

"Lee refused medicine and nourishment the next day, even from his daughter, but despite the confusion of his mind, self-discipline still ruled, and when either of his doctors put physic to his mouth he would swallow it. During the morning he lapsed into a half-delirium of dreams and memories."...His mind wandered to those dreadful battlefields." He muttered unintelligible words — prayers, perhaps, or orders to his men. Sometimes his voice was distinct. "Tell Hill he *must* come up," he said, so plainly and emphatically that all who sat in the death-chamber understood him.

"His symptoms now were aggravated. Mrs. Lee, in her rolling-chair, took her place by his bed for the last vigil and held his moist hand. His pulse continued weak and feeble; his breathing was worse. By the end of the day the physicians admitted that the fight was lost: the General was dying. They could only wait, not daring to hope, as he lay there motionless, save for the rapid rise and fall of his chest. His eyes were closed. When he talked in his delirium he did not thresh about. The words, though now mingled past unravelling, were quietly spoken. The darkened skies danced a sad refrain.

"At last, on October 12, daylight came. The watchers stirred and stretched themselves and made ready to give place to those who had obtained a little sleep. Out of the windows, across the campus, the students began to move about, and after a while they struggled down to the chapel to pray for him. Now it was 9 o'clock, and a quarter past. His old opponent, Grant, was sitting down comfortably to breakfast in the White House. With axe or saw or plough or pen, the veterans of Lee's army were in the swing of another day's work. For him it was ended, the life of discipline, of sorrow, and of service. The clock was striking his last half-hour. In some corner of his mind, not wrecked by his malady, he must have heard his marching order. Was the enemy ahead? Had that bayoneted host of his been called up once again to march through Thoroughfare Gap or around Hooker's flank or over the Potomac into Maryland . . . moving . . . moving forward? Or was it that the war was over and that peace had come? "Strike the tent," he said, and spoke no more." (Lee; Freeman, Douglas Southall; An Abridgment by Richard Harwell of the Pulitzer Prize Winning four-volume Biography; Touchstone; New York; 1991)

"The Angels Flooded the Earth with Their Tears"

General Robert E. Lee died on Wednesday morning, October 12, 1870, at 9:30, in the President's house at Washington College. His body was taken to the chapel on Thursday, October 13, 1870, at noon and the funeral services were held at 1:30 P.M. on Saturday, October 15, 1870. The angels flooded the earth with their tears as the general began his final passage. Due to the flooding all the metallic caskets belonging to C.M. Koones & Brother had been swept downstream. A search was conducted and one of the casements was located on an island entwined in a pile of brush, lodged in the forks of a tree, just below the first dam. J.L. Root and W.P. Hartigan worked for Koones and Brother and were given the task of bringing the casket to Lexington.

"The Remains are consigned to the Grave"

The Lexington Gazette published the following article on October 21, 1870. In it is offered a lasting tribute to the man and the level of respect that was afforded to his memory by all.

"It is done. The remains of the brave soldier, the peerless hero, the great and good man, our noble and beloved President, have been consigned to the grave! We have looked for the last time upon all that was mortal of him, and he now belongs to immortality and to fame. It is our mournful duty here to record the last tribute of respect that has just been paid to his memory.

"According to arrangements of the printed program, at 10 o'clock Saturday, October 15, 1870, the procession was formed at the Episcopal Church, in front of the late President's residence, and, to the sound of solemn music, it moved in appointed order. We here present the order of procession: escort of honor, consisting of officers and soldiers of the Confederate army; chaplain and other clergy, hearse and pall-bearers, General Lee's horse, the attending physicians, trustees and faculty of Washington College, dignitaries of the State of Virginia, visitors and faculty of the Virginia Military Institute, other representative bodies and distinguished visitors, alumni of Washington College, citizens, cadets of Virginia Military Institute, students of Washington College as guard of honor.

"Bells Toll and Minute Guns Salute"

"The procession moved, to the sound of solemn music (furnished by the band of the Military Institute), down Washington Street, up Jefferson Street to Franklin Hall, thence to Main Street. In front of the hotel the ranks were opened, and the committee from the Virginia Legislature, the representatives of the faculty and students of the University of Virginia and other distinguished guests, took their appointed place. Moving on, in front of the courthouse, it was joined by the large body of citizens, and thus the long line moved slowly and solemnly down to the Military Institute. Meanwhile all the bells were tolled, and minute guns were fired from the parapet of the institute. In front of the institute the whole corps was drawn up, with presented arms, and as the procession slowly defiled past, it was joined by the visitors and faculty, who took up their places immediately behind the legislative committee, and by the cadets, who took their places just in front of the students of the college, to whom, as a post of honor, had been assigned the duty of closing the procession. Moving up to the college chapel, the front of the procession was then halted, and while its front was at the chapel door the rear was still in the institute grounds, so great was the number of those that had crowded to do honor to the lamented chief. After the procession had halted, the students, and after them the cadets, were marched to the front and proceeded into and through the chapel, past the remains, where they were drawn up in two bodies on the southern side of the chapel. The procession then moved in and was seated by the marshals. On the platform were the officers of the college and of the Military Institute, the legislative committee and other representatives from abroad. The body of the chapel was appropriately filled by the officers and soldiers who had followed the dead hero through the shocks of battle. The gallery and side blocks were filled with ladies and citizens, while the students and cadets held their post of honor outside in front of the tomb.

"The funeral service of the Episcopal Church was then read with impressive solemnity by Rev. W.N. Pendleton, D.D., the pastor of the church to which General Lee belonged, himself a distinguished officer who had served under him throughout the war in the Army of Northern Virginia. The congregation was vast and impressive, and the deepest solemnity pervaded the entire multitude. When the services in the chapel were concluded the corpse was removed by the pallbearers and conveyed to the vault in the basement of the chapel, which had been prepared for its reception. The coffin had been literally strewed with flowers, which had to be removed separately. The body was then solemnly deposited in its last resting place, and amid the tears of the countless multitude the venerable minister pronounced the solemn words, 'dust to dust' from the lofty bank in front of the tomb."

The Pallbearers Were:

1. Judge F.T. Anderson and David E. Moore, Sr., trustees of Washington College.
2. Ex-Governor John Letcher and Commodore M. F. Maury, for Virginia Military Institute.
3. Professor W. Preston Johnston & Professor J. Randolph Tucker; professors.
4. William L. Prather and Edward P. Clark, students of Washington College.
5. Captain J. C. Boude and Captain J. P. Moore, soldiers of Confederate States of America.
6. William G. White and Joseph G. Steele, citizens of Lexington." (Southern Historical Society Papers; Vol.41; page188)

"To Sit Up With the Remains of General Robert E. Lee"

The following request was submitted by several cadets asking for permission to be the honor guard at the great general's remains. Five of them were granted permission. Cadet William Nalle was one of them selected. He was a resident of Culpepper, Virginia and graduated from the Institute in 1872.

V.M.I.
October 14, 1870

"We the undersigned cadets respectfully apply for permission to be absent from Barracks from 7 P.M. today until 8 A.M. tomorrow, as their services have been kindly accepted by the Chief Marshall at Washington College to sit up with the remains of General Robert E. Lee tonight. Respectfully Submitted by Cadets Hamilton, Alex.; Morgan, J.H.; Hawkins, N.D. Taylor, S.M.; Taylor, Z.; Sullivan,

A.R.; Nalle, Wm., W.H.; Harrison, N.M.; Farrar, Walton."

"He Looked to be Reduced to Half His Original Size and Desperately Thin"

The following is a letter written by Virginia Military Institute cadet regarding the funeral of General Lee. It is dated October 16, 1870. In the correspondence, the cadet captures the entire sober scene including the weather, his appearance, and the homage paid by those that loved and revered his memory.

"Dear Mother,

Expect you have been looking for a letter from me for some time and in fact I would have written but about the time I thought of writing the rains & the flood came on, destroying bridges canals, & cutting off communication generally.

"I suppose of course that you have all read full accounts of Gen Lee's death in the papers. He died on the morning of the 12th at about half past nine. All business was suspended at once all over the country and town, and all duties, military and academic suspended at the Institute, and all the black crape and all similar black material in Lexington, was used up at once, and they had to send on to Lynchburg for more. Every cadet had black crape issued to him, and an order was published at once requiring us to wear it as a badge of mourning for six months. The battalion flag was heavily draped in black, and is to stay so for the next six months. The Institute has been hung all around with black. The College buildings were also almost covered with black. All the churches and in fact the town looked as if they had been trying to cover everything with festoons of black cambric, and every sort of black that could be procured.

"The morning after his death we marched up and escorted the remains from the house to Washington College Chapel, where they lay in "state" until the burial yesterday morning.

"After the remains were placed in the Chapel on the morning of the 13th the entire procession was marched through the Chapel, past the corpse, which they were allowed to look at. The lid of the coffin having been taken off for that purpose. I saw the General after his death, and never saw a greater change than must have taken place in him a short time before he died. Some days before he was taken I met him in the path leading into town, coming in direction of the barracks. He was walking, and seemed to be the picture of health, and when I saw him in his coffin, he looked to be reduced to half his original size, and desperately thin. When first taken with the paralytic stroke or whatever it was, he fell on his dining room floor, a bed was placed under him and he died where he fell. The doctors forbid anyone to move him. Myself and four other cadets with Gen Smith's permission sat up all night with the corpse on Friday night, perfect silence was kept the whole night, no one speaking except in a low whisper. It was considered a great honor to be allowed to sit up with the remains, and a great many applied for the privilege but one of the college professors on arrival took only five of us, whom he requested to stay.

"The day following the funeral procession after marching all around town and through the Institute grounds, formed around the college chapel and he was buried in the chapel under the floor of the basement. The procession was a very large one, a great many persons from a distance being here. Our brass band with muffled drums, went ahead of the hearse playing the dead march. Cannon of our stationary battery were fired & the hearse however was perfectly empty the corpse being all the time in the Chapel where it was placed at first.

"The flood of which I spoke, did a great deal of damage in this part of the country, carrying off some ten or fifteen houses, some dwelling houses some ware houses situated at the canal boat landing near here all the bridges in the river were carried off and the canal running to this place entirely ruined, all the locks being torn up and carried off. It was a rare sight to see large houses, bridges, mills & every sort of lumber go sailing at a rapid rate, down the river. Up to a week or two since, we could get no mails or any thing that had to come from a distance, and it is still very difficult to get provisions. Mails come and go regularly now, as they have fixed ferries for stages &&.

"I was made a sergeant in Co A about three weeks ago, and the evening after the first appointment, I was appointed color sergeant. I have to carry the battalion flag and have charge of the color guard, do not wear any such accoutrements as cartridge box and bayonet scabbard, when I am in charge of the guard, as the other sergeants have to do, but wear only a sword and sash, go to church in the staff, and enjoy various other privileges Jessie is getting along very well, he seems to be a great favorite. I had him put in a room, with the best new cadets that I could find. One of them is a son of Col. Dulaney of Loudoun, the others seem very nice little fellows, and they are all about the same size.

390

"I am getting along pretty well I think, and I have written about all that I can think of at present. Let me hear from you soon and let me know whether or not Gen Smith sent pa the receipt for the deposit."

Your affectionate son
Wm Nalle

"Tributes to the Fallen Hero of Our Dreams"

The nation was in mourning, for he walked the earth no more. This Christian leader that followed to the best of his ability the teachings of Christ, this humble man who loved working with the young minds of tomorrow, this warrior of God that sought His guidance in all things, this husband and father would rest among the ages. Tributes came from all over the world. Even those that had called him an enemy of America and a traitor paid homage to this man of moral Christian character. *The New York Sun* stated that, "In the death of General Lee an able soldier, a sincere Christian, and an honest man has been taken from the earth." *The Halifax Nova Scotia Chronicle* voiced that he was the greatest General of the Age. A Canadian paper (*The Montreal Telegraph*) heralded him as the greatest general of all times stating that, "Prosperity will rank Lee above Washington or Napoleon, before Saxe or Tureene, above Marlborough or Frederick, before Alexander, or Caesar... {Lee was} the greatest general of this or any other age. He has made his own name, and the Confederacy he served, immortal." *The Cincinnati Enquirer* honored him by saying that, "He was the great general of the 'Rebellion.' It was his strategy and superior military knowledge which kept the banner of the South afloat so long." *The London Standard* spoke of Lee as in mystical proportions, equating him to King Arthur. "{A} country that has given birth to men like him, and those who followed him, may look the chivalry of Europe in the face without shame: for the fatherlands of Signy and of Byard never produced a nobler soldier, gentleman, and Christian than Gen. Robert E. Lee." *The New York Herald* praised his military leadership and more importantly recognized his Christianity. The writer of the proclamation stated that, "{I}n {Lee} the military genius of America was developed in a greater extent than ever before. In him all that was pure and lofty in mind and purpose found lodgment. He came nearer to the ideal of a soldier and Christian general than any man we can think of, for he was a greater soldier than Havelock, and equally devout a Christian." *The Philadelphia Age* stated that, "As a great master of defensive warfare Lee will probably not be ranked inferior to any general known in history."

"The Loss of the Bayard of America"

On October 13, 1870, in an editorial from the New York Herald a day after Lee's death the significance of Lee is captured. I quote it in its entirety so that the reader can feel the full impact of Lee's life on the nation.

"On a quite autumn morning, in the land he loved so well, and, as he held, served so faithfully, the spirit of Robert Edward Lee left the clay which it had so much ennobled, and traveled out of this world into the great and mysterious land. The expressions of regret which sprang from the few who surrounded the bedside of the dying soldier, on yesterday, will be swelled today into one might voice of sorrow, resounding throughout our country, and extending over all parts of the world where his great genius and his many virtues are known. For not to the Southern people alone shall be limited the tribute of a tear over the dead Virginian. Here in the North, forgetting that the time was when the sword of Robert Edward Lee was drawn against us-forgetting and forgiving all the years of bloodshed and agony-we have claimed him as one of ourselves; have cherished and felt proud of his military genius as belonging to us; have recounted and recorded his triumphs as our own; have extolled his virtue as reflecting upon us-for Robert Edward Lee was an American, and the great nation which gave him birth would be today unworthy of such a son if she regarded him lightly.

"Never had mother nobler son. In him the military genius of America developed to a greater extent than ever before. In him all that was pure and lofty in mind and purpose found lodgment. Dignified without presumption, affable without familiarity, he united all those charms of manner which made him the idol of his friends and of his soldiers, and won for him the respect and admiration of the world. Even as, in the days of his triumph, glory did not intoxicate, so, when the dark clouds swept over him, adversity did not depress. From the hour that he surrendered his sword at Appomattox to the fatal autumn morning, he passed among men, noble in the quiet, simple dignity, displaying neither bitterness nor regret over the irrevocable past. He conquered us in misfortune by the grand manner in which he sustained himself, even as he dazzled us by his genius when the tramp of his soldiers resounded through the valleys of Virginia. And for such a man we are all tears and sorrow today. Standing beside his grave, all men of the South and men of the North can mourn with all the bitterness of four years of warfare erased by this common bereavement. May this unity of grief-this unselfish manifestation over the loss of the Bayard of America-in the season of dead leaves and withered branches which this death ushers in, bloom and blossom like the distant coming of spring into the flowers of a heartier accord."

One of the greatest tributes to Lee came from a man that never actually knew him yet had studied him and later wrote of him. Douglas Southall Freeman was captivated by the essence of Lee's character and gave the answer to the quest of why are we so intrigued by this mortal man. As we study Lee, we take a part of his Christian character with us and are the better for his existence. Mr. Freeman simply stated that, "I have been fully repaid by having the privilege in live, as it were, for more than a decade in the company of a great gentleman." In his classic book, Dr. J. W. Jones states that, "Robert Edward Lee of Virginia, of America, of the world, will be recognized as one of the finest specimens of the soldier and the man whom God ever gave to bless the world. He had first hand knowledge of Lee and was counted by the general as a dear friend. What greater tribute than to be hailed by friend and foe as being a man of God. (Life & Letters of Gen. Robert Edward Lee; Jones, W.J.; Sprinkle Publications; Harrisonburg, Virginia; 1986; @ by Neale Publishing Company in 1906; pages 482-486)

"Here He Now Sleeps in the Land He Loved so Well"

His greatest tributes came from those that knew and loved the man. One of the greatest would come from the one and only Confederate President ever to be elected as President of the Confederacy and the other would come from the person that knew him so well, Mrs. Robert E. Lee. On November 3, 1870, the largest concentration of Confederate Generals since the war had ended attended a memorial service to honor their commanding general. It was held in Richmond, Virginia. Jefferson Davis, the former President of the Confederacy, was the keynote speaker and offered a eulogy of "rare eloquence" paying reverence to the fallen hero. Mr. Davis's passion and heart felt admiration for his general of generals is quite evident. The following is an excerpt from that tribute: (Life & Letters of Gen. Robert Edward Lee; Jones, W.J.; Sprinkle Publications; Harrisonburg, Virginia; 1986; @ by Neale Publishing Company in 1906; page 482)

"Here he now sleeps in the land he loved so well, and that land is not Virginia only, for they do injustice to Lee who believe he fought only for Virginia. He was ready to go anywhere, on any service for the good of his country, and his heart was as broad as the thirteen States struggling for the principles that our forefathers fought for in the Revolution of 1776. He sleeps with the thousands who fought under the same flag-and happiest they who first offered up their lives. He sleeps in the soil to him and to them most dear. That flag was furled when there was none to bear it. Around it we are assembled a remnant of the living, to do honor to his memory, and there is an army of skeleton sentinels to keep watch over his grave. This good citizen, this gallant soldier, this great general, this true patriot, had yet a higher praise than these, he was a true Christian. The Christianity which ennobled his life gives to us the consolatory belief that he is happy beyond the grave.

"But, while we mourn the loss of the great and the true, drop we also tears of sympathy with her who was a help mate to him-the noble woman who, while her husband was in the field leading the Army of the Confederacy, though an invalid herself, passed the time in knitting socks for the marching soldiers! A woman fit to be the mother of heroes- and are descended from her. Mourning with her, we can only offer the consolations of the Christian. Our loss is not his, for he now enjoys the rewards of a life well spent, and a never-wavering trust in a risen Saviour. This day we unite our words of sorrow with those of the good and great throughout Christendom, for his fame is gone over the water- his deeds will be remembered; and when this monument we build shall be crumbled into dust, his virtues will still live, a high model for the imitation of generations yet unborn."

"To Lose the Strong Arm & Caring Heart"

On November 15, 1870, Mary Randolph Custis Lee (sometimes referred to as Mollie by friends) wrote a letter to her friend Lettie. One can ascertain the strength and character of this physically disabled lady of dignity by her comments. In the contents of the correspondence, she offers her sympathy for the passing of a baby, talks of her physical ailments, reflects upon her late husband, and provides insight into the darkest moments before the dawn as her husband hesitated between the thresholds of two worlds. Her love and adoration for her soul mate is apparent. She would join him across that great divide and rest among the shade of those heavenly trees; reunited on November 5, 1873.

"I have long intended to write to you my dear Lettie ever since I heard of the death of Rosa's dear little boy but was prevented by many things. What a sorrow it must have been to them & to you all & you never saw him. I know what a joy a baby is in a house & it was her first. You must give my affectionate love to her & tell her I have often thought of her. Will she not come & see you all this winter or some of you go to her? The sympathy of friends is very grateful to us when we know it is sincere & in my trouble dear Lettie I feel that it is all heartfelt that there is no feigned grief for him who all mourn who could appreciate true excellence & though it is very sad for me to lose the strong arm & caring heart on which I have leaned for so many eventful years, yet I mourn not for him but for myself. It never crossed my mind for one moment that I would outlive him, that a life so valueless as mine could be spared & his taken, so important to his family & country, but God knows what is best for us all & I am content. I would not recall him if I could. The toils of his crowded and eventful life are ended & had he succeeded in gaining the cause which cost him so much labor & sacrifice, he could not have been more beloved & lamented than he is now. Only the Hero of a lost cause yet as the blood of the Martyrs built up the Church so may the sacrifice of this Martyr yet produce fruit for his country that we know not of. "God moves in a mysterious way, His wonders to perform".

"My husband's last day on earth was crowded with cares & labors for others & when late in the evening he reached home and sank back in his chair unable to articulate a word I saw in the look of resignation on his face as he sat perfectly calm & upright waiting the arrival of the physicians that he knew the summons had come & though from the nature of his disease he did not express his feelings, never smiled & rarely spoke, yet he never expressed a single thought or anxiety for aught but lay calmly & quietly awaiting his end. Once when Agnes urged him to take some medicine, which he always seemed to take with great repugnance, he said quite plainly "tis no use" but took it as it was ordered. When he came so much better that they were very hopeful of his recovery, the Dr said "you must soon mount your favorite grey." He shook his head very emphatically & looked upward. He knew us all, welcomed us with a warm pressure of the hand & seem to like us around him, especially Custis who was a most efficient nurse. He slept a great deal & the last 48 hour the Dr. assured us was insensible to all pain & after a long night of breathing heavily awoke to rest with one deep long sigh. I cannot even now realise that he has gone. I listen for his step at the usual time & when he does not enter feel my sad disappointment. We had determined to remain here this winter & if Custis accepts the Presidency of the College may continue to make it our home for more years. I have been quite sick for more than 3 weeks first with a bilious attack & then a violent inflammation of my leg ankle & foot which was so painful that I could scarcely turn in bed & had to be lifted in & out of it, & still though it is much better, I spend part of every day in bed & out with my limbs spread out before me in such an uncomfortable position that I write with difficulty which must be my apology for this letter. The girls all desire to be particularly remembered to you & all your family & to Rosa to express their deep sympathy - also remember us to Mrs. Meredith & other kind friends. Do you ever hear anything of the Bufords now? Or of from Nat Burwell. Did he ever get the little dress? We have had the most beautiful weather ever known since that dreadful storm which commenced just about the hour when my husband was taken as if the very elements were in convulsive thrusts weeping with us, & since the skies have been radiant with beauty as rejoicing over the freed spirit in his glorified mansion. I would I had been able my dear Lettie to detail to you all the circumstances attend his last moments but I cannot now & will only subscribe myself your faithful friend, M.C. Lee"

THE FINAL CURTAIN

Upon a visit to the Stonewall Jackson Cemetery, located in Lexington, Virginia, I became keenly aware of the significance of that particular sacred sight. Here, within the confines of that hallowed ground surrounded by cut stones, rest the remains of so many that believed in a cause that they were willing to give their lives. It is a place of reverence and reflection, a sheltered place in which inspiration is drawn.

While paying my respects to as many sites as possible, I meandered back to the original burial site of Stonewall Jackson. The plot is surrounded much as it was in the 1860's, with the original wrought iron fence still protecting the immediate families of the general (they have been reinterred beside the monument at the apex of the hill). I remembered reading of how General Lee would ride at different times during the day to spend time with his friend and fallen comrades at the cemetery. A sense of reflection overcame my being. What was he saying in the unspoken language of prayer, what were his thoughts, and was the man thinking in terms of his own mortality?

The following poem was roughly scribbled while standing in the area in which so many others have stood. It is my attempt of not only paying homage to the greatness of Lee, or to those interred at that particular site, but also to offer insight into how all of us address those moments of mourning as we attempt to look beyond the long black veil. (Poetry of the Civil War: Poems for a Bygone Era; Chaltas, David; Copyrighted; 2006)

The Final Farewell

As he bowed his head to heaven
With knees upon the ground.
His thoughts were all unleavened
But words could not be found.

His eyes were filled with sorrow;
Reflections of the past.
He thought of his tomorrow
And going home at last.

He thought of his shocked alarm
In the middle of that night,
When Jack had lost his left arm
But he had lost his right.

He reflects upon their meeting
On the second day in May.
Their final farewell greeting
As ole Sorrel rode away.

Awakened by a sudden chill,
He closed the Iron Gate.
Riding Ole Traveller down the hill,
He sees his looming fate.

(Taken inside the chapel at Washington and Lees College.
Author is paying a mark of respect to all soldiers while at the marble
statue of General Lee resting on the battlefield.)

FINAL TESTIMONY ON LEE'S CHARACTER

"Let Us Take to Heart the Lesson of His Bright Example"

One of the greatest victories conceptualized upon the battlefield was also considered by some to be the greatest tragedy of all times. At the apex of his brilliant military career General Lee received word that his dearest general, the ravages of the war had smitten his right arm. The following is a detailed account given by Colonel Marshall, Lee's Aide-De-Camp, a year after Lee's death describing the moment of victory and the agony Lee expressed at the loss of so many men. In his words, he eloquently captures the essence of General Lee's character. The speech was given in Baltimore, Maryland. (Lee's Aid-De-Camp; Marshall, Charles; University of Nebraska Press; Lincoln and London; @1927; First Bison Books printing: 2000; pages 171-176)

"In present the Resolutions of the Committee, I cannot refrain form expressing the feelings inspired by the memories that crowd upon my mind, when I reflect that these resolutions are intended to express what General Lee's soldiers feel towards General Lee. The Committee are fully aware of their inability to do justice to the sentiments that inspire the hearts of those whom they speak. How can we portray in words the gratitude, the pride, the veneration, the anguish, that now fill the hearts of those who shared his victories and his reverses, his triumphs, and his defeats? How can we tell the world what we can only feel ourselves? How can we give expression to the crowding memories called forth by the sad event we are met to deplore?

"We recall him as he appeared in the hour of victory-grand, imposing, awe-inspiring, yet self-forgetful and humble. We recall the great scenes of his triumph when we hailed him victor of many a bloody field, and when, above the paeans of victory, we listened with reverence to his voice as he ascribed "all glory to the Lord of Hosts, from whom all glories are." We remember that grand magnanimity that never stooped to pluck from the tree of victory those meaner things that grow nearest the earth, but which, with eyes turned to the stars and hands raised towards heaven, gathered the golden fruits of mercy, pity, and holy charity, that ripen on its topmost boughs, beneath the approving smile of the God of Battles.

"We remember the sublime self-abnegation of Chancellorsville, when in the midst of his victorious legions, who, with the light of battle still in their faces, hailed him conqueror, he thought only of his great lieutenant lying wounded on the field, and transferred to him all the honour of that illustrious day. I will be pardoned, I am sure, for referring to an incident which affords to my mind a most striking illustration of one of the grandest features of his character.

"On the morning of May 3, 1863, as many of you will remember, the final assault was made upon the Federal lines at Chancellorsville. General Lee accompanied the troops in person, and as they emerged from the fierce combat they had waged in the depths of that tangled wilderness, driving the superior forces of the enemy before them across the open ground, he rode into their midst. The scene is one that can never be effaced from the minds of those who witnessed it. The troops were pressing forward with all the ardour and enthusiasm of combat. The white smoke of musketry fringed

402

the front of the line of battle, while the artillery on the hills in the rear of the infantry shook the earth with its thunder, and filled the air with the wild shrieks of the shells that plunged into the masses of the retreating foe. To add greater horror and sublimity to the scene, Chancellor House and the woods surrounding it were wrapped in flames. In the midst of this awful scene, General Lee, mounted upon that horse which we all remember so well, rode to the front of his advancing battalions. His presence was the signal for one of those outbursts of enthusiasm which none can appreciate who have not witnessed them.

"The fierce soldiers with their faces blackened with the smoke of battle, the wounded crawling with feeble limbs from the fury of the devouring flames, all seemed possessed with a common impulse. One long, unbroken cheer, in which the feeble cry of those who lay helpless on the earth blended with the strong voices of those who still fought, rose high above, the roar of battle, and hailed the presence of the victorious chief. He sat in the full realization of all that soldiers dream of-triumph; and as I looked upon him in the complete fruition of the success which his genius, courage, and confidence in his army had won, I thought that it must have been from such a scene that men in ancient days rose to the dignity of gods.

"His first care was for the wounded of both armies, and he was among the foremost at the burning mansion where some of them lay. But at that moment, when the transports of his victorious troops were drowning the roar of battle with acclamations, a note was brought to him from General Jackson. It was brought to General Lee as he sat on his horse, near the Chancellor House, and, unable to open it with his gauntleted hands, he passed it to me with directions to read it to him. The note made no mention of the wound General Jackson had received, but congratulated General Lee upon the great victory.

"I shall never forget the look of pain and anguish that passed over his face as he listened. With a voice broken with emotion, he bade me say to General Jackson that the victory was his, and that the congratulations were due to him. I know not how others may regard this incident, but to myself, as I gave expression to the thought of his exalted mind, I forgot the genius that won the day in my reverence for the generosity that refused its glory.

"There is one other incident to which I beg permission to refer, that I may perfect the picture. On the 3rd day of July, 1863, the last assault of the Confederate troops on the heights of Gettysburg failed, and again General was among the baffled and shattered battalions as they sullenly retired from their brave attempt. The history of that battle is still to be written, and the responsibility for the result is yet to be fixed.

"But there, with the painful consciousness that his plans had been frustrated by others, and that defeat and humiliation had overtaken his army, in the presence of his troops he openly assumed the entire responsibility of the campaign and of the last battle. One word from him would have relieved him of the responsibility, but that word he refused to utter until it could be spoken without fear of doing the least injustice.

"Thus, my fellow soldiers, I have presented to you our great commander in the supreme moments of triumph and defeat. I cannot more strongly illustrate his character. Has it been surpassed in history? Is there another instance of such self-abnegation among men? The man rose high above victory in the one instance, and, harder still, the man rose superior to disaster in the other. It was such incidents as these that gave General Lee the absolute and undoubting confidence and affection of his soldiers.

"Need I speak of the many exhibitions of that confidence? You all remember them, my comrades. Have you not seen a wavering line restored by the magic of his presence? Have you not seen the few forget that they were fighting against the many, because he was among the few?

"But I pass from the contemplation of his greatness in war to look to his example under the oppressive circumstances of final failure-to look to the example which is most useful for us not to refer to for our guidance and instruction. When the attempt to establish the Southern Confederacy had failed, and the event of the war seemed to have established the indivisibility of the Federal Union, General Lee gave his adhesion to the new order of affairs.

"His was no hollow truce; but with that pure faith and honor that marked every act of his illustrious career, he immediately devoted himself to the restoration of peace, harmony, and concord. He entered zealously into the subject of education, believing, as he often declared, that popular education is the only sure foundation of free government. He gave his earnest support to all plans of international improvement designed to bind more firmly together the social and commercial interests of the country; and among the last acts of his life was the effort to secure the construction of a line of railway communication of incalculable importance as a connecting link between the North and South. He devoted all his great energies to the advancement of the welfare of his countrymen, while shrinking from public notice, and sought to lay deep and strong the foundation of the new fabric of government which it was supposed would arise from the ruin of the old. But I need not repeat to you, my comrades, the history of his life since the war. You have watched it to its close, and you know how faithfully and truly he performed every duty of his position.

"Let us take to heart the lesson of his bright example. Disregarding all that malice may impute to us, with an eye single to the faithful performance of our duties as American citizens, and with the honest and sincere resolution to support with heart and hand the honor, the safety, and the true liberties of our country, let us invoke our fellow-citizens to forget the animosities of the past by the side of this honored grave, and joining hands around this royal corpse, friends, now, enemies no more, proclaim perpetual truce to battle."

"The Religion of Christ Had Ordered All His Ways"

Upon word of his death spread across the country, several people met to form committees to eulogize Lee. Maryland sent her delegates to the Richmond Lee Monumental Convention. The Honorable Reverdy Johnson (1796-1876), a well-known senator and statesman attended the meeting and spoke after General Trimble. Senator Johnson rose to the occasion and offered the following tribute to the fallen general. The date was October 29th.

"Mr. Chairman and Gentlemen: I am here in compliance with the request of many gentlemen present, and I not only willingly complied with that request, but I am willing to do all I am able, to show my appreciation of the character, civil and military, of Robert E. Lee. It was my good fortune to know him before the Mexican War, in those better days before the commencement of the sad struggle through which we have recently passed. I saw in him every thing that could command the respect and admiration of men, and I watched with peculiar interest his course in the Mexican War. It was also my good fortune to know the late Lieutenant-General Scott. In the commencement of the struggle to which I have alluded, I occupied in Washington the position of quasi-military adviser to him, and was, in that capacity, intimately associated with him. I have heard him often declare that the glorious and continued success which crowned our arms in the war with Mexico was owing, in a large measure, to the skill, valor, and undaunted courage of Robert E. Lee. He entertained for him the warmest personal friendship, and it was his purpose to recommend him as his successor in the event of his death or inability to perform the duties of his high position. In April, 1861, after the commencement of hostilities between the two great sections of our country, General Lee, then lieutenant-colonel of cavalry in the Army of the United States, offered his resignation. I was with General Scott when he was handed the letter of resignation, and I saw what pain the fact caused him. While he regretted the step his most valuable officer had taken, he never failed to say emphatically, and over and over again, that he believed he had taken it from an imperative sense of duty. He was also consoled by the belief that if he was placed at the head of the armies of the then Confederation, he would have in him a foeman in every way worthy of him, and one who would conduct the war upon the highest principles of civilized warfare, and that he would not suffer encroachments to be made upon the rights of private property and the rights of unoffending citizens.

"Some may be surprised that I am here to eulogize Robert E. Lee. It is well known that I did not agree with him in his political views. At the beginning of the late war, and for many years preceding it, even from the foundation of this Government, two great questions agitated the greatest minds of this country. Many believed that the allegiance of the citizen was due first to his State, and many were of the opinion that, according to the true reading of the Constitution, a State had no right to leave the Union and claim sovereign rights and the perpetual allegiance of her citizens. I did not agree in the first-named opinion, but I knew it was honestly entertained. I knew men of the purest character, of the highest ability, and of the most liberal and patriotic feelings, who conscientiously believed it. Now the war is over, thank God! and to that thank I am sure this meeting will respond, it is the duty of every citizen of this land to seek to heal the wounds of the war, to forget past differences, and to forgive, as far as possible, the faults to which the war gave rise. In no other way can the Union be truly and permanently restored. We are now together as a band of brothers. The soldiers of the Confederacy, headed by the great chief we now mourn, have expressed their willingness to abide by the issue of the contest. What a spectacle to the world! After years of military devastation, with tens of thousands dead on her battle-fields, with the flower of her children slain, with her wealth destroyed, her commerce swept away, her agricultural and mechanical pursuits almost ruined, the South yielded. The North, victorious and strong, could not forget what she owed to liberty and human rights.

We may well swear now that as long as liberty is virtuous we will be brothers.

"Robert E. Lee is worthy of all praise. As a man, he was peerless; as a soldier, he had no equal and no superior; as a humane and Christian soldier, he towers high in the political horizon. You cannot imagine with what delight, when I had the honor to represent this country at the court of Great Britain, I heard the praises of his fame and character, which came from soldiers and statesmen. I need not speak of the comparative merits of General Lee and the Union generals who opposed him; this is not the place or time for a discussion of their respective successes and defeats; but I may say that, as far as I was able to judge of the sentiments of the military men of Great Britain, they thought none of the Union officers superior to General Robert E. Lee. Their admiration for him was not only on account of his skill on the battle-field, and the skilful manner with which he planned and executed his campaigns, but the humane manner in which he performed his sad duty. They alluded specially to his conduct when invading the territory of his enemy--his restraint upon his men, telling them that the honor of the army depended upon the manner of conducting the war in the enemy's country--and his refusal to resort to retaliatory measures. I know that great influences were brought to bear upon him, when he invaded Pennsylvania, to induce him to consent to extreme measures. His answer, however, was, 'No; if I suffer my army to pursue the course recommended, I cannot invoke the blessing of God upon my arms.' He would not allow his troops to destroy private property or to violate the rights of the citizens. When the necessities of his army compelled the taking of commissary stores, by his orders his officers paid for them in Confederate money at its then valuation. No burning homesteads illumined his march, no shivering and helpless children were turned out of their homes to witness their destruction by the torch. With him all the rules of civilized war, having the higher sanction of God, were strictly observed. The manly fortitude with which he yielded at Appomattox to three times his numbers showed that he was worthy of the honors and the fame the South had given him. This is not the first time since the termination of the war I have expressed admiration and friendship for Robert E. Lee. When I heard that he was about to be prosecuted in a Virginia court for the alleged crime of treason, I wrote to him at once, and with all my heart, that if he believed I could be of any service to him, professionally, I was at his command. All the ability I possess, increased by more than fifty years of study and experience, would have been cheerfully exerted to have saved him, for in saving him I believe I would have been saving the honor of my country. I received a characteristic reply in terms of friendship and grateful thanks. He wrote that he did not think the prosecution would take place. Hearing, however, some time after, that the prosecution would commence at Richmond, I went at once to that city and saw his legal adviser, Hon. William H. McFarland, one of the ablest men of the bar of Virginia. Mr. McFarland showed me a copy of a letter from General Lee to General Grant, enclosing an application for a pardon which he desired General Grant to present to the President, but telling him not to present it if any steps had been taken for his prosecution, as he was willing to stand the test. He wrote that he had understood by the terms of surrender at Appomattox that he and all his officers and men were to be protected. That letter, I am glad to say, raised General Lee higher in my esteem. General Grant at once replied, and he showed his reply to me. He wrote that he had seen the President, and protested against any steps being taken against General Lee, and had informed him that he considered his honor and the honor of the nation pledged to him. The President became satisfied, and no proceedings were ever taken. General Grant transmitted to the President the application of General Lee for pardon, indorsed with his most earnest approval. No pardon was granted. He did not need it here, and, when he appears before that great tribunal before which we must all be called, he will find he has no account to settle there. No soldier who followed General Lee could have felt more grief and sympathy at his grave than I would, could I have been present upon the mournful occasion of his burial. I lamented his loss as a private loss, and still more as a public loss. I knew that his example would continue to allay the passions aroused by the war, and which I was not surprised were excited by some acts in that war. I love my country; I am jealous of her honor. I cherish her good name, and I am proud of the land of my birth. I forbear to criticise the lives and characters of her high officers and servants, but I can say with truth that, during the late war, the laws of humanity were forgotten, and the higher orders of God were trodden under foot.

"The resolutions need no support which human lips can by human language give. Their subject is their support. The name of Lee appeals at once, and strongly, to every true heart in this land and throughout the world. Let political partisans, influenced by fanaticism and the hope of political plunder, find fault with and condemn us. They will be forgotten when the name of Lee will be resplendent with immortal glory.

"Mr. Chairman and gentlemen, in the course of Nature my career upon earth must soon terminate. God grant that when the day of my death comes, I may look up to Heaven with that confidence and faith which the life and character of Robert E. Lee gave him! He died trusting in God, as a good man, with a good life and a pure conscience. He was consoled with the knowledge that the religion of Christ had ordered all his ways, and he knew that the verdict of God upon the account he would have to render in heaven would be one of judgment seasoned with mercy. He had a right to believe that when God passed judgment upon the account of his life, though He would find him an erring human being, He would find virtue enough and religious faith enough to save him from any other verdict than that of 'Well done, good and faithful servant.' The monument will be raised; and when it is raised many a man will visit Richmond to stand beside it, to do reverence to the remains it may cover, and to say, 'Here lie the remains of one of the noblest men who ever lived or died in America.'"

"We Have a Sacred Duty"

On January 19, 1872, two years to the day that General Lee had crossed through the turbid vale, General Jubal Early gave a speech in Lee's Chapel, Lexington, Virginia. Custis was now the president of the college and the college had been renamed Washington and Lee University. From General Early's speech, the following excerpt summates our commitment to remember.

"We have a sacred duty to discharge. It is…proper that the tomb of our beloved Commander, in this chapel, shall be suitably decorated and honored. Let it be our especial charge to see that the pious work is accomplished." (Lee, The Soldier; Gallager,

412

Gary W.; University of Nebraska Press; Lincoln, Nebraska; 1996; page 620) We have been given the Charge by Stephen D. Lee and with this one engrained upon our spirit, let us honor the especial charge given to us by General Jubal A. Early.

The old Christian Warrior now rides the wind on his beloved horse, leading the army that he loved so well with his family waiting every evening for his return. And there are joyful shouts, warm cheers and a rebel yell from the angels as they proclaim, "Well done thy good and faithful servant..." And destiny's child once again takes off his hat as he bows and bids us all an affectionate farewell.

THE AFTER SHOCK

As I came to the realization that I had completed my mission (though I could have written for years on the Christian servant) it dawned upon my being the impact that the man who had died over 136 years ago had on my life. You see dear reader, through researching Lee's life, legend, and legacy, I have reached a point in which I wish to follow his lead and become an example for others to follow me towards Christ. There have been so many blessings and there is not a day goes by that I do not thank God for allowing me this opportunity at not only writing about a Christian but giving me a chance to in attempting to immolate the virtues that set forth by Lee's example. I know I am unworthy, for we all are but through God's forgiveness and grace we are more than conquerors. The following excerpts from my life hopefully will give you a glimpse into how a man of antiquity molded me into the person wishing to be more than I was.

"Why General Lee"

While at a recent dedication/memorial service I was asked the question. "Why General Lee? Why did you choose to portray him?" Well the simple truth of the matter is that I didn't choose to represent him. I was chosen! I was first introduced to the idea when we were dedicating a soldier's grave and I was in line as a private ready to obey the commands of, "Ready, aim, fire!" with no thought of anything else except honoring a man that had gone before. After the volley and taps was offered, I heard a lady talking on my right flank. I dared not look over in that direction for the dismissed command had not been given nor the benediction. "When is Lee going to speak?" I heard her say. That was confusing since I knew Lee was not

414

amongst us. I wondered what she was talking about. After the dedication, I heard that familiar voice beckoning in my direction and I turned to see her walking towards me. She said, "Sonny, why didn't you speak as General Lee". I explained that I was but a lowly private slow of tongue and was not worthy to speak for him. She looked at me with a glare that puzzled me and then from her mouth came wonderment: "You have been given a gift of representing the Christian Lee and it is your duty to discover who you really are!" and simply turned and walked away. I must say I was quite taken back but her words haunted me.

A few weeks later I was yet at another location wearing my kepi and private's attire when a lady came up to me and said, "General Lee, will you honor us with some words?" I was quite embarrassed as I did not know what to say nor did I feel knowledgeable on the subject of Lee's Christian character. I declined the offer but felt poorly for my slowness of tongue and reluctant nature. But I thought to myself that I needed to be prepared just in case this happened again and I started studying what turned out to be the fascinating life of Lee. Some time expired but a wonderful lady that I refer to as my second mom approached me. She matter-of-factly stated that she was having a reunion and that I was going to be the guest speaker in the form of a persona. Since I possessed his features I was to speak. Now this is the first dawning that I resembled the general! What could I say but yes and I began to panic before even leaving the room. I prayed for deliverance. "I am unworthy," I protested but yet a stronger voice persisted. I am slow of tongue," yet an inner voice said I shall give you the words. Well the night came and to my horror there were over 200 people assembled and all of them were kin.

Strangers I don't mind but kin! I spoke and within 30 seconds I noted that I had a stirring of the spirit that I had never experienced and found myself sharing not only the words of the general but also what I felt were the emotions that he possessed. My eyes filled with tears, my voice quivered and I spoke from a spirit that I will never fully comprehend. The crowd was mesmerized and I was in a state of shock. It was upon that night that I vowed that if I was to portray the man, I must become the man.

The more I studied the more I realized that God was doing for me what I could not do for myself. Moses had made his excuses but God persisted. Jonah had made his excuses but God persuaded. Sometimes the voice of God cannot be heard in our lives but must be felt and then we are to step out of faith in order to find the will of God in our lives. I am so humbled by the honor of representing the Christian man known as R E Lee and had it not been for a few ladies and gentlemen encouraging me I do not feel that I would this day be in the will of God. God works in mysterious ways. Won't you listen to that inner voice as He guides you? Won't you do His bidding even if you think you are not worthy? Whenever you follow God's will, the path will not always be smooth but when you stumble, you will have the touch of the Master's Hand in yours. I am humbled by the honor of being your obedient servant in Christ, The Old General

"Without Thought of Reward"

Recently a friend gave me the prayer that he said General Robert E. Lee carried in his pocket. It was said that every morning he would unfold the paper, read it, fold it back and then return it to its original resting place. Late at night as the candles and

416

lanterns offered the only light except for an occasional moon light night he would be seen reading his Bible, closing it, and praying. Then prior to going to bed he would reach into his pocket unfold the little paper, read it, fold it back and then return it back into his pocket. He was known to give out Bibles and shared his belief in that, "The Bible was the Book of Books". In all things, Robert Edward Lee sought the guidance of his Creator. He believed that the Bible was the divine revelation to man and that within the old ragged book that he always carried was all the answers to the questions of life. He was an avid reader of the Bible and believed in its truths. He had a practice of reading it in the morning, the evening and sharing its wisdom during family devotionals. But he also prayed and dwelt upon the Word of the Lord. What were those words that were said to be his daily source of renewal? Where did the words come from and was this something he performed daily? We will never know the answers to these questions but this we do know; it was of his nature and Christian character to do so. For the general believed in denying himself and living an honorable Christian life following the example of Christ in all matters WITH the realization that we mortals can never live up to His truths. For He is God and Lee was merely a man of God. But a man earnestly seeking God's guidance as so many others have done once they find the path and the Light that shines upon it. The prayer that was shared with me I now share with you. May it bless you in its simple complexity. "Help me to be, to think, to act what is right, make me truthful, honest and honorable in all things; make me intellectually honest for the sake of right and honor and without thought of reward to me."

Saying of the Week: "There are many things in the old Book which I may never be able to explain, but I accept it as the infallible Word of God, and receive its teachings as inspired by the Holy Ghost." R. E. Lee

"The Speak Rule"

Recently I had the privilege of visiting the campus of Washington Lee College. My morning started at 6:30 as I paid my respects to General Jackson, Pendleton, Governor Letcher and the other brave men and women of yesterday. The morning mist clung to my persona as General Lee walked once again on the hallowed soil of the Jackson Cemetery. As I exited the cemetery a mother and her child stopped and asked if I was General Lee. The child was 4-5 years old and the mother stated that her idol was the ole General. At first I thought that I would say yes but then I thought it best to be diplomatic and simply stated that I was nothing more than a voice of the past representing the great general. That satisfied her young mind and she came up and offered me a hug. What a grand way to start the morning. I drove down to the chapel around seven thirty and went to Traveller's gravesite. An apple was already placed upon his marker and I left my token of love for the great steed of the South. I decided to walk to the chapel where the general used to attend church and as I walked a couple of college professors walked by. I nodded and spoke with my usual, "Good Morning" blessings to each as our paths crossed. The first one grunted and walked swiftly by this 'familiar stranger'. The other one did not even recognize my salutations. Was I on the same campus in which our general had implemented the 'speak rule'? The rule is simple. Each person you encounter, you offer a cordial greeting to and try to know the names of all your students as well as faculty. In fact it corresponds to the Golden Rule of life.

418

I sat by the Lee's Episcopal Church trying not to be irked but feeling despondent over what had transpired and the changes of tradition when a very lovely black girl with a cute terrier came by. Upon seeing me sitting upon a bench in my attire, she immediately came over and said, "Good Morning General Lee" and began to share her smile. Her smile was contagious. She talked of her ambitions, the beautiful campus and of VMI. Not once did she offer up a negative statement on life and even told me of places to visit around the area. A breath of fresh air permeated my being as I realized that this young lady was carrying on the tradition and following the Golden Rules of life. She was practicing the rule of being kind to strangers, speaking to them, the rule of being a Good Samaritan, and the rule of human kindness. She renewed my spirit and as I left the campus after speaking to so many wonderful students and adults, I could not help but note the number of beings that were utilizing the speak rule.

When was the last time you were kind to a stranger? When was the last time you spoke to someone that you did not know or knew but simply was to busy to address as you walked by? When can you utilize the speak rule of life and maybe, just maybe brighten another person's day by your ray of sunshine? Upon my next visit to my beloved Washington/Lee College I will recommit myself to simply sitting on the bench and greeting all that I encounter with a hardy, "Good Morning" or "A great day for ducks!" AND I shall continue my endeavors in implementing the speak rule to whomever I may encounter, for this is what I feel Christ would do. This life, live well as I shall remain your obedient servant, RELEE

419

"Lee and the Speeding Ticket"

I perform a soliloquy as General Robert E. Lee and was to perform in Knoxville at the Confederate Memorial Museum (Bleak House) for the Knoxville Chapter of the United Daughters of Confederacy. It was a beautiful morning so I decided to take the long way and have a leisurely drive through Virginia. The air was crisp but the sun made the day seem 10 degrees warmer. I stopped at a local gas station and purchased some gas. I decided to go ahead and put on my new coat. When I reentered my jeep, I thought that I might as well wear my hat and get into character by practicing my speech in full regalia. I found my tape of my friends Dixie Grey performing 'Dixie' and other period songs and I guess that I let my foot become heavy upon the gas pedal. I came over the top of a hill and I saw a Virginia State Trooper with his lights rotating going down the other lane. I wondered who the unfortunate person he was chasing was. When I looked in my rearview mirror, to my horror I saw him turn in the medium in my direction. I immediately pulled the reins on ole Traveller but it was too late. I pulled over and a very pleasant young state trooper steps up to my window and says, "Good morning sir, may I see your drivers license and registration." I reciprocated the greeting and noted the odd look on his face. I began to dig through my glove compartment and could not find my registration form. He politely stated that he would step back in his cruiser and if I found it to wave it at him. After nervously digging through a ton of useless paper, I found the item. Then it dawned on me that I must be quite a unique looking figure driving up and down the road in my uniform! I smiled to myself and wondered just what this young man was thinking. Momentarily he got out of his vehicle and had his citation book with him. My heart sank but I knew I was guilty. He came up to my window and looked at me and stated, "Sir you were speeding but I did not inform you of that when I first stopped you and I was writing a summons for you because you did not have a registration. But then I thought what would my fellow troopers, my Captain, my family as well as the state of Virginia think of me if I gave General Lee a ticket!" He bid me an affectionate farewell and off I went.

Is it not strange how a man that followed God's principles until his death on October 12, 1870, still is so revered today? It is said that one man can sometimes touch seven generations but a few touch eternity. I think the character that Lee tried to emulate was Christ like and the people saw it shine through him. When you accept Christ, you become a new creature. Lee said it and lived it best when he stated, "I am nothing but a poor sinner trusting in Christ alone for my salvation." And then he lived the life in which his Savior directed him to do. When you live a life of following the teaching of Christ people will remember. Honor, honesty, duty, virtue, chivalry all are words that Christ lived by and set the example for us to live up to. Great men of God are not born, they are created by seeking, knocking, and asking for guidance. Then they lead by example. What will people say of you after your time on this earth has gone? Will they remember you as a Christian or will they even remember? Our southern heritage calls for us to be southern gentlemen but more importantly, our heritage beckons us to embrace the 'Book of books' as did our ancestors. There is a reason that we are known as the Bible belt. I remain your obedient servant, East Kentucky Chaplain Chaltas/General R.E. Lee

Saying of the Week: "Be true, kind and generous, and pray earnestly to God to enable you to keep

His commandments and walk in the same all the days of your life." R.E. Lee

"General Lee and the Train Conductor"

I was just returning from what I considered a very successful reenactment in Columbia. The Battle for Columbia was what I call a reenactor's reenactment. The people were so nice (as they had been in Charleston two weeks prior) and the hospitality was truly southern in nature. I must admit that I was filled with a sense of pride in my representation of General Lee and how well that persona was received. I was thinking of all the pictures and all the people talking to me and I found my chest swollen with an emotion bordering on arrogance. I thought how great it is to be so respected, forgetting the true nature of General Lee as a Christian; that of humbleness of spirit. I thought wherever I go I am recognized as General Lee, forgetting that we must maximize the message while minimizing the messenger. That is what false pride can do to a normal human being not focusing on his calling and mission. I must have been thinking for a few hours because my warning light for being low on gas came on and I decided to stop. I found a gas station close to Johnson City and stepped out in all my glory. I had on my gray vest, time piece, gray pants, boots, and white shirt. I filled up my tank and went in to pay for my gas. I decided to purchase a snack and went to the counter to pay for my items when a nice cashier greeted me with a warm welcome. We talked a couple of minutes and then he said, "I think I know who you are." Well, I was in my glory and stated, "Really, who am I?" But I need not ask such a question, I just knew he would recognize me! "You're that railroad conductor from CSX that stops here ever now and then!" Well, the ego burst and I was humbled.

I drove a few miles and found an area where I could contemplate what had transpired. I opened my Bible or should I say it opened to St. Luke 21:46-47. "Beware of the scribes, which desire to walk in long robes, and love greetings in the markets, and the highest seats in the synagogues, and the chief rooms at feasts; which devour widow's houses, and for a show make long prayers: the same shall receive greater damnation." I realized my error of not giving God the glory for being allowed to represent Him in the persona of General Robert E. Lee. I realized that my pride must not overtake my purpose of serving the principles that I am duty bound to honor. I realized that I must as a voice from the past serve the people of the present as well as those of the future. I realized that I can only accomplish this through prayer as I seek guidance in that my performance. In all things, I must acknowledge God, glorify God, and serve Him while denying myself. It is my destiny to follow the old path and to deviate from it would make me one of the scribes. I asked for forgiveness and left that chapter behind at a lonely rest stop, feeling forgiven and once again walking with my destiny.

Sometimes in life we get so wrapped up in our own importance that we forget to humble ourselves in the sight of God and let Him guide our steps. My persona and my life is not for show but to help others see a Christian model that they can follow. General Lee believed in humbleness of spirit, denying himself, believing that Christ was his redeemer and to acknowledge God in all endeavors. We must remember that the way we conduct ourselves is being scrutinized by those that doubt and we must conduct ourselves in such a manner that others will want what we have. General Lee knew this. So, did General Jackson as was evidenced when he and General Ewell were in a bitter argument. General Ewell stormed out of General Jackson's tent in anger and decided to go back to finish the argument. To his surprise when he reentered the tent he found General Jackson on his knees praying out loud for Ewell. General Ewell exclaimed, "If this is religion I must have it." and was led to Christ by Jackson's humbleness and piety. By example, ladies and gentlemen we can make a difference. Let us take off the old coat and put on the new as we follow our destiny no matter where it may lie or wherever we are led. Let our lives be that of humbleness of spirit and servitude to others as Christ taught us to walk in humility. Luke 14:8-14: "For whosoever exalteth himself shall be abased; and He that humbleth himself shall be exalted." Sometimes a lesson in eating humble pie is the best medicine in keeping us spiritually healthy. I owe that young man a debt of gratitude. That is what is great about life, we learn from it daily or we are doomed to repeat our patterns again until we ultimately fail. Remember that we must maximize the message while we minimize messenger. Rejoice in all things this day as I remain your humbled servant in Christ, The Old General

Lee and the Train Conductor
Lesson of Humbleness

I was just returning from what I considered a very successful reenactment in Columbia. The Battle for Columbia was what I call a 'reenactor's reenactment'. The people were so nice (as they had been at the Battle of Charleston two weeks prior) and the hospitality was truly southern in nature.

I must admit that I was filled with a sense of pride in my representation of General Lee and how well that persona was received. I was thinking of all the pictures and all the people talking to me and I found my chest swollen with an emotion bordering on arrogance. I thought how great it is to be so respected, forgetting the true nature of General Lee as a Christian; that of humbleness of spirit. I thought wherever I go I am recognized as General Lee, forgetting that we must maximize the message while minimizing the messenger. That is what false pride can do to a normal human being not focusing on his calling and mission.

I must have been thinking for a few hours because my warning light for being low on gas came on and I decided to stop. I found a gas station close to Johnson City and stepped out in all 'My glory'. I had on my gray vest, time piece, gray pants, boots and white shirt. I filled up my tank and went in to pay for my gas. I decided to purchase a snack and went to the counter to pay for my items when a nice cashier greeted me with a warm welcome.

We talked a couple of minutes and then he said, "I think I know who you are..." Well, I was in my glory and stated, "Really, who am I?" I need not ask such a question; I just knew he would recognize me! "You're that railroad conductor from CSX that stops here ever now and then!" Well, the ego burst and I was humbled.

I drove a few miles and found an area where I could contemplate what had transpired. I opened my Bible or should I say it opened to St. Luke 21:46-47. "Beware of the scribes, which desire to walk in long robes, and love greetings in the markets, and the highest seats in the synagogues, and the chief rooms at feasts; which devour widow's houses, and for a show make long prayers: the same shall receive greater damnation." I realized my error of not giving God the glory for being allowed to represent Him in the persona of General Robert E. Lee. I realized that my pride must not overtake my purpose of serving the principles that I am duty bound to honor. I realized that I must as a voice from the past serve the people of the present as well as those of the future. I realized that I can only accomplish this through prayer as I seek guidance in that my performance. In all things, I must acknowledge God, glorify God, and serve Him while denying myself. It is my destiny to follow the old path and to deviate from it would make me one of the scribes. I asked for forgiveness and left that chapter behind at a lonely rest stop, feeling forgiven and once again walking with my destiny.

Sometimes in life we get so wrapped up in our own importance that we forget to humble ourselves in the sight of God and let Him guide our steps. My persona and my life is not for show but to help others see a Christian model that they can follow. General Lee believed in humbleness of spirit, denying himself, believing that Christ was his redeemer and to acknowledge God in all endeavors. We must remember that the way we conduct ourselves is being scrutinized by those that doubt and we must conduct ourselves in such a manner that others will want what we have. General Lee knew this. So, did General Jackson as was evidenced when he and General Ewell were in a bitter argument. General Ewell stormed out of General Jackson's tent in anger and decided to go back to finish the argument. To his surprise when he reentered the tent he found General Jackson on his knees praying aloud for Ewell. General Ewell exclaimed, "If this is religion I must have it." and was led to Christ by Jackson's humbleness and piety. By example, ladies and gentlemen we can make a difference. Let us take off the old coat and put on the new as we follow our destiny no matter where it may lie or wherever we are led. Let our lives be that of humbleness of spirit and servitude to others as Christ taught us to walk in humility. Luke 14:8-14: "For whosoever exalteth himself shall be abased; and He that humbleth himself shall be exalted." Sometimes a lesson in eating humble pie is the best medicine in keeping us spiritually healthy. I owe that young man a debt of gratitude. That is what is great about life, we learn from it daily or we are doomed to repeat our patterns again until we ultimately fail. Remember that we must maximize the message while we minimize messenger.

"The Essence of One's Character"

I feel that my closing story of Lee captures the essence of the man. There was a group of young men gathered talking and as young men do, began discussing a topic that was off color. The man speaking did not note an older officer that had stepped from the shadows and was within hearing distance. As the man began to make an inappropriate statement, he paused and stated that since he noted that there were not any ladies present that he would continue. At that juncture the older officer stepped forward and said that he was indeed correct in his assumption that there were no ladies present but need he be reminded that there were gentlemen present. The crowd dropped their heads and silently walked off convicted by the presence of a righteous man's soft words and deeds. May we all walk as tall and be humble men of great character.

BIBLIOGRAPHY

A Diary From Dixie; Chesnut, Mary Boykin; Edited by Williams, Ben Ames; New York; 1906, 1949

A Commitment to Valor: A Character Portrait of Robert E. Lee; Gragg, Rod; Rudledge Hill Press; Nashville; 2001

A life of General Robert E. Lee; Cooke, John E.; Kessinger Publishing Company; New York; originally published in 1871; Project Gutenberg on line at http://www.gutenberg.org/etext/10692

A Month's Visit to the Confederate Headquarters; Wolseley, Colonel; Blackwood's; January 1863

Advance and Retreat; Hood, John Bell; Hood Orphan Memorial Fund; New Orleans; 1880

Battles and Leaders of the Civil War; Bradford, Ned; First Meridian Printing, December 1989

Battles and Leaders of the Civil War; edited by Johnson, Robert Underwood and Buel, Clarence Clough; editorial staff of The Century Magazine; Castle N. J; Volume III; pages 420-423

Call To Duty: The Sterling Nobility of Robert E. Lee; Wilkins, J. Steven; Cumberland House Publishing; 1997; page 94

Christ in the Camp: Religion in the Confederate Army; Jones, J. William; Martin and Hoyt Company; Atlanta; 1904

Co. Aytch a Side Show of the Big Show; Watkins, Sam R.; Touchstone, Rockefeller Center, 1230 Ave. of the Americas, N.Y.; copyright 1962

Fading of the Grey; Chaltas, David; Lulu Publishing; 2006

Fighting for the Confederacy: The Personal Recollections of General Edward Porter Alexander; Alexander, Edward Porter; The University of North Carolina Press; Chapel Hill; 1989

Four Years with General Lee; Taylor, Walter H.; D. Appleton-Century Company; New York; 1878

Four Years Under Marse Robert; Stiles, Robert; The Neale Publishing Company; New York and Washington; 1904

From Manassas to Appomattox; Longstreet, Major General James; Chapter XLIII, Appomattox

General Lee; Lee, Fitzhugh; Premier Civil War Classics; Fawcett Publications, Inc.; Greenwich, Conn., 1961

General R.E. Lee as a College President; Ashley, T.; Confederate Veteran; Volume XIII; No.8; Nashville, Tennessee; August, 1905

General Robert E. Lee after Appomattox; Riley, Franklin L.; New York; MacMillan Company; 1930

Grey Fox: Robert E. Lee and the Civil War; Davis, Burke; Wings Books, an imprint of Randon House Value Publishing; New York; 1956

Growing Up in the 1850s: The Journal of Agnes Lee; Edited by and with a forward by deButts, Mary Custis Lee; Robert E. Lee Memorial Association, Inc.; University of North Carolina Press; Chapel Hill and London; 1984

Gunner with Stonewall: Reminiscences of William Thomas Poague, a Memoir, Written for His Children in 1903; Poague, William Thomas; ed. Cockrell, Monroe F.; McCowat-Mercer Press; Jackson, Tennessee; page 181

History of the Life of Rev. Wm. Mack Lee, Body Servant to Robert E. Lee Through the Civil War-Cook from 1861-1865; Still Living Under the Protection of the Southern States; Lee, William Mack; copyright 1918

In the Footsteps of Robert E. Lee; Johnson, Clint; John H. Blair Publisher; Winston-Salem, North Carolina; 2001; page 12-13

Jackson & Lee; Legends in Gray; Kunstler, Mort, paintings of; Text by Robertson, James I., Jr.; Rutledge Hill Press; Nashville, Tennessee; 1995

Lee; Freeman, Douglas Southall; An Abridgment by Richard Harwell of the Pulitzer Prize Winning four-volume Biography; Touchstone; New York; 1991

Lee; Freeman, Douglas Southall; Touchstone Book; Simon & Schuster; New York; 1961, 1991

Lee's Adjutant: The Wartime Letters of Colonel Walter Herron Taylor; Taylor, Walter H.; Edited by Tower, R. Lockwood; University of South Carolina Press; 1995

Lee and Grant at Appomattox; Kantor, Mackinlay; Random House; New York; 1950

Lee In Battle; Bradford, Gamaliel; Jubille Jr.: One Hundred Years of the Atlantic; Little, Brown & Company; Boston; 1957

Lee of Virginia; Freeman, Douglas Southall; Charles Scribner's & Sons; New York; 1958

Lee Papers; Lee to Charles Carter Lee; Washington and Lee College; April 18, 1870

Lee, The Last Years; Flood, Charles Bracelen; Houghton Mifflin Company; New York; 1981

Lee, The Soldier; Gallager, Gary W.; University of Nebraska Press; Lincoln, Nebraska; 1996; page 620

Lee's Aid-De-Camp; Marshall, Charles; University of Nebraska Press; Lincoln and London; @1927; First Bison Books printing: 2000

Lee's Dispatches: Unpublished Letters of General Robert E. Lee, C. S. A., to Jefferson Davis and the War Department of the Confederate Sates of America 1862-1865; Lee, Robert E.; From the private Collection of Wymberley Jones de Renne, of Wormsloe, Georgia (edited by Freeman, Douglas S. Freeman); G.P. Putnam's Sons; New York; 1915;

Life & Letters of Gen. Robert Edward Lee; Jones, W.J.; Sprinkle Publications; Harrisonburg, Virginia; 1986; @ by Neale Publishing Company in 1906

May I Quote You General Lee?; Bedwell, Randall; Cumberland House Publishing; Nashville; 1997

Medical Histories of Confederate Generals; Welsh, Jack D.; Kent State University Press; Kent, Ohio, 1995; page 297

Memoirs of Robert E. Lee; Long, A.L.; Blue Gray Press, Secaucus, N. J.; 1983

Official Records; Volume 19; series 1; part 2; page 722

One of Jackson's Foot Cavalry, His Experience and What He Saw During the War 1861-1865; Worsham, John H.; New York; The Neale Publishing Company; 1912

Personal Reminiscences, Anecdotes and Letters of General Robert E. Lee; Jones, J. William; Appleton; New York; 1875

Poetry of the Civil War: Poems for a Bygone Era; Chaltas, David; Lulu Publishing; 2006

Recollections and Letters of General Robert E. Lee; Lee, Robert E. Lee Jr.; Garden City Publishing Company; Garden City, New York; 1904

Recollections of a Confederate Staff Officer; Sorrel, Moxley; McCowat-Mercer Press; Jackson, Tennessee; 1958

Reflections of a Confederate Staff Officer; Sorrel, G. Moxley; Neale Publishing Co.; New York; 1905; page 315

Recollections of My Father's Death; Lee, Mildred; deButts-Ely Collection; Library of Congress

R. E. Lee: A Biography; Freeman, Douglas Southall; Charles Scibner's Sons; New York; 1934-1935; 4 volumes; 2,398 pages

Reminiscences of the Civil War; Gordon, Major General John B.; C. Scribner's Sons; New York; 1904

Robert E. Lee, A Biography; Thomas, Emory M.; W.W. Norton & Company; New York-London; 1995

Robert E. Lee, A Life Portrait; Eicher, David J.; Taylor Trade Publishing; Lanham, New York; 2002

Robert E. Lee and the Road of Honor; Carter, Hodding; Randon House; New York; 1955

Robert E. Lee Man and Soldier; Page, Thomas Nelson; Charles Scribner's sons; New York; 1926

Robert E. Lee on Leadership; Executive Lessons in Character, Courage, and Vision; Crocker III, H. W.; Forum, an Imprint of Prima Publishing; Rocklin, California; 1999

Southern Historical Society Papers; Volume 41; page188

The Boys' Life of Robert E. Lee; Horn, Stanley F.; Harper Brothers Publishers; New York and London; 1935

The Campaign to Appomattox; Davis, William C.; Civil War Times Illustrated; Volume XIV, Number 1; April, 1975; pages 1-50

The Christian Character of Robert E. Lee; Weaver, John; Chaplain in Chief; Confederate Veteran; Volume Three 2002

The Civil War: A Narrative: Red River to Appomattox; Foote, Shelby; First Vintage Books Edition; Random House; New York; 1986

The Court Martial of Robert E. Lee: a Novel; Savage, Douglas; Warner Brothers

The Encyclopedia of Civil War Usage; Garrison, Webb; Cumberland House Publishing; Nashville, Tennessee; 2001

The Fremantle Diary, A Journal of the Confederacy; Fremantle, James, Lt. Col.; edited by Walter Lord; Burford Books; 1954

The Gentleman Commander: A character Portrayal of Robert E. Lee; Bishop, Merrill & Roemer, Joseph; The Economy Company: Oklahoma City; 1936: pages 14-18

The Harper's Weekly: Journal of Civilization; New York, Saturday, July 25, 1863; Vol. VII; No. 343

The Funeral Procession of Lee; The Lexington Gazette; October 21, 1870

The Maxims of Robert E. Lee for Young Gentlemen; Williams, Richard G.; Pelican Publishing Company; Gretna, Louisiana; 2005

The Memoirs of Colonel John S. Mosby; Mosby, John Singleton; Edited by Russell, Charles W.; Little, Brown, and Company; Boston; 1917

The Revolutionary War Memoirs of General Henry Lee; edited by Robert E. Lee; DaCapo Press Incorporated; New York, New York; 3rd edition 1869; new introduction-1998

The Robert E. Lee Reader; edited by Stanley f. Horn; Smithmark Publishing Company; New York, New York; 1995; page 42)

The Soul of Lee; McKim; Randolph H.; New York; Longmans, Green & Co.; 1918

The War Between the Union and the Confederacy; Oates, William C.; Neale Publishing Company; 1905; page 808

The Wartime Papers of Robert E. Lee; Dowdey, Clifford and Manarin, Louis H.; De Capo Press; Commonwealth of Virginia; 1961

The Wit and Wisdom of Robert E. Lee; edited by Cannon, Devereaux D.; Pelican Publishing Company; Gretna, Louisiana; Third Edition; 2000

Traveller; Adams, Richard; Alfred A. Knopf; New York; 1988

Unveiling of Valentines's Recumbent Figure of Lee; Daniel, John W.; Southern Historical Society Papers

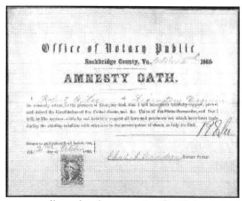

(Lee's Amnesty Oath)

The following public law restored citizenship to Lee that had been denied him for over one hundred five years. President Ford rectified an injustice to a Lee family that had been forgotten and hidden away in a box until rediscovered. *NOTE: President Gerald Ford spoke on August 5, 1975, at 2:12 p.m. at the Arlington House, Arlington, Virginia. Arlington House, formerly known as the Custis-Lee Mansion, was the home of General Lee. As enacted, S.J. Res. 23 is Public Law 94-67 (89 Stat. 380).

"Governor Godwin, Senator Byrd, Congressman Butler, Congressman Harris, Congressman Satterfield, Congressman Downing, and Congressman Daniel, distinguished guests, ladies and gentlemen:

"I am very pleased to sign Senate Joint Resolution 23, restoring posthumously the long overdue, full rights of citizenship to General Robert E. Lee. This legislation corrects a 110-year oversight of American history. It is significant that it is signed at this place.

"Lee's dedication to his native State of Virginia chartered his course for the bitter Civil War years, causing him to reluctantly resign from a distinguished career in the United States Army and to serve as General of the Army of

Northern Virginia. He, thus, forfeited his rights to U.S. citizenship.

"Once the war was over, he firmly felt the wounds of the North and South must be bound up. He sought to show by example that the citizens of the South must dedicate their efforts to rebuilding that region of the country as a strong and vital part of the American Union.

"In 1865, Robert E. Lee wrote to a former Confederate soldier concerning his signing the Oath of Allegiance, and I quote: "This war, being at an end, the Southern States having laid down their arms, and the questions at issue between them and the Northern States having been decided, I believe it to be the duty of everyone to unite in the restoration of the country and the reestablishment of peace and harmony."

"This resolution passed by the Congress responds to the formal application of General Lee to President Andrew Johnson on June 13, 1865, for the restoration of his full rights of citizenship. Although this petition was endorsed by General Grant and forwarded to the President through the Secretary of War, an Oath of Allegiance was not attached because notice of this additional requirement had not reached Lee in time.

"Later, after his inauguration as President of Washington College on October 2, 1865, Lee executed a notarized Oath of Allegiance. Again, his application was not acted upon because the Oath of Allegiance was apparently lost. It was finally discovered in the National Archives in 1970.

"As a soldier, General Lee left his mark on military strategy. As a man, he stood as the symbol of valor and of duty. As an educator, he appealed to reason and learning to achieve understanding and to build a stronger nation. The course he chose after the war became a symbol to all those who had marched with him in the bitter years towards Appomattox.

"General Lee's character has been an example to succeeding generations, making the restoration of his citizenship an event in which every American can take pride.

"In approving this Joint Resolution, the Congress removed the legal obstacle to citizenship which resulted from General Lee's Civil War service. Although more than a century late, I am delighted to sign this resolution and to complete the full restoration of General Lee's citizenship." President Gerald R. Ford

"He possessed every virtue of the great commanders, without treachery; a private citizen without wrong; a neighbor without reproach; a Christian without hypocrisy, and a man without guile." B. H. Hill

"A leader of men in war and peace, a champion of principles, a humanitarian, a man who devoted his entire life to the benefit of others without regard to himself." President Woodrow Wilson

"I have taught my sons (I have not my daughter) my friends and neighbors to love General Lee and honor his memory. I have never seen his equal upon this earth and never expect to. What he was, I ardently wish all men to be." W. W. Estill, Lexington, Kentucky, a student under Lee

"Character is invincible-that, it seems to me, is the life of Robert E. Lee in three words." Douglas Southall Freeman

"How is it, that his shadow lengthens daily? The answer is to the honor of mankind. A generation sometimes mistakes the theatrical for the dramatic, the specious for the serious, the pretender for the defender...The 'hero of the hour' may not have deserved his place even for that hour; he who is a hero when his century is done has qualities that are timeless." Freeman

"We have been daily witness to his quiet, unostentatious, Christian life; we have seen him prove that him no adversity could ever move, nor policy at any time entice to shrink for God and from his word." Eulogy given by Rockbridge County, Virginia Confederate Soldiers

"I was raised by one of the greatest men in the world. There was never one born of a woman greater than Gen. Robert E. Lee, according to my judgment. All of his servants were set free ten years before the war, but all remained on the plantation until after the surrender." Reverend William Mack Lee

"Hold yourself above every mean action. Be strictly honorable in every act, and be not ashamed to do right." R. E. Lee

"I think it better to do right, even if we suffer in so doing." R. E. Lee

"We made a great mistake in the beginning of our struggle, and I fear, in spite of all we can do, it will prove to be a fatal mistake. We appointed all our worst generals to command our armies, and all our best generals to edit the newspaper." R. E. Lee

"Our hardest lesson is self knowledge, and it is one perhaps that is never accomplished." R. E. Lee "

"In all my perplexities and distresses, the Bible has never failed to give me light and strength." R. E. Lee

"All is bright if you will think it so. All is happy if you make it so." R. E. Lee

"We cannot undo the past; that is forever gone; but the future is in our hands." R. E. Lee

"Nothing is more instructive than the perusal of the deeds of men in other ages." R. E. Lee,
April 8, 1869

"They do not know that they say. If it came to a conflict of arms, the war will last at least four years. Northern politicians will not appreciate the determination and pluck of the South, and Southern politicians do not appreciate the numbers, resources, and patient perseverance of the North. Both sides forget that we are all Americans. I foresee that our country will pass through a terrible ordeal, a necessary expiation, perhaps, for our national sins." R. E. Lee

"You can have anything you want-if you want it badly enough. You can be anything you want to be, have anything you desire, accomplish anything you set out to accomplish-if you will hold to that desire with singleness of purpose." R. E. Lee

"We failed, but in the good providence of God apparent failure often proves a blessing."
R. E. Lee

"We poor sinners need to come back from our wanderings to seek pardon through the all-sufficient merits of our Redeemer. And we need to pray earnestly for the power of the Holy Spirit to give us a precious revival in our hearts and among the unconverted." Robert E. Lee

"We owe it to our dead, to our living and to our children to preserve the truth and repel the falsehoods, so that we may secure just judgment from the only tribunal before which we may appear and be fully and fairly be heard, and that tribunal is the bar of history." R. E. Lee

"Fear not the toils of gaining knowledge, but embrace them instead-for with knowledge comes the key to success, and the number of doors it opens is only limited by yourself." R.E. Lee

(Mary Custis Lee)

200th BIRTHDAY ADDRESS

(Author at Col Alto prior to the 200TH Birthday address on Robert E. Lee)

He Stands Upon a Shadow
David Chaltas, Keynote Speaker
200th Birthday of Robert E. Lee
January 13, 2007, Lee's Chapel, Lexington, Virginia

As I stand in awe of the honor bestowed on me and even more HUMBLED by the location in which I address the 'Citizen's of the South', my mind's eye catches a glimpse of the greatness of the silhouette that lies behind me and I am lost for words to those that walk upon the wind. We assemble on hallowed ground. We are sitting and standing inside the chapel that was built by Lee, supervised by his very eye, and lovingly crafted by his love of God. It reminds me of his mission. In Joshua 4: 4-9, the Book of Books states that when Joshua began crossing the Jordan he instructed twelve men representing the twelve tribes of Israel to take twelve stones from the water and place them as a sign that, "When your children ask in times to come, saying, 'What do these stones mean to you.' Before Then you can answer them that, 'the waters of the Jordan were cut off before the ark of the covenant of the Lord; when it crossed over the Jordan, AND these stones shall be for a memorial to the children of Israel forever.'" So, it is with this sanctuary, this chapel. It is a breathing tribute to Lee's love for Christ. AND in Proverbs 22:28, the Bible says," Do not remove the ancient landmark which your fathers have set." This is our charge!

With unfazed laurels, he rests. With untainted merit his shadow lengthens. With untarnished duty, he stands upon a shadow, lingering. His un-compromised virtues, his humble spirit, his very signature is upon our land. Tecumseh stated, 'When you were born, you cried but the world rejoiced. So, you must live your life in such a manner that when you die, the world cries but YOU rejoice", be as a warrior going home. Such is the legend and legacy of Lee. We call him a hero. We call him a legend. We say he is a man of marble. But I must beg leave of you this day to say it is not that he was an undaunted hero, but that he represented the essence of Christian character that MADE him a hero to all. He represents each of our ancestors and their sacrifices. DUTY, HONOR,

INTEGRITY, HUMBLENESS OF SPIRIT AND TRUE CHRISTIAN LOVE.

While we stand in the shadow of legends, let us take a moment and envision those men and women that suffered the hardships of war and yet remained loyal to their cause. Even when it cost them everything, yet they tarried. And though our general would be appreciative of all your praise and recognition on this his birthday, he would gently ask you to recall others. Please recall the names of your ancestors that served so gallantly in the greatest army ever to march upon this earth. An army outnumbered (sometimes 5 to 1), an army out manufactured, an army out mechanized but an army never outfought. I tell you this: never was a general prouder of his men than he, as he stood in awe within the shadow of THEIR greatness. As I raise my hand to heaven and lower it to earth, I ask that you say your ancestors' name, as we honor their memory. Let us not forget that his old warhorse, ole Pete was born on JAN. 8, 1821. Stonewall, his right arm was born on JAN 21, 1824, 2 days after (being 16 years his junior) and of course General Pickett was born in this month in 1825.

LISTEN; can you not hear it, the fading sound of wagons, horses, wheels upon the plankton and the soft murmur of indistinguishable voices permeating the essence of our spirits? LOOK yonder across the meadow; do you not see our glorious flags dancing in the wind, as they slowly rise above the hill as the fog yields to their colors? Do you not SEE the gray images as they march by in all their colorless glory? Can you not TASTE the coffee, beans, and hardtack? Can you not taste the gunpowder as it weds the dew and softly floats upon the fields of honor? SMELL the aroma of the

445

wood as it carries the prayers of the people skyward? Can you not FEEL the presence of those giants of yesteryear as they once again walk upon the shadows, pleading that their stories be passed on to future generations? This is our calling, this is our duty and by the honor of all that we hold sacred, we must remember, lest the world forget the greatness of the southern soldier.

Let us rekindle the pride that POLITICAL CORRECTNESS is attempting to take from us. For the war is not over; INDEED, the enemy is waiting outside the chapel walls. IGNORANCE, APATHY, HATRED, ARROGANCE, PREJUDICE AWAITS. But this war that we are currently engaged in is not fought with bullets, but with ballots. We fight ignorance and arrogance in every school that has an author unwilling to tell the truth of the cause. We fight to save the truth of the cause and our heritage, for it is the northern pen that now currently writes it. But we must remember that WE are armed with FORTITUDE OF DETERMINATION, we are armed with BIBLICAL principles, we are armed with LOVE and we are armed with the TRUTH and it shall set us free. We must remember whom they were, in order for us to know who we are and for our youth to understand who they will become. I charge you to remember. We must pass the torch, for they stand upon a shadow, listening...

They Stand Upon a Shadow

They stand upon a shadow
Beyond the turbid vale.
They've fallen from their saddle:
A foreign sea they sail.

They mingle with the shadows
And scurry on the wind.
They've witnessed their last battle
But walk the land again.

At times, we feel their presence
As we stray all alone.
Their spirit is effervescent
Trying to make it home.

With trails of tears behind them
They walk upon the haze.
Their memories remind them
Of spring and winter days.

Like fog upon the mountain;
Like the morning dew.
As water from a fountain
Must run to be renewed.

They stand upon the shadows,
Just barely out of sight.
With rolling thunder's rattle
They walk the fields tonight.

Is it not strange how a man that followed God's principles until his death on October 12, 1870, still is so revered today? It is said that one man can sometimes touch seven generations but a few touch eternities. I think the character that Lee tried to emulate immolate was Christ like and the people saw it shine through him. When you accept Christ, you become a new creature. Lee said it and lived it best when he stated, "I am nothing but a poor sinner trusting in Christ alone for my salvation." And then he lived the life in which his Savior directed him to do. When you live a life of following the teaching of Christ, people will remember. Honor, honesty, duty, virtue, chivalry all are words that Christ lived by and set the example for us to live up to. Great men of God are not born but are created by seeking, by knocking and asking for guidance. Then they lead by example. What will people say of you after your time on this earth has gone? Will they remember you as a Christian or will they even remember. Our southern heritage calls for us to be southern gentlemen but more importantly, our heritage beckons us to embrace the 'Book of books' as did our ancestors. There is a reason that we are known as the Bible belt...

I remember during a review, a young parson from the Carolinas made a statement to Lee's adjutant about how proud the general must be regarding the devotion of his men. The adjutant turned and stated, "Not proud sir, it awes him." On several occasions, General Lee could not help from breaking down in reverence of men willing to do his bidding at the cost of their lives.

I remember the Texan who visited Lee after the war. Our general had left word not to be disturbed due to being tired from all the well-wishers, but after a lapse of time, his beloved went up stairs and knocked. Lee restated that he was tired and did not wish to be disturbed but his son told him that it was a Texan that was downstairs, wishing to bid him farewell before his ride home. Lee descended the stairs and extended his hand. The Texan grasped it tightly, staring into each other's eyes, without one word being spoken. The Texan put his hand over face and with tears streaming down his face, left his captain. I remember.

I remember his uncles: Richard and Francis Lee were signers of the Declaration of Independence. I remember his father, General Henry "Light Horse" Lee, a patriot, a hero, a Governor of Virginia, and a man that helped approve the final draft of the US Constitution. I recall his worlds at Washington's funeral; "First in war, first in peace, first in the hearts of men". I recall his unpopular stance against the War of 1812, and how he was beaten. I see him leaving his beloved Virginia never to grace its sacred soil again and died at Cumberland Island, Georgia (Nathaniel Greene home) on the evening of 25 March 1818. He was buried there in the Greene family cemetery. General Lee didn't see the grave of his father for 42 years until he was in Georgia in 1862.

I remember Ann Hill Carter Lee, his sainted mother, that instilled within his being honor, faith, duty, and servitude to his fellow men. I remember her infirmaries and how her beloved son cared for her during her declining years.

I recall Robert E. Lee entered West Point in 1825, and ending his career as a cadet with no demerits, being second in his class. Due to his well-polished traits and demeanor, he was known as the man of marble by others that admired him. <u>Lee once stated</u>, *"There is true glory and true honor, the glory of duty done and the honor of integrity and principles."* He also wrote, *"Duty is the sublimest word in the language. You cannot do more than your duty; you should never wish to do less."*

I recall Lee's marriage to Mary Randolph Custis, the heiress to Arlington, Shirley, Roanoke, and the White House. She was the step great granddaughter of the father of our country, George Washington. A man that held the Lee family in such high esteem and selected "Lighthorse" Lee to be his right arm during America's first revolution. The marriage yielded seven children and several thousand letters endorsing their love for God, family, and each other.

I reflect upon his appointment as assistant to the chief of engineers in Washington, and how he was selected to supervise projects such as Fort Monroe, changing the course of the Mississippi River, New York, settling a boundary dispute between states and the Atlantic coastal fortification projects masterminded by Lee.

I can see the fall of 1846, when Lee learned of military expeditions that were being sent to Mexico. I next followed Lee when he was at the city of Vera Cruz, hiding underneath a log to avoid capture, staying awake for over 2 days to give a report, and collapsing after giving the report to General Winfield Scott from loss of blood from a wound received on September 13, 1847. I read of him receiving three brevet promotions in twenty months.

I remember his service to Westpoint for three years in which his family was beside him. I recall his service in Texas and his being called to the defense of the United States by the President during the infamous Harper's Ferry raid by John Brown. I can still see that gallant Lt. Stuart that would become forever entwined with the general due to his chivalry. I recall the emotions that permeated his soul when he had to decide whether to follow the course that he had served so admirably for over thirty years or submit to a higher calling; that of following the voice of his Virginia. He chose Virginia.

Do you recall that it was upon Lee's shoulders that fell the arduous task of building the army, strengthening the coastal defenses, and offering his advice, talents, and experience as a military leader? Through four years of war, Lee moved down the haunting trail of tears led from the Cheats Mountain, Seven Days' Battle and Second Manassas, past Sharpsburg, and Fredericksburg, to Chancellorsville, Gettysburg, Petersburg, Richmond, Sailor Creek ending at the Appomattox Courthouse in Virginia, due to Lee's great compassion for his brave men in gray.

I remember that sad date when all the masses cried and the Lee family was destitute. The white house had been burned, Shirley had been ransacked and their home, their lovely Arlington, had been turned into a cemetery. Though accused of treason, Lee put aside his animosities and began the arduous task of rebuilding the South through education. The Board of Trustees at Washington College in Lexington, Virginia, selected him as their president. Through Lee's vision, the college that had been ravaged by war went from a fading memory to one of the leading educational institutes in the nation. Lee envisioned adding subjects such as agriculture, commerce, engineering and the teaching of duty, honor, and unwavering devotion to God. We are now assembled in his creation devoted to his love of our God. Here, at Lexington, Virginia he lived. Upon the sacred soil of heritage known as Washington and Lee College, he built his greatest legacy. He set the example in which every American should attempt to obtain. I remember God being in the forefront of this wondrous institution and Lee's earnest wish that all become sincere Christians.

As a parting thought to the Citizens of the South here today, remember it is our Duty to stand for these fallen heroes, we took an oath to do no less. We MUST carry the torch and pass it on to future generations. Remember these words of General

Lee "You cannot do more than your duty; you should never wish to do less". This was the man called Lee. Denied his citizenship and almost tried for treason, Lee clung to the Christian virtues that his mother had ingrained within his heart. It took over 100 years for the 'oversite' of Lee's citizenship to be rectified. I think it only fitting to share it with you to honor our general and the last president to recognize the achievements of Lee

The following are President Gerald R. FORD's remarks upon signing a bill restoring rights of citizenship to General Robert E. Lee. As enacted, S.J. Res. 23 is Public Law 94-67 (89 Stat. 380). The President spoke at 2:12 p.m. at on August 5, 1975, at Arlington House (formerly known as the Custis-Lee Mansion) in Arlington, Virginia. This was the home of Mr. and Mrs. Lee for over thirty years.

'Governor Godwin, Senator Byrd, Congressman Butler, Congressman Harris, Congressman Satterfield, Congressman Downing, and Congressman Daniel, distinguished guests, ladies and gentlemen:

"I am very pleased to sign Senate Joint Resolution 23, restoring posthumously the long overdue, full rights of citizenship to General Robert E. Lee. This legislation corrects a 110-year oversight of American history. It is significant that it is signed at this place.

"Lee's dedication to his native State of Virginia chartered his course for the bitter Civil War years, causing him to reluctantly resign from a distinguished career in the United States Army and to serve as General of the Army of Northern

Virginia. He, thus, forfeited his rights to U.S. citizenship.

"Once the war was over, he firmly felt the wounds of the North and South must be bound up. He sought to show by example that the citizens of the South must dedicate their efforts to rebuilding that region of the country as a strong and vital part of the American Union.

"In 1865, Robert E. Lee wrote to a former Confederate soldier concerning his signing the Oath of Allegiance, and I quote: "This war, being at an end, the Southern States having laid down their arms, and the questions at issue between them and the Northern States having been decided, I believe it to be the duty of everyone to unite in the restoration of the country and the reestablishment of peace and harmony."

"This resolution passed by the Congress responds to the formal application of General Lee to President Andrew Johnson on June 13, 1865, for the restoration of his full rights of citizenship. Although this petition was endorsed by General Grant and forwarded to the President through the Secretary of War, an Oath of Allegiance was not attached because notice of this additional requirement had not reached Lee in time.

"Later, after his inauguration as President of Washington College on October 2, 1865, Lee executed a notarized Oath of Allegiance. Again, his application was not acted upon because the Oath of Allegiance was apparently lost. It was finally discovered in the National Archives in 1970.

"As a soldier, General Lee left his mark on military strategy. As a man, he stood as the symbol of valor and of duty. As an educator, he appealed to reason and learning to achieve understanding and to build a stronger nation. The course he chose after the war became a symbol to all those who had marched with him in the bitter years towards Appomattox.

"General Lee's character has been an example to succeeding generations, making the restoration of his citizenship an event in which every American can take pride.

"In approving this Joint Resolution, the Congress removed the legal obstacle to citizenship, which resulted from General Lee's Civil War service. Although more than a century late, I am delighted to sign this resolution and to complete the full restoration of General Lee's citizenship.

I recall many men of stature that song the laurels of the man. President Theodore Roosevelt described General Robert E. Lee as, "The very greatest of all the great captains that the English-speaking peoples have brought forth."

Prime Minister Winston Churchill wrote of Lee: "His noble presence and gentle, kindly manner were sustained by religious faith and an exalted character." Of his army, Churchill observed: "It was even said that their line of march could be traced by the bloodstained footprints of unshod men. But the Army of Northern Virginia 'carried the Confederacy on its bayonets' and made a struggle unsurpassed in history."

Georgia Senator Ben Hill immortalized Lee with his passionate words: "He possessed every virtue of other great commanders without their vices. He was a foe without hate; a friend without treachery; a victor without oppression, and a victim without murmuring. He was a public officer without vices; a private citizen without reproach; a Christian without hypocrisy and a man without guile. He was a Caesar without his ambition; Frederick without his tyranny; Napoleon without his selfishness, and Washington without his reward. He was obedient to authority as a servant, and loyal in authority as a true king. He was gentle as a woman in life; modest and pure as a virgin in thought; watchful as a Roman vital in duty; submissive to law as Socrates, and grand in battle as Achilles!"

Citizens of the South, do you recall your heroes? Do you remember our fathers and mothers? This day is a day of remembrance, for when we honor one, we honor all. Our general would have wanted it that way...

South Carolina (Dec 20, 1860), Recall the home of succession and General Richard Anderson!
Mississippi (January 9, 1861), Do you remember the gallant charge of General W. Barksdale?
Florida (January 10, 1861), Remember the Osceola Rangers and General Joseph Finegn!
Alabama (January 11, 1861), 3rd Alabama, Cullen Battle; Major Genrl William Mahone
Georgia (January 19, 1861), Edward Porter Alexandria calls upon you to honor the South!
Louisiana (January 26, 1861), Do you remember Richard Taylor?
Texas (February 1, 1861), Do you recall A. S. Johnston and General Hood?
Virginia (April 17, 1861); Do recall the immortal Stonewall Jackson?
Arkansas (May 6, 1861), Do you remember Patrick R. Cleburne
Tennessee (May 7, 1861), Nathan Bedford Forrest reaches from the grave to our hearts!

North Carolina (May 20, 1861), Remember Daniel Harvey Hill and James Johnston Pettigrew* Missouri, Recall your warriors, the brave Choctaw Brigade, and Cherokee Partisan Rangers Kentucky, Do you remember the martyred John Hunt Morgan? Do you recall President Davis? Maryland, Can you not hear the cries of your brothers, as the fight each other at Dunker's Church.

**Sons and daughters, do you recall Lee's words regarding black soldiers as he says, "When you eliminate the black Confederate soldier, you've eliminated the history of the South." quoted from General Robert E. Lee, in 1864. Pray God please remember!

One of my favorite quotes by R.E. Lee was his statement regarding slavery. Listen to his words and ask yourself of his character.

"So far from engaging in a war to perpetuate slavery, I am rejoiced that Slavery is abolished. I believe it will be greatly for the interest of the South. So fully am I satisfied of this that I would have cheerfully lost all that I have lost by the war, and have suffered all that I have suffered to have this object attained.

Finally, as I bid you adieu, let us bring to mind that terrible day when the colors were no more and the last order that was given, as the glorious gray army faded into the shadows to walk upon the wind.

April 10, 1865-GENERAL ORDER #9

After four years of arduous service marked by unsurpassed courage and fortitude, the Army of Northern Virginia has been compelled to yield to overwhelming numbers and resources.

I need not tell the brave survivors of so many hard-fought battles who have remained steadfast to the last that I have consented to this result from no distrust of them.

But feeling that valor and devotion could accomplish nothing that could compensate for the loss that must have attended the continuance of the contest, I determined to avoid the useless sacrifice of those whose past services have endeared them to their countrymen.

By the terms of the agreement, officers and men can return to their homes and remain until exchanged. You will take with you the satisfaction that proceeds from a consciousness of duty faithfully performed; and I earnestly pray that a Merciful God will extend to you His blessings and protection.

With an unceasing admiration of your constancy and devotion to your Country, and a grateful remembrance of your kind and generous consideration for myself, **I bid you all an affectionate farewell**."

(Portrayal of Lee after the surrender)

(Photo by Randy Seal)

"They do not know what they say. If it came to a conflict of arms, the war will last at least four years. Northern politicians will not appreciate the determination and pluck of the South, and Southern politicians do not appreciate the numbers, resources, and patient perseverance of the North. Both sides forget that we are all Americans. I foresee that our country will pass through a terrible ordeal, a necessary expiation, perhaps, for our national sins."

(Joseph Johnson and Robert E. Lee)

(Interior Christ Church, Alexandria, VA)

During the twilight years of his life, Union Major General Joshua Lawrence Chamberlain would say of Robert Edward Lee, "As to personal qualities, Lee's utter unselfishness, in fact his whole moral constitution, appeared to us singularly fine. In his high characteristics as a man he compelled admiration among those who knew him, - even as we did, - and he will command it for all the future."

"There is a terrible war coming, and these young men who have never seen war cannot wait for it to happen, but I tell you, I wish that I owned every slave in the South, for I would free them all to avoid this war."

"We must expect reverses, even defeats. They are sent to teach us wisdom and prudence, to call forth greater energies, and to prevent our falling into greater disasters." R. E. Lee

http://www.citelighter.com/history/history/knowl edgecards/robert-e.-lee

461

"My experience of men has neither disposed me to think worse of them, or indisposed me to serve them; nor in spite of failures, which I lament, of errors which I now see and acknowledge; or of the present aspect of affairs; do I despair of the future."

"The truth is this: The march of Providence is so slow, and our desires so impatient; the work of progress is so immense and our means of aiding it so feeble; the life of humanity is so long, that of the individual so brief, that we often see only the ebb of the advancing wave and are thus discouraged. It is history that teaches us to hope."

"Everyone should do all in his power to collect and disseminate the truth, in the hope that it may find a place in history and descend to posterity. History is not the relation of campaigns and battles and generals or other individuals, but that which shows the principles for which the South contended, and which justified her struggle for those principles."

"The interests of the State are therefore the same as those of the United States. Its prosperity will rise or fall with the welfare of the country. The duty of its citizens, then, appears to me too plain to admit of doubt. All should unite in honest efforts to obliterate the effects of war, and to restore the blessings of peace. They should remain, if possible, in the country; promote harmony and good feeling; qualify themselves to vote; and elect to the State and general Legislatures wise and patriotic men, who will devote their abilities to the interests of the country, and the healing of all dissensions. I have invariably recommended this course since the cessation of hostilities, and have endeavored to practice it myself."

"Knowing that intercessory prayer is our mightiest weapon and the supreme call for all Christians today, I pleadingly urge our people everywhere to pray. Believing that prayer is the greatest contribution that our people can make in this critical hour, I humbly urge that we take time to pray—to really pray. Let there be prayer at sunup, at noonday, at sundown, at midnight—all through the day. Let us all pray for our children, our youth, our aged, our pastors, our homes. Let us pray for our churches. Let us pray for ourselves, that we may not lose the word 'concern' out of our Christian vocabulary. Let us pray for our nation. Let us pray for those who have never known Jesus Christ and redeeming love, for moral forces everywhere, for our national leaders. Let prayer be our passion. Let prayer be our practice." *Robert E. Lee*

"You see what a poor sinner I am, and how unworthy to possess what was given me; for that reason it has been taken away.

(From archives of Washington & Lee University)

463

(From archives of Washington & Lee University)

(Mary Custis Lee)

(Eleanor Agnes Lee)

(Portrait of Anna Carter Lee)

(Mildred Childe Lee)

(George Washington Custis Lee)

(William Henry Fitzhugh Lee)

(Robert E. Lee Jr.)

(Mary Custis Lee, wife of R. E. Lee)

54728850R00281

Made in the USA
Columbia, SC
07 April 2019